Nyerges - POEMS OF ENDRE ADY

STATE UNIVERSITY OF NEW YORK

COLLEGE AT BUFFALO

Program in Soviet and East Central European Studies
Publication Number 1.

POEMS OF
ENDRE ADY

Introduction and translations

by

ANTON N. NYERGES

———— ▬ ————

Prepared for publication

by

JOSEPH M. ÉRTAVY-BARÁTH

———— ▬ ————

Illustrated with Photographs

HUNGARIAN CULTURAL FOUNDATION
Buffalo, New York
1 9 6 9

Library of Congress Catalog Card Number: 74—75423

Two hundred numbered copies of this book in de luxe edition
are autographed by the translator.

Orders may be addressed to
Hungarian Cultural Foundation
P. O. Box 16 — Buffalo, N. Y. 14225

Printed by
Classic Printing Corp. — 9029 Lorain Avenue, Cleveland, Ohio 44102

Contents

ENDRE ADY

(1877—1919)

Commemorative Edition

Published on the 50th anniversary
of the Poet's death

Foreword

ENDRE ADY's life and work is the quintessence of the Hungarian spirit, and his greatness is akin to that of his two friends, Béla Bartók and Zoltán Kodály.

While the music of Bartók and Kodály gained international renown, Ady's art remained a prisoner of the non-Indo-European Magyar language in which he wrote. Throughout Hungarian history it has always been the non-verbal creative men (composers, conductors, instrumentalists, sculptors, painters, moviemakers, and scientists) who established the legend of the extraordinary achievements of Hungarian art. The reputation of Hungarian men of letters, however, has been sadly confined to the national boundaries.

The Hungarian literati have for long entertained a myth that the poems of the great lyricist Endre Ady are especially difficult, nay impossible, to translate. This myth is now shattered. Anton N. Nyerges—American diplomat, linguist, poet in his own right, and now professor at Eastern Kentucky University—labored over two decades to prove Endre Ady belongs to the World. Equipped with a thorough and earthy knowledge of both Hungarian and English from childhood, he has succeeded in capturing the essence of Endre Ady's poetic genius. With his work the Hungarian Cultural Foundation proudly presents the first comprehensive volume of Endre Ady's poetry in a foreign language.

Joseph M. Értavy-Baráth

State University of New York
at Buffalo

7

Acknowledgments

Selected bibliography of Ady literature
was compiled by

Dr. Elemér Bakó,
Library of Congress

The jacket was designed by

József Vudy

Preface

This book is designed to open perspectives on a summit of achievement hitherto concealed from Western eyes and to serve as a point of reference in East-West contacts. The spirit of Ady's poetry is aesthetically summed up in Ezra Pound's beautiful lines:

> *". . . high deeds in Hungary*
> *to pass all men's believing."*

But even more it presents firm evidence of the complexity of Hungarian political and social life and demonstrates, as does Bartók's music, that the Hungarian genius of the century moves in the forefront of European art.

The preparation of the translations extended over more than two decades. I cannot avoid putting it less starkly than saying I was faced with incredible difficulties which could frequently be overcome, if at all, only by living with the original poems over long periods of time.

The first fruits appeared in a booklet entitled T h r e e - s c o r e   P o e m s   o f   A d y published for the American Hungarian Federation by the Indiana University Press in 1946. This publication saw the light of day largely through the personal efforts of Mr. Béla P. Báchkai and Professor Charles C. Bajza now on the faculty of Texas A & I University, Kingsville, Texas, who were both in Bloomington at that time.

Without mentioning everyone who helped move the translation to its present state of completion in one important way or another, it is necessary to make special mention of two outstanding musicians and musicologists, now deceased: Professor Carl Mathes of the University of Notre Dame in South Bend, Indiana, and László Lajtha (early collaborator of Kodály and Bartók), whom I met in Budapest in 1955-1957; and of my wife, Helen Nyerges.

Special heartfelt thanks go to Joseph M. Értavy-Baráth — Bibliographer at SUNYAB, Visiting Associate Professor at the

State University of New York, College at Buffalo and President of the Hungarian Cultural Foundation — for devoting his talents and his time to making this publication a real fact; and to Dr. Béla Kardos of Washington, D.C. for his counsel and unwavering faith. To the State University of New York, College at Buffalo, the translator extends his warmest thanks for sponsoring the book as part of its Program in Soviet and East Central European Studies headed by Professor Walter Drzewieniecki. The translator's sincere appreciation goes to Tibor Kerekes, Professor emeritus, Georgetown University, Washington, D. C.; to Professor John Lotz, Director of the Center for Applied Linguistics in Washington, D. C.; and to Dr. Emmi Szörényi of Rosary College, Chicago, Illinois for their sustained interest in the work; to Reverend Stephen Csernitzky of Bridgeport, Connecticut, now deceased; to Dr. Elemér Bakó of the Library of Congress for his work in preparing the Bibliography.

For an unusual interest in the production of this book the translator expresses his heartfelt appreciation to Mr. László Berta, owner of the Classic Printing Corporation in Cleveland, Ohio.

Anton N. Nyerges

Tehran, Iran
January, 1969

ENDRE ADY

The World of Gog and God

The Seven Plum Trees

Endre was born in the thatch-roofed home of Lőrinc and Mária Ady on November 22, 1877, at Érmindszent, a village in the eastern part of the old Hungarian Kingdom where most of the land-holdings were so small that, as the saying went, there was room for only seven plum trees. At birth he had six fingers, which folk wisdom regarded as a sign of extraordinary powers since the time of those six-fingered Árpád kings who founded the country. The supernumeraries were amputated by the midwife, leaving only two white scars which the youthful Endre called his wizard marks. The village with the queer, obscure name he left behind except for periodic visits. But wizard marks and plum trees symbolized his entire career. One of the most mystically creative of poets, he unceasingly strove to conjure up new forms of life. One of the most fervid of revolutionaries, he consistently saw life from the lower social levels.

Although of higher standing prior to the sixteenth century, the Ady family had lived for generations like the peasantry. The poet's paternal grandfather, Dániel, might with some truth be described as a John Durbyfield were it not that Érmindszent was populated almost entirely by Durbyfields. Of the nine hundred inhabitants in the village about seven hundred were of a genteel class living in circumstances similar to those of the Ady's. They had received titles and small land-holding for their bravery in the innumerable wars fought in this area known as the Partium, a buffer zone between Hungary proper and Transylvania.

On his mother's side Ady came from a long line of Calvinist ministers and school-teachers. Calvinism was known in the Partium as the "Magyar religion", for in the eyes of Protestantism the Catholic Church was identified with the ethnic Germans and the Greek Orthodox Church with the Romanians. Severely plain churches, characterized by white-washed walls and simple pews, dotted the area. The dourness of Calvinism as well as the grayness of poverty lay on the land. When the mature Ady wrote of his native village, he recalled a life of secret hurts and long-repressed hopes.

In a prose work that is a mixture of fact and fancy Ady gives us this description of his paternal and maternal lines under the names of Tas and Gáborián:

"On my father's side I can refer only to simple men, although at one time they included some *homines regii* ... On the other hand, I am not indebted to my paternal ancestors for my ability to write poetry, for basically the Tases were a helpless lot. The warlike Magyar nobles, with whom I understand they were related, plundered them as much as they wished. I have heard that a half villageful of Tases lives somewhere in Transylvania. They are peasants who ever since the coming of phylloxera have drunk whiskey. No matter how much my father tried to deny it with his gentry hauteur, I am certain they are my relatives.

"On my mother's side my ancestors were Calvinist ministers and teachers, but the family name is Gáborián which causes me to suspect that they are not thousand-year-old Magyars. They were driven here probably by a restlessness greater than that of the ancient Magyar horsemen. There is a legend in this family, which has pursued anointed occupations but is not itself anointed, that before Calvinism came to Hungary the Gáboriáns were Armenian and Catholic.

"The Gáboriáns were always restless, a characteristic unbecoming ministers and school-teachers, but they could not help themselves. Ádám Gáborián, my grandfather, was a scribbler of poetry, and even though his poems were not exactly majestic, he died a beautiful death when drunkenly and sorrowfully he plunged into the Szamos River. By that time he was no longer a minister. Although at times he was unbelieving and unfaithful in thought to the Lord of Hosts, he still could not live without Him—he was a poor, crazy man.

"In general, the Gáboriáns could no more find their equilibrium in the spiritual realm than the Tases in the material. Against these dissimilar troubles they found a similar remedy in drinking. The Gáboriáns, it seems, drank with a talent that was not entirely Magyar, and this probably explains why one or two madmen other than Ádám came from my mother's family. This was an exalted, demented, and apparently non-Magyar line which vibrated, trembled, and suffered in order to bring forth a genius, which, no matter how conceited I am, does not mean that I was the ultimate goal."

Endre's father was small, steely, and powerful of frame, with no trace of the softness that was to appear in his adult son's own imposing physique. He loved the soil, which he tilled from boyhood, worshiped horses, and delighted in the virgin home-grown tobacco he stuffed into his long-stemmed pipe. The only one of five brothers who did not acquire some higher education (he left school because of an incapacity to accept discipline), he nevertheless pursued the traditions of the family in his determination to secure a good education for his children. In his declining years he sought for diversions among the village women and brought on himself the scoldings of his own wayward son. It was his father whom

14

Ady resembled in temperament, in his love for wine and women and moody music, in his impatience and tyranny.

Mária was the only person whom Endre regarded throughout his life with an unmixed love. Even as an adult he addressed and referred to her as "sweet", the manner in which the peasant children of the area were wont to call their mothers. From her he inherited his creole skin, large brown eyes, and wavy hair. On Mária's lips a sad smile frequently appeared, and the poet's favorite word of "sombre" seems to have been created for her sake.

As a young girl Mária was exceptional for her beauty, but she was undifferentiated from the village girls in educational and cultural attainment. After she completed her elementary schooling, the world of letters, except for the Bible and the provincial newspaper, was closed to her. But she loved her son with an emotion that raised her above her formal attainments. This little educated but infinitely tender woman, the very antithesis of the polished and city-bred Léda who was to become the poet's great love, was a faithful reader of her son's writings. Throughout his life he sent her copies of his works, and Mária, in turn, not only provided him with physical comforts whenever it was in her power but also followed his career with jealous attention, familiarizing herself with the literary and political struggle that raged about him and carefully learning the identity of his friends and enemies.

Mária was Ady's link to the peasantry with whom he knew an enduring bond. Like Béla Bartók, he had a profound interest in the realities of this ancient civilization, and its infusion by these two great creative workers into the bloodstream of Western music and literature was a principal revolutionary act of the twentieth century. The urgency of this infusion after centuries of self-containment has a meaning our century has not yet fully grasped or interpreted. But it dispelled forever the *am haaretz* and Thersites image which had been foisted on the bearers of this civilization by the aristocratic principles of our society, and after the dispersal of Hungary's old ruling class at the tremendous price of the upheavals following World War II it pointed toward the assumption of a leadership role by this people.

The poet once said, "Two of us, my father and I, tormented the saddest woman in the world." That his mother and her ancestors had never found marital happines and the family thus owed life a debt of love was an obsession of Ady's. This is the theme of a short story he wrote in the year 1909 under the title of *Éva Eszterkuthy's Sister*, in which truth and fiction are obscurely mingled in the description of a traumatic experience. The characters are Éva, who represents Ady's grandmother; Krisztina and Sára, who represent his great aunts; and a little boy who represents Ady himself.

Grandmother Éva, as described in the story, was a half-genteel, half-peasant woman married to a Calvinist minister, whom she despised but endured for eight years, bearing seven children before she died an early death. Krisztina was a woman madly jealous of her husband, and Sára was morally loose and mentally demented, the shame of the family and the talk of the village. Endre was forbidden to visit the house where Sára was detained, but like other boys in the village he would frequently approach her window in the hope of catching a glimpse of the strange creature. On one such occasion Sára caught sight of him and called out:

"...You, you have eyes like Éva's. Aren't you the grandson of Éva Eszterkuthy, my sister, the minister's wife?" She pressed her head against the grating. "How small you are, how much of a child you are, how long before you will be a man, and how bad you will be when you grow up and have things to do with women."

Endre stood with beating heart, straining his body and craning his neck that by some miracle he might grow into a man and learn what women say to men. But Sára returned to her couch, talking and singing to herself. Her speech was a song, sacred and devotional like ministers use on Sundays. Her voice rang with God, wordly vanity, life, sorrow, sin, flowers, birds, time, and death. But it also rang with curses, kisses, complaints, escape, love, secrets, and woes, many, many woes. She sang that she had never loved her husband, that she waited in vain for the man she loved, that love is good but men are bad. She sang that she had loved not her husband but the father of her daughter and that her lover had forsaken her.

Late that night Endre slipped from his bedroom, went to Sára's house, and broke the lock on her door. The following morning she was found stabbed to death, apparently the deed of some drunks who had run across her in the night. Endre kept to himself his secret of the broken lock. His mother, contrary to her former silence, spoke to him thereafter a great deal about his grandmother. At bedtime Grandmother Éva would appear with sweets, stroke his face, kiss him, and say "God bless you." In a curious passage foreshadowing his tortuous struggles with the problem of belonging and of the relationship of creativity to security and acceptance, Ady writes: "Unfortunate is the man who knows his grandmother only as a name... I don't know why it is that life is more kind to the man whom it receives from the arms of a grandmother." From the facts of Ady's life all that appears certain is that his grandmother died at an early age broken by sorrows and that he had a mentally aberrant aunt who had some fateful influence on him as a boy. He alludes to her in an autobiographical sketch with the remark that his first book

16

of poetry was given to him by a "fateful aunt" on his eighth birthday.

In these obscure years is to be found a shaping influence not only on his later strange treatment of love but also on some of his other major themes. The Ady household stood on the outskirts of the village near a cemetery, and the early impressions gained in this surrounding may well have predisposed him to a taste for rumination on death, reinforcing a Transylvanian genius for the macabre. His predilection for alcohol was also developed during these early years as relatives, following a provincial practice, dosed the somewhat weak and sickly youth with red wine.

The farther Ady's career took him from his native village the more prominently emerged the personality which his background stamped on him. The natural timidity of a villager before the great outside world plays a curiously important role in the poetry of this twentieth century writer, who arrogated as his own whatever was new and modern. Ady once wrote of himself: "Fundamentally I was not born to be a man of great presence because I am a coward, and I am terrified by the mere fact that there are so many other men and women, each of whom is an infinitely haughty god on earth. I might dub myself an inverted Victor Hugo who sees a lion in every other man .. If the whole world is a lion, why should I make my own faint voice be heard?" Time and again his poetry deals with the feeling of comfort he experienced behind the curtain of mist lying over his native area where the plains rise into the Transylvanian Alps and an endlessly unchanging life is concealed from the kaleidoscopic changes of the outer world.

Among his playmates was a neighbor girl by the name of Rosie, whom over a quarter of a century later he immortalized in the *Altar of Hagar* with the lines:

> *I felt this sinful love arise*
> *one time upon a sorrel lea.*
> *Rosie, the little neighbor girl,*
> *was playing hide-and-seek with me.*

It is clear Ady remembered her as the alpha of his bizarre sexual life. When she was visited by an Ady biographer many years later, Rosie admitted to mutual story telling as the favorite game of the two playmates. The biographer gives the following account of the meeting:

"My dear, I was passing by this way and decided to visit you. I have been thinking of the days long ago when Endre Ady was a little boy and he liked you."

Rosie's face lit up.

"I liked him very much also," she replied without hesitation.

I listened closely. This was not a common voice; it was gentle and somewhat reserved. Intelligence was obvious.

"Do you recall him clearly, I mean as a little boy?"

Amazement appeared on her face as if to parry the suggestion that she might have forgotten. Her face revealed that Endre had been an important, probably the most important, experience of her childhood.

But she said simply, "Of course I do. He was a good looking boy with black hair, dark eyes, and a pale face. He would often sit in a corner and read. He didn't like boys, because all the other boys at school were stronger. He was a bit weak and sickly. The boys often beat him. Because of this he looked to girls for friends. Girls he liked."

"You went to elementary school together?"

"Yes, boys and girls went to school together in the first four grades. We went to the school beside the church, which was razed a long time ago ... I remember he always wanted to tell stories. He would begin by telling a story, and after he had finished he would ask me to tell one. But I was stupid. I always told stories I had read in books. But he would always make up stories. He would be very angry with me for not being able to make up my own."

Rosie's face changed. Her cheeks reddened, her eyes shone a bright blue; the entire woman seemed to become young again.

"He would say, 'make up your own story, Rosie, make up your own story, Rosie, like me. Don't tell stories you read in a book.' "

She laughed shyly.

"But I could never make up a story. I wasn't clever like he was. And he scolded and complained, 'you stupid one, you stupid one.' "

And then as if feeling it necessary to round out her thought, she quickly added, "But he was a very good boy. He never hit anybody. The boys would hit him, and often they would lie in ambush to catch him."

Because his father had a quarrel with the local Calvinist authorities, Endre was taken from the Calvinist elementary school at the age of nine years and placed in the local Catholic school, a move which caused almost as great a family scandal as when grandfather Dániel became a Catholic convert. It was here he wrote his first poem, which was an account of how his younger brother fell into the mud on the way to school. A mocking, Beelzebub-like attitude toward friends and companions characterized him throughout his life.

Two years later Ady enrolled in the Piarist (Catholic) gymnasium at Nagykároly, located about eleven miles from Érmindszent. He completed four years among the accomplished and scholarly Piarist fathers. When Endre was fourteen years old, the school authorities complained of his frequent associations with girls, and it was exactly at this time that the parents, worried about the Catholic influence on their son, decided to send him to the near-by Calvinist college at Zilah. In an autobiography written in 1913, over twenty years later, Ady asserted that his parents' fears of Catholic influence were groundless. However, in light of his tendency to integrate each new experience into his background, it is reasonable to suppose that the Catholic school had a deep effect on him and that to the consternation of his father he may have knelt at mass.

The release from Piarist discipline was welcome at a time when the disturbances of puberty were plaguing him to such an extent that he required medical attention, but he responded to the free air of the Protestant college, and the four years he spent at Zilah were, as he frequently recalled, the happiest of his life. The city had a genuine charm, and the school was infused with a spirit of liberalism common only to the Protestant schools in Hungary at that time. A sign of this liberalism was the fact that the students in the two highest forms were permitted to smoke and carry canes. Drinking by the older students, although not officially permitted, was tolerated by custom.

In his second year at Zilah, Endre was threatened with expulsion for frequenting a tavern, and the threat was serious enough for a few weeks to cause him to apply to a Jesuit college for permission to enter as a novitiate. Later in life he complainingly boasted in verse that "in a dark hour of my life I almost became a priest at Kalocsa."

As he advanced to higher forms, Ady took full advantage of the liberties at Zilah and became noted as the school's best drinker. However, he was also the school's outstanding student and its acknowledged poet. The former distinction he gained even though he scarcely studied but merely glanced at his lessons in textbooks borrowed from schoolmates. The latter distinction he gained by becoming the poetry editor of a student journal and writing a number of poems for a local newspaper. His first published piece of verse, a patriotic poem on Lajos Kossuth, appeared when he was nineteen years old. It is at least an interesting footnote to Ady's biography that he was Béla Kun's private tutor at Zilah. According to an anecdote related by the poet's younger brother, Kun's father recommended that Endre should insure Béla's attentiveness by belaboring him with a cane, preferably over the head, before each lesson.

In *The Returned Flag*, a poem published in 1913, Ady wrote it was from Zilah that he carried his ideals into the world and first sensed that

> on bloody Protestant battlefields
> I am the Gustaf Adolph of this age.

He made no mention in poetry of his years spent at the Catholic gymnasium but in a short story written in 1906 spoke in unflattering terms of the Piarist fathers excepting only one favorite teacher. It is probable that he was influenced to write as he did by the tastes of his reading public, for the story in question appeared in a popular mouthpiece of the politically progressive elements of Budapest. Despite this article and others like it, Ady's lifetime work does not exhibit continuity of interest in anticlericalism, the overwhelming majority of his articles of this nature having appeared early in his career.

Ady concluded his fourth year at Zilah without a definite vocational goal, a common plight of gentry youth whose parents had neither sufficient land nor capital for their children to undertake a promising rural or urban pursuit. Hoping to improve the family's position, the father insisted Endre prepare himself to become a county magistrate. Accordingly, he enrolled in the law school at Debrecen at the age of nineteen years.

With law studies Ady's interest in academic pursuits deteriorated into desultory cramming for examinations at the same time that his interest grew in love affairs, tavern entertainment, and writing. He barely managed to pass his first year's law examination, and it was obvious he lacked the discipline necessary to become a jurist in a country where legal studies and practices were advanced to a high level of sophistication.

Debrecen and the surrounding livestock raising region of eastern Hungary, where some of the flavor of the nation's nomadic past was retained, later served Ady with materials for his most characteristic genre poems on the "Asiatic" backwardness of the country. The city, known as the "Calvinist Rome", was the center of a narrow gentryism and conservatism which aroused Ady's animadversion. The difference between Debrecen and his native Partium and the reasons for his dislike of the former were described by the poet's brother as follows: "Here the Protestants were burghers who had bribed Tartars, Turks, and Germans into appeasement: there they were a race that drove back invaders with the force of arms. Here they were merchant dynasts; there they were poor, déclassé but proud gentrymen who had lost everything on battlefields. Here the greatest Protestant figure was Melius-Juhász, the iron-hatted "Pope Peter"; there it was Ferenc Dávid, the fiery reformist. Here winds swept up the sands, darkened the city, and stifled the air; there fresh breezes from the Transylvanian mountains were redolent with the scent of flowers and forests."

After a year in Debrecen Ady spent a year in Temesvár, a city of strong Teutonic character where he did not feel at ease. Although he makes some reference in his writings to all other towns in which he lived, he scarcely so much as alludes to the period of his life in this city where the feudal lords in the sixteenth century burned the peasant rebel George Dózsa on a fiery throne and forced his followers to eat of his flesh and where subsequently Turks and Teutons successfully cowed the population for centuries. After Temesvár and a period in Budapest he returned to Debrecen with a final promise to his parents to complete his law examinations. However, on accepting a position with a Debrecen newspaper, he soon resolved to abandon law once and for all.

Ady published his first book of verse in Debrecen, little of which is interesting in and for itself. However, a certain prose article which he wrote during this period rings with an unmistakable Ady voice. This piece, which foreshadows so many of his later visions, reveals that the reporter who covered the police and courthouse beats of Debrecen and who wrote up divorce cases and petty thefts was dwelling on some of the most flamboyant thoughts of his time:

"I am not inspired by anything in the world... I am sick, feverishly sick. I am sick, I see visions. Thousands and thousands of visions pass before my eyes like a kaleidoscope... I see a hungry crowd of men fighting over bread. The struggle is most fierce at the point where the largest piece of bread lies in the dust. This piece has been trampled into the dirt and sullied with blood, and yet with what hellish triumph the strongest man runs away with it after overcoming his rivals. The crowd howls and cries like an animal... But now I see a host of crucifixes, among them a familiar one. Above it are four letters—I.N.R.I.... The champions of truth were crucified on these crosses. The great crowd assembled here is glorious mankind leaping in ecstasy at the sight of innocent blood. I see madonna-faced women with voluptuously vile and inviting looks. I see virgins with sullied foreheads, angels of temptation standing at their backs. I see a poet in whose heart is a flame capable of cleansing the world, but who lies abandoned and reviled on a bed of rotten straw. I see a marble-faced woman in a purple robe holding a delicate pair of scales in her hands. Her name is a glorious one and is written above her head in letters of flame—Justitia. But this beautiful woman has no heart, only a crude instinct. Her eyes do not see the truly wretched, her ears are bribed by the clinking of gold... Oh, even if I had no heart these visions would drive me mad."

Before leaving Debrecen he had a brief but passionate affair with an actress and a number of duels, one of which was widely publicized and resulted in a five-day jail sentence. In

January 1900 he accepted a position as a newspaper writer in the city of Nagyvárad, an industrial and commercial center. This half-Jewish, half-Christian and half-gentry, half-capitalist town, sensitive to the newest currents of European life and thought, affected him with the acuteness of a sunstroke, and here began the metamorphosis that eventually led to his bitter cry:

> *a patch of grief like this is sewn*
> *on no one in the whole wide world*
> *but Magyars who outgrow their kind.*

In the three and one-half years that Ady spent at Nagyvárad he wrote some fifty poems, most of which appeared in a volume called ONCE MORE published shortly before his first visit to Paris. Only few of these poems give any indication of striking originality. That at the age of twenty-five he should produce so little promise of his later genius is an intriguing literary puzzle. There is probably some truth in the theory that he was unable to find his true voice until he had lived through his Parisian experience. But perhaps it is even more likely that the brilliant and superficial Nagyvárad infused him with a cynicism that caused him to look on poetry as something of a liability to a writer seeking fame. About his lack of poetic creativity at this stage of his career he wrote, "A kind of haughty cynicism cramped my fingers. I did not feel it was worth while to become a József Kiss" (a capable but second-rate poet). Ady hoped, at least in his Nagyvárad period, to become the kind of writer that some of his contemporaries—Ferenc Molnár, Lajos Biró (famous in Hollywood for *Hotel Imperial* with Pola Negri) and Menyhért Lengyel (famous for the play *Typhoon*)—were destined to become and who made Hungarian stage pieces and scenarios sought-for products in Berlin and Vienna, and especially in New York and Hollywood. That he was deterred from this kind of writing was due to his own natural talents which inevitably led him into lyrical poetry and to the fact that as he grew older he became more and more bound to the Hungarian scene, which Molnár, Biró, and Lengyel abandoned. Arthur Koestler's comments in *The Invisible Writing* (page 173, published by The Macmillan Company, New York, 1954) are to the point: "... to abandon his native language and traditions means in most cases death to the writer, and his transformation into a nondescript, cosmopolitan journalist or literary hack. Hungary's main export since the first World War has been reporters, script writers, film producers, magazine editors, commercial artists, actresses, and manufacturers of topical best sellers—the international demimondes of the arts and letters. They were strewn all over the world by that centrifugal force which is generated when an exceptional amount of talent is cooped up without means of expression in a small country. Though I had the good fortune to be brought up bilingually and to leave Hungary as a child, I have paid the penalty which the loss of one's cultural roots entails through a long time."

A year after his arrival in Nagyvárad Ady entered into a major affair with a local singer. He addressed her with a poem, *My Bride*, the opening lines of which,

> *though she be a strumpet of the streets*
> *let her but follow me into my grave,*

startled his friends into comic action to release him from the singer's net. A kidnapping plot, in which the victim participated, was concocted, and Ady, concealed in a near-by town, was permitted to appear on the streets only under the cover of night. For five days he was safe but on the sixth day the singer moved into town, the secret hiding place having been revealed apparently by Ady himself. The affair, however, came to an end just prior to the arrival of Léda and the beginning of the poet's *grande passion*.

It was in Nagyvárad that Ady contracted syphilis, resulting in the most fateful consequences for his poetry. As a writer he was probably never mentally or spiritually free from the festering and fermenting effects of his illness, and not a single one of his main themes—love, death, God, genius, revolution—is without an intimate connection with its overpowering effects.

In a short story entitled *Rozália Mihályi's Kiss*, Ady wrote an account, factually fantastic but psychologically revealing, of how he contracted syphilis. According to the story he had besieged Marcella Kun, a blue-eyed and dark-haired singer without success over a prolonged period. Finally he delivered an ultimatum, and she yielded saying:

"I know you men, I know it is useless for me to talk, cry, resist. All right. I don't want this, it doesn't make me feel good, it hurts. But you men are like that. I've always had reason for regret whenever I've had anything to do with any of you, especially with one whom I detested. But I had to, and he destroyed me."

Ady went on to describe the situation:

"I heard and did not hear her words, for I was already kissing her slippers. Man is a very sad animal who can make love even when he does not desire it. I looked into her eyes and face. I thought I must have gone mad. Her eyes were not blue, but dark. Her hair was red, her lips were red, so red. A metamorphosis had taken place, and we were under a spell.

23

"I know now that it was Rozália Mihályi who had come and cast a spell on us. I know this from descriptions given to me by people who knew, indeed all too well, Rozália Mihályi, the most important woman in my life.

"I never became tired of Marcella Kun, but I did not want her although her kiss was very good, something which I confess and dare to confess even today. At the same time her kisses were sad and pathetic, and a man like me pursues the kiss only to free himself from sadness. I was with her one night when my blood seemed like a chalice which perceives too late it must overflow. My blood gave birth to roses, large, dark, fiery, roses of love. Marcella Kun bent her head over me, kissed me, and said, 'It doesn't matter any more. You asked for it. I told you.'

"It terrifies me to think—I can see her now— that Marcella Kun again looked like the Rozália Mihályi who was later described to me. We made love thereafter; however, I no longer loved Marcella Kun, but a chimera, a red-haired, heavy-lipped and dark-eyed woman. Marcella Kun was there, but Rozália Mihályi played the main role. And it seemed that someone else was there, someone all three of us detested."

With questioning Ady learned that the transmitter was a newspaperman who lived in the city of Győr. He succeeded in finding him and obtaining a confession of his relations with Marcella Kun and Rozália Mihályi. Visiting the town where the latter was reported to live, Ady learned that she had died the previous winter of a horrible disease. The story concludes with the following lines:

"It is no longer possible for me to find the woman who greeted me with an unfortunate kiss. I cannot talk with Rozália Mihályi, I cannot question her. Only one thing remains for me to do, I must make Rozália Mihályi the muse of life and love. I did not know her well, but she defiled my life well enough. Indeed, who knows otherwise how long I would have had to seek the person who sent me sorrowful greetings of love by way of Marcella Kun as a reward for my male animality? On the following day in the bright of morning I took a wreath to Rozália Mihályi's grave, and there on her stone I read these lines: 'Here lies Rozália Mihályi. She lived twenty-six years. Peace unto her dust. I desire to depart and be with Christ for He is better than all things.' Oh, indeed it would be better to die but what is one to do who cannot die? He must live on, as long as he can, suffering the sickness that ended Rozália Mihályi's life. Red hair, red, red lips, dark eyes. As long as I live I shall see them, I must see them. I shall kiss even though I know that this is simply an exchange of greetings and every now and then we receive a greeting of sorrow."

The Asian Bacchus

Although not his most profound works, NEW VERSES and BLOOD AND GOLD are the most vivid books of poetry Ady wrote. As yet unabsorbed in god-seeking or profoundly ethical and political writings, he appeared on the literary scene as an unencumbered pagan, an Asian Bacchus with brown tormented eyes and a trace of mockery on his lips. The poems of this period bear some resemblance to the works of the French symbolists, but even more they have the outlandish color of the old wandering days on the Eurasian steppes and the truculence brought into Europe a thousand years earlier by the nation of Magyars. The more he asserted his newness and sympathy with French liberalism the more he retreated into the gray of Magyar antiquity until his later poetry appears to be a recreation of the lost mythology of the small group of horsemen who almost alone among Eastern people succeeded in securing a lasting place in the heart of the West.

Ady threw with NEW VERSES the challenge of rebellion at the literary tastes of the ruling class. That the book was also a blow aimed at the heart of an aristocratic political authority which for a thousand years had successfully withstood the temerity of rebellion and the erosion of change was almost submerged in a deeply personal and introspective character that was to mark Ady's entire poetical output. The *I* of the poet forever held up a mirror before the *me*, reflecting countless images in the gallery of the self. As he grew, searching for God and groping for a philosophical system, he peered further inside seeking the most faint and distant reflections.

In NEW VERSES Ady merely sensed the role he later made his mission, but he unfailingly found his voice. With the opening line of a remarkable but probably untranslatable title poem he proclaimed himself the son of Gog and Magog, described in Ezekiel and Saint John the Divine as a remote northern people or, alternately, their princes serving in the army of the Prince of Darkness. He never thereafter ceased to attack any form of authority or society that shackles human progress, to search the inner Abel-Cain duality of the soul, and to claim the tribute due his lonely genius that sought an unmanageable meeting of love with others. At the same time, his identification with Gog was accompanied by a feeling of guilt and martyrdom with strongly masochistic overtones.

NEW VERSES is divided into four cycles, each of which deals with a single theme and the individual poems are variations on that theme. Never content until he had experienced an idea in all its Protean forms and striven toward a synthesis of the spiritual contradictions, Ady continued to use and develop this technique. His poems are linked to cycles, cycles to books, and books to books in a manner that makes it literally true his thousand-odd poems form a vast single work. Without an understanding of this intricate structure a reading of the poems as individual entities leads to a world of disintegration and chaos.

Over the book hovers a Bergsonian atmosphere of the "ceaseless upspringing of something new" and a mystic morrow which is forever consumed in the fever of the present. A sense of unpredictability and emergent evolution is combined with the determinism and messianic fervor of Nietzschean philosophy. Like some of the Russian symbolists Ady saw himself as the prophet of a new era in which mankind would become strong and glorious under the guidance of a great poet or superman.

Ady states in a striking dedicatory conceit to the NEW VERSES that poetry is no more than a presentiment of the morrow destined to perish in its own conflagration and that the sixty-six perfervid poems of the book were spared from destruction for the sake of the Woman. The woman was Léda, his suggestive anagrammatic name for Mrs. Ödön Diósi née Adél Brüll, the comely and cultured wife of a Hungarian merchant with a modest business in Paris. Ady and Mrs. Diósi first met in 1903 in Nagyvárad, where her family was engaged in business activity. While an intimacy quickly developed, the sophisticated thirty-one year old woman gave no indication of wishing to become seriously involved with the twenty-six year old provincial poet-journalist, even though he addressed her with a poem as lovely as *Her Ladyship of Tears*. At any rate, her attention at the time was centered on a certain man-about-town, and the early Ady-Léda correspondence witnesses that the young poet was subjected in a Budapest hotel to a "tragic revelation." Nevertheless, after her return to Paris he followed her and during a thirteen month visit a triangle destined to endure for eight years was established. Neither a Madame Bovary bent on ruining herself for romantic love nor a woman content to be closed in the compartment of marriage, Léda did not consider tying her economic lot to that of the impecunious Ady, but she entered without reservation into an unconcealed and impassioned love affair and lived a dual life as Léda-Adél. With expert guidance she introduced the young writer to the latest currents in French cultural life, and her educational devotion was soon apparent in the expanding horizons of his writings. Devoted to his wife and impressed by the young poet, Mr. Diósi stood by with unstinting hospitality.

Ady's dependence on Léda was heightened by a progression of his syphilitic condition, for neglect and taboo had led him to disregard the early warning signs. When the sores appeared, the Diósis made no attempt to disentangle themselves, and the husband took Ady to leading Parisian specialists for treatment. During the worst phase of the disease the Diósis moved him to their own apartment, where Léda personally cared for him.

A sadness lurks in the poems written shortly after the diagnosis as when in *A Parisian Dawn* he wrote

> *this kiss-fed Paris never knew*
> *kisses more sad, more like a malady.*

At times he was terrified, and once like other frightened or superstitious Parisians he went to Madame Thebe, a famed clairvoyant of the day, and mockingly but curiously presented his palm for a reading. She disturbingly foretold that by the age of thirty he would be tremendously successful in his career or totally insane. But as the disease cleared, his self-confidence returned and in the later poems of the NEW VERSES there are indications that his illness was to become a creative stimulus.

Ady made no reference in the *Psalms for Leda* to his mistress's acts of tenderness. With dithyrambic madness he concentrated on all that was excruciating in the relationship. Breaking with the romantic tradition and its theme of subjection to the will of the beloved, he portrayed a man subjected to his own ideal. For the marvels that had been a part of the romantic tradition since the revival of Ovid, he substituted one marvel, his psychic self. For the traditional romantic love of solitude and privacy he substituted a desire to exhibit in the habiliments of dream imagery the privatissima of his emotional life. The meaning of his love he expounded in the light of Nietzschean heroism, declaring it to be the power that would conceive a child (his poetry) whom others would bring to fruition.

In his relations with Léda as well as with certain Parisiennes Ady was the eternal bachelor in pursuit of or flight from women. The exciting love acts he conceived of as invitation and arrival or dismissal and departure. In *Leda Aboard Ship*, for example, a state of intense excitement is attained because Léda is hovering in sight. Between arrival and departure, however, he experienced long periods of spiritual impotence.

Léda awoke the poet's awareness not of herself but of the realm of his own unconscious. With almost the first psalm the white ghost of an idealized Léda walks a castellated dreamland. The psychal guards, the eyes, fearfully watch the outer world, and only at midnight when the guards grow lax do the repressed emotions come to the surface. Whenever the poet studies Léda it is only because her eyes mirror the blessed marvels of himself. In *My Leda's Heart* her power to look into his soul creates love, which in turn sees her as no more than a symbol from the "grove of sombre marvels."

With the birth of this dual love the poet's conscious and unconscious forever haunt each other. The conscious as nemesis of the unconscious is the theme of *In Vain You Shadow Me* (which at first glance appears to treat of naked sadism) and of *The White Silence,* which is a confession that the furious struggle produces symptoms of madness. In the conflict between the ideal and the real, Léda, the voluptuous object of pleasure, is associated with pain, and in *The Fiery Sore* the poet expressed the desire to fuse the torments of love and syphilis into one intensely emotional experience. The peculiar Ady world of love is nowhere more breathlessly displayed than in *The Hackney Coach,* which depicts a vehicle of fantasy bearing the lovers to vicarious pleasures. But in the real world their relations were the exhausting storms of hedonism. On their own wings, unaided by conveyances of fantasy, they sail

> ... *into the autumn gloom*
> *shrieking, pursuing and pursued,*
> *two hawks with languid, drooping wings.*

In *A Woman's Lap* Ady identified woman as the material or life force and man as the polarized death force. This identification is also significantly implicit in the fact that nowhere does he ever represent woman as seeking the solution of death whereas for him it may seem the only solution. The difficulty of rubricating Ady's poetry is evident, however, in that in subsequent books the life force of woman becomes more and more a killer force akin to death.

The spiritual disharmony of this early phase of Ady's life is nowhere more evident than in his poems on money. Tied as he was to gentry attitudes, the underlying principles of capitalism were alien and perhaps even repugnant to him. Nevertheless, he was irresistibly drawn toward an adulation of this source of power. In 1806 Wordsworth had written his famous sonnet accusing his fellow men of giving their souls away and thinking of nothing but making money and spending it. The core of the poem is the idea that the nineteenth century was a great time for money-makers but not for thinkers or artists. Almost exactly a hundred years later Ady repudiated the intellectual's sublimated attitude and acknowledged the power of money over the soul of the artist. The two attitudes reflect one poet's recession from socially revolutionary ideas and the other's advance toward them, although for the time being Ady anticipated only what F. Scott Fitzgerald was to develop into a view of life—the struggle between fluid income and wealth as a solid possession.

Ady's longing for gold grew into an obsession as his struggle for meager honoraria from newspaper articles continued. A trip to the Riviera with Léda only whipped up the fury of his longing, and finally he wrote *The Yellow Flame* and *Lord Swine Head*. The latter poem, perhaps the peak of his achievement in the NEW VERSES, is comparable in its anguish to the Laocoon. The statuary magnificence of the poem is grounded in a Parisian experience. On having seen The Thinker at the Grand Palais, he said it was a pity Rodin had not created a statue of Money, for this would have been an awsome and appalling work. Some months later *Lord Swine Head* erupted into being as the poet wrote feverishly in a Budapest cafe, from where a friend rushed the poem stanza by stanza to a newspaper printer. The myth-making powers of the poet are utilized in this work for the revelation of eternally modern forces in primordial garb and for the description of life as being under constant pressures that allow no room for the expression of individuality. The clean-shaven physiognomy of a banker lurks behind the bristled snout of Lord Swine Head as surely as the Old Faun masks a poet.

The inner conflicts over money and love were not resolved in the NEW VERSES, and for some time thereafter the poet continued to be dominated by them. The solutions, however, are foreshadowed in poems that deal with the poet's dream-making or creative powers. One of the most remarkable of these poems is the *Scion of Midas*, in which the poet claims descent from the ass-eared Phrygian king and gives an imagistic illustration of the power the saint had observed in the "low and despised in the world, even things that are not, to bring to nothing things that are."

Although Ady occupied himself with the realm of the unconscious, he avoided the sterility with which complete absorption in introspectiveness threatens the creative mind and stood at an opposite pole from those European symbolists who made a literary dogma of abstention from political affairs. A red chariot pausing in the "misty mauve" of the NEW VERSES was a portent of at least one line of his thinking. It was also during this period that he became identified with the Social Democrats' support for an attempt of the Hapsburg Emperor to introduce universal suffrage into Hungary, a move designed by the Crown to counter the demands of the Independence Party for the creation of a national army.

The most overtly political aspect of the NEW VERSES, however, was its attack on a prime convention of "Magyar morality", namely, adherence to the picture drawn of Hungary by the great nineteenth century poets who in epic and song had given the Magyars that feeling of self-confidence in their national distinctiveness which national states have regarded as necessary to cultivate. The sure statements of Petőfi, who loved and stood squarely on the broad and open expanse of the steppes, gave way in Ady to a view of life from the ridges of doubt and paradox. This is evident, for example, in *The Hortobagy Poet*. Also, *On the Tisza*, which foreshadows many neopagan poems, boasts in the first stanza of the poet's measurelessly deep roots tapping the phylogenetic childhood but decries in the second stanza a scene from contemporary rural Hungary. The symbolism of the first stanza is intensely personal in origin. Upon first visiting the Louvre, Ady marveled at finding what seemed his own strange, swart face among the reliefs in the Assyrian-Egyptian collection. Thereafter he repeatedly spoke of his discovery, examining his features before a mirror and exclaiming in self-mockery that Ramses had not been more handsome.

In the localism of the Magyar poems with their trenchant criticism of the Hungarian scene the universality of their significance was all but lost on everyone. But the cry of the poet of Hortobágy that he could have been a "holy bard on any other part of earth" was like the cry of other European poets and artists of the late eighteenth and early nineteenth century who had turned against the life they saw around them. For the West European poet the cry was against the ugliness of industrial cities, slums, clatter, and tawdriness, and for Ady against an anachronistic social and political order.

The year following the publication of NEW VERSES was an *annus mirabilis* in Ady's creative life. Having fled once more to Paris, which he had come to regard as a Sherwood Forest (or in Ady's word Bakony, the legendary woodland hideaway of highwaymen) he plundered his striking originality to the full in creating a new book to which he gave the unchristian title of BLOOD AND GOLD.

In Budapest and the provincial strongholds the appearance of the new book augmented the fears of aristocrats and gentry that the poet was helping prepare a holocaust. This impression was strengthened by a declaration of faith which Ady published in a defiant challenge to his detractors: "I believe and vow that the revolutionary renovation of Hungary is inevitable. The blessed and marvelous storm is heralded by sacred gulls. Only a shrill restlessness is heard in social and political affairs, but in literature, art, and science the lightning bolts of certainty are here." The air thus cleared, little room existed to mistake the intent of BLOOD AND GOLD or to underestimate the seriousness of its contribution to the political reform movement.

The new book developed further the cyclical structure of NEW VERSES. However, BLOOD AND GOLD shows a striking advance toward a synthesis in that above all it is a treatment of the sources of creative power and the inter-mingling elements. Although from the point of view of poetic development NEW VERSES and BLOOD AND GOLD may be regarded as a unit, a spiritual alteration is perceptible as the "coltish flame" of the earlier work gave way to more sombre hues. The ineluctable whiteness that earlier envel-oped Léda deepened into black and scarlet, and the struggle against the "white satanic veil" was replaced by a strug-gle with a black and unbearably fecund creativity.

The interplay of the fear of death with love for the excite-ment of living is the subject of the opening cycle, *Kinsman of Death*. The presentimental arrival of death is described in *The Ghost Got Into Paris*, aesthetically one of Ady's most gratifying poems. The first stanza, referring in the external world to some early autumn-like days that actually occurred in Paris during the summer of 1906, states that the chill of death came during the dog-days as the poet walked along the Boulevard of Saint Michel. The second stanza reveals that the events in the external world corresponded with an anxiety suppressed in the poet's inner world:

> *small, twiggy songs within my spirit burned—*
> *purple and pensive, strange and smoky-hued.*

In the third stanza the repressed emotion comes to the sur-face as both the internal and external world speak of death. In the final stanza the anxiety is once more repressed and only the memory of a psychic disturbance, corresponding to the moan of trees in the outer world, remains in the con-scious mind. The tremulous subtlety of the poem derives from the delicate weaving of conscious allegory and uncon-scious symbolism into the expression of an almost impercep-tible mood half clearly and half unclearly understood. Beneath this Freudian world of symbols and allegories, however, there is an even stranger world of religious mysteries, and the autumn is less the month of August than of the mystical Ab.

Once the thought has risen to the surface, death is there-after recognized as the never plumbed depth of the unconscious from where arise the phantasmagorias that die in the shackles of life. Death is the subjective world that would make desires manifest without the distortions imposed on them by life. The poet describes himself as the kinsman of death because like death he loves those who refuse the distorted offerings of life.

The dream thoughts about death as the realm of creativity are the subject of *My Sons' Fate,* which describes the formation of poetry as the interplay between resistance to death and the evasion of this resistance. Beneath this theme lies Ady's continuous struggle with himself as an unfettered dreamer and a formal artist. The poetry resulting from this struggle is like that which Nietzsche imagined Greek art to be, namely, the outgrowth of a tension between the artistic sense, represented by Apollo, working not on objective materials but on savage unconscious urges, represented by Dionysus. This duality has escaped those critics who have tended to regard Ady as a writer incapable of conscious planning and living in a world where unconscious symbolism is the tyrant lord of creation. Ady is *par excellence* the genius of Coleridge's definition—the power of acting creatively under laws of its own origination.

My Sons' Fate is an abstract and non-pictorial representation of the dream thoughts about death which in *My Coffin Steed* and *The Black Piano* are translated into concrete dream imagery. In the first poem the unconscious is symbolized by a black coffin on which the conscious is commanded to ride by dreams symbolized as laconic (compare the dream condensation of Freudian terminology) and weak-eyed urchins who drum the coffin as they arrive at midnight and shuttle around with the speed of unfettered thought. As the poet rides his black mysterious coffin he sits on the closed lid, which is the dividing line between the world of dream and death. In his left hand he holds a bloody rein and in his right hand a whip, the pictorial representation of the line "I seek and shun the storm" in *My Sons' Fate.* The flames of sulphur, an allusion to the Hadean world, are reminders of the indeterminate distinction between the world of the preternatural and the supernatural. The laughter in the final stanza is the dream-translated weeping of a poet creating under the spell of cruel demons who come from an unknowable world. The black piano symbolizes the same psychic substratum as the black coffin. The instrument, however, is played not by dreams, which can see even though they are weak of sight, but by the completely blinded conscious which has abandoned its role of guiding the unconscious. The resultant music is the melody of life, which is made bearable only by the use of intoxicants. To the beat of this music, which like the original chaos lies at the very base of existence, the poet expends his life's blood, that is, gives himself up to death through creativity.

In the midst of his preoccupation with death Ady does not fail to keep in touch with reality. This is demonstrated in the curious poem *The Hotel Lodger* wherein he reflects on the contrast between his cheap Parisian hotel, symbol of the outer world, and the magic of his room number, the symbol of his poetic afflatus. (He did, in fact, live for a period in room thirty-six on the third floor in his favorite hotel at 15 Rue de Constantinople in Paris). The waiter who will some day announce his death, he states with almost amused detachment, will be aware only of his physical demise but will have no notion of the meaning of the magic numerals or of all the poet's intellectual struggles with death. Few poets since Dante have occupied themselves with the number three to the same extent as Ady, who also utilized tripartite titles for almost all his poems and frequently employed tricolon constructions of syntax.

The *Kinsman of Death* cycle deals with that substratum of the conscious which, if it were to triumph, would cause the utter annihilation or death of the conscious. *The Demon Guile* cycle deals with this same substratum but offers as a means of access to it not death but a state of self-forgetfulness induced by alcoholic draughts or other media. This state is characterized by the orgiastic impulse of Dionysian emotions which incite the poet to a frenzy of his symbolic powers. The symbols thus evolved are music and dance, non-concrete symbols which annihilate ordinary experience and penetrate into the true meaning of existence. These dithyrambic symbols are projections of the poet's very own self. The white creatures of the *Widow Bachelors' Dance* are such projections who under religious and civic interdiction carouse in the poet's soul during the spring fertility rites on Saint George's eve. The ecstasies of intoxication are followed by a dream-state in which the drunken realities of Dionysian emotion are translated into the Apollonian world of appearances or concrete images:

> *Saint George's day — the dance is done.*
> *Each widow bachelor turns and goes*
> *into a midnight yawning grave*
> *where bloom the woman and a rose.*

The final three stanzas symbolize the sudden awakening from the dream with the report of the "swift-sinewed spies", the quick effort of the partially awakened conscious to review and interpret the dream and finally the translation of the images when orgy and dream are done into the work of man. The explication of the *Widow Bachelors' Dance* as a creative process involving the emergence of concrete from non-concrete forms through a Delphian intoxication is strengthened by a passage in one of Ady's prose works, *The Magyar Pimodan* (after the Hotel Pimodan, where Gautier and Baudelaire chewed and smoked hashish): "Two states of ecstasy are to be found in alcohol, but only persons with very sensitive nervous systems are able to experience both of them. The first state is common to everyone who drinks; it inflames every inclination toward ecstasy and invests us with a feeling of great power. Toward dawn or day we undergo a period of sleep that is interrupted by queer periods of awakening. When we awake our head feels taut, we are the very soul of restless alertness, and we can link the most antipodal ideas together. Then all of a sudden at twilight, wherever we are, eternity envelops our still restless brain and heart. With this we have come completely to the sensation of art, and it is only at such times that I love Homer and that I am able to conceive Michelangelo as he should be conceived. I emphasize that this state of sensitivity, the period of an hour or two which reveals and betrays the greatest secrets, comes on the following evening. This state has no direct relation with alcohol poisoning or ecstasy; it is the perverse and magic manifestation of the nerves from which only these exclamatory words are lacking—we thank our dear master for having given us such sweet sorrows."

Ady created his most complex symbolization of the Dionysian and Apollonian worlds in the title poem to *The Demon Guile* cycle. The characteristics of Dionysus and Apollo are masked in the demon into one symbol of a psyche with twofold aspects, a deeper and more primitive one which would express without distortion the naked realities of self-forgetfulness and a more recent one which would give representation to these realities through art (or dreams in Ady's terminology). The first five stanzas of the poem are a depiction of this dual inheritance from an archaic world that came into existence with the dawn of civilization when the two elements began a struggle in the arena of the poet's psyche symbolized as a tavern beneath the windows of which the outer world swirls by and clamors for admission. During this struggle, Demon Guile on one hand prompts the poet to the ecstasies of intoxication and on the other hand wrestles with him in an effort to transform these ecstasies into presentable dreams or art. On the table where the poet drinks are a cross and two candles, funereal symbols that indicate the table top is all which separates the world of self-forgetfulness from the world of death. Stanza six depicts Demon Guile as forever having his steed ready to depart, a symbolization of the evanescent nature of ecstasies. The realization of this evanescence causes the poet in the following nine stanzas to reflect on the barrenness and absurdity of the world outside the tavern to which he must return when ecstasy and dream are done, and he longs to be released from the struggle that is waged on behalf of life. In the final two stanzas the demon departs for a new rebirth in the westward course of civilization, and the poet sinks beneath the table into final death.

The close relationship of creativity to death is also the theme of the *Good Prince Silence,* in which the *I* is the poet's symbolization of his own conscious self wandering in the realms of the unconscious where in psychic unrest it creates midst forces beyond understanding. Here the conscious is forever stalked by fear of the disintegration of creative sanity and the abandonment of the conscious to the final curse of silence.

The following cycles, *Money, Our Lord* and *Leda's Golden Statue,* deal with the life forces of materialism and love. Even as Jesus had renounced, without rejecting, the materialistic world with his magnificent "Render unto Caesar" so Ady renounced, without rejecting, the world of Christ with his *Judas and Jesus.* The renunciation came after a grievous struggle:

> *Upon basalt of Golgotha*
> *I gash my heart-beat's anguished plea.*
> *O Christ, my poet, holy Form,*
> *I bartered Thee.*

The justification follows:

> . . .
> *A woman longs for money, silk,*
> *and waits for me.*

Ady cannot accept Christianity to the exclusion of all else because Christ's renunciation of life and his dreams of a Kingdom of Heaven would have forever blocked the realization of his own dream of knowing in life the freedom of creative activity he associated with death. The state of being poor in spirit is incompatible with the state of being a poet.

In NEW VERSES Ady stated his obsession for gold and gave one possible solution, complete and absolute gratification. With BLOOD AND GOLD the struggle becomes more complex and the professed solutions increasingly subtle. In *Only One Moment* he feigns to be content with brief moments of plentifulness that come like the light of inspiration and make everything burn in an "immortal blaze." In *Lazarus Before the Palace* he resigns himself to the role of a beggar pampered by the wealthy because they fear his revolutionary powers. In *The Usurer's Garden* he feigns contentment with his lot as one of the "lads of Athens" who founder that the usurer's flowers may bloom. The rationalization is that it matters little who enjoys life as long as someone enjoys it to the full. *Flight from Worry* is the romanticized notion of a previous existence in a nomad society not based on a money economy from where the black stallion of his creativity had been lured into pursuing the guldens of the "bright Western heaven."

Finally, in *Monk of Mammon* with its diabolically inverted symbol of monkhood Ady arrives at a solution which abandons wish-fulfilment for the infinite resignation of a person who antithetically holds fast to that which he has given up. Thus with one compromise he satisfies the varied demands of his psychic life, and without rejecting the world of life he places his reliance on a world beyond the senses. The contrast between the icy sculpture of the monk and his burning passion for life is like the contrast between Homer's blindness and the brightness of the Odyssean world. It was to such a contrast that Ady looked for an intensification of his own creative powers. Unlike the wise man who prayed to have neither poverty nor riches, he prayed to have both.

With BLOOD AND GOLD Ady abandoned the theme of money, and in his following book the cycle corresponding to *Money, Our Lord* is of a bright socialist red. Nevertheless, money remained a disturbing factor in his life, as evinced by his pursuit of gambling during frequent visits to the Riviera with Léda. In a prose work, *Portus Herculis Monoeci*, he laid bare the meaning that gambling held for his creative life: "We must love the Gamble, the Chance, the Either/Or because if a spirit of life exists we can discover and understand it only in this formless, holy form. We must feel we are free beggars, the ragged descendants of gods, perhaps the victims of a gambling loss who must keep on playing. He who plays does so not with a bank or with another rich or poor Lazarus but with the Lord into whose bosom the biblical Lazarus departed."

With the title poem to the cycle *Leda's Golden Statue* Ady fuses the two life forces of materialism and love into one aesthetic projection of his obsession for gold and for Léda. Just as in the *Monk of Mammon* he saw himself transformed into ice in contrast to the heat and passion of life, so he sees Léda transformed into a glacial image of gold contrasting with his own burning body. This is the solution that was promised in the *Scion of Midas* with the prophecy of the gold-making powers of the poet's dream.

With *On Dead Seas*, the first poem of the new Léda cycle, the white ghost of the Psalms is reintroduced but surrounded by a black and scarlet aureole and bearing objective characteristics. Following a prophecy that she will die within his soul, the white ghost disappears from the Léda poems and her place is taken by a lifelike symbol of beauty and ugliness, love and hate, mother and mistress. The seed of the later Ady-Léda tragedy is already evident in that she exists for him not as an objective reality but as what he says she is.

Advancing beyond his trenchant criticism of Hungary in the NEW VERSES, Ady describes in *The Magyar Messiahs* those mystic souls who attract society in their wake but are treated with indifference by a society subject to traditional requirements. He sees in the legendary character of Saint Margaret, represented as a personality who had developed a sensitivity exceeding that of her contemporaries, a messiah who would shape the rough materials of life into new and delicate patterns. In the poet at the court of King Matthias he sees a dreamer who would give shape to a truly national culture. In *City of Clouds* the visionary Magyar character is portrayed in imagery of breath-taking beauty and stirring insight into the genius and weaknesses of a people. *I Am Not a Magyar?* asserts the genuineness and antiquity of the poet's national character and puts him in a place of honor in the gallery of the preceding messiahs.

Although Ady was profoundly immersed in the problem of a Hungarian renascence, among his most endearing traits was one that placed him side by side with Béla Bartók as a creative artist interested in Hungary's non-Magyar elements and neighbors. Given the traditional East European propensity for cultivation of a strictly national culture or for leap-frogging, in a cultural sense, to Paris, Vienna, or London, the phenomenon of Ady and Bartók is a refreshing one and re-grettable only in that so few East European artists have followed their lead. The cultural disarray of the region and its counterpoint in historic Hungary was the reflection, as Ady sensed, of a political weakness that was to produce the seeds of tragedy for both Eastern Europe as a whole and Hungary as well.

BLOOD AND GOLD concludes with the cycle *Toward Tomorrow*, a paean of praise to the poet's creative powers that bear him on one level swiftly ahead of his contemporaries toward a mystic morrow and on another level from his private universe toward a never converging universe of mankind.

The God-intoxicated Man

The period from 1907 to 1913 in which he wrote ON ELIJAH'S CHARIOT, LONGING FOR LOVE, OF ALL MYSTERIES, and THIS FUGITIVE LIFE marks the development of Ady as a religious and social poet. The Dionysian who appeared in BLOOD AND GOLD perched atop a black piano yielded to a poet seeking a dialogue with God. In this search he examined the central problems of evil, as he saw them, the inner duality of man, which he had earlier portrayed so vividly, and the effect on man of a degrading social and political system.

At the beginning of this period Ady took only faltering steps toward developing his political philosophy. Having fled Budapest in the summer of 1906, he returned in the autumn of the following year to reassess his positon and reflect on the possibility of coming to terms with Hungarian conservatism and rehabilitating his house of Rahab. The importance he attached to securing his position at home is indicated by the fact that he spent the following eight months in Hungary, his longest home stay during the years 1904 to 1912.

Ady clearly felt himself caught between individualism and tradition. In the period of NEW VERSES and BLOOD AND GOLD he could well have accepted Emerson's statement on self-reliance: "No law can be sacred to me but that of my nature. Good and bad are but names very readily transferable to that or this; the only right is after my constitution, the only wrong what is against it." But by the time he wrote ON ELIJAH'S CHARIOT his desire to be accepted and understood by the Hungarian reading public as a whole presented him with the problem of reconciliation with the dominant social group.

Both as a newspaperman and a poet he felt the constant need of a public and openly desired acclamation to a degree few writers have before or after him. But his first two books had gained for him only the recognition of the more progressive urban Jews, a few intellectual proletarians, and a younger generation of writers, artists, and women. Barred to him were the traditionally important classes and consequently denied to him, at least such was his reaction, his rightful place of prestige in the country's cultural and political world.

Not only had Ady failed to win for himself a wide reading public but in 1907 he found himself without a mass publishing outlet. Ownership of the progressive daily newspaper which had provided him with a reading public passed into conservative hands. Of the remaining half dozen or so publishers of large dailies only the Social Democrats and the Freemasons opened their columns to him, although not without reservations about his usefulness or reputation.

To find a way out of the publishing dilemma he participated with some writers of kindred mind in self-help measures. The first of these was the establishment of a literary journal by a small group of writers in Nagyvárad. Appearing under the name of *Tomorrow*, the first issue was a sensation, and it seemed a literary movement as important to Hungarian literature as *Lyric Ballads* to English literature had been launched. However, Ady was well aware the country was not large enough to support co-axial Budapest-Nagyvárad literary movements, and he quickly lost interest in further participation. But in 1908 a similar group of kindred literary men established in Budapest an enduring periodical called the *West*. Thereafter the literary history of the country was dominated by the rivalry between this periodical and the *New Times*, a traditional journal headed by Ferenc Herczeg, a prose writer and dramatist, and Jenő Rákosi, publisher of an influential daily newspaper and advocate of a policy of "magyarization" of the minorities to create a state of thirty million Magyars. The members of these two groups were separated by a social gulf paralleled by a less distinct nonetheless real ethnic difference. Both Herczeg and Rákosi, like the majority of writers clustered about the *New Times*, were of the German middle class. The editors, propagandists, and financial supporters of the *West*, on the other hand, were urban middle class Jews and bourgeois "radicals", while its outstanding writers were mostly of Magyar gentry background. It was in this avant garde group that Ady found his most enduring friends.

Ironically, Ady first gave vent to his dissatisfaction in an essay published in the *West*, combining his expression of malaise with a phillipic against some of his more fanatical followers:

"I was useful, indeed very useful, for a battering ram at the beginning of my career in this Budapest which is united only in its lack of culture, in this sassy city which is false although filled with zeal. I had a good hard head that possessed the *passe-partout* of a sombre and, for the nonce, harmless Magyar who by accident was also of the right religion. I rose against every wall, first against that of the Scythians and the analphabets because I had first claim on them, but I also rode against the Hebrews whenever it was necessary. I made a breach or two, dispelled a superstition or two, and perhaps conquered a man or two. But a miracle is a miracle only for two days. People sobered up and cleared me away along with the fallen. My head is a bit battered, but my eyes are clear and see how those who most passionately urged me to jump now walk into the breach. It is my fate to be born a man who smooths the way for others and for the future. Even more than by this fate I am hurt by the fact that no one sees my bloody head and breast. In the days when all this happened I had to choose madmen or buffoons as my companions whenever I wanted a bit of relief or a friend besides alcohol. Those who according to the external order of things should have stood by me as brothers pretended to be busied with other affairs and looked forward with pleasure to the days when they no longer would find it necessary to concern themselves with my person. Perhaps my feminine soul dominates me and compels me to perform many unfair deeds, but my anger is just. I anticipate with laughter the philosopher who will try to comfort me in the light of domestic and foreign examples by saying it has always been so. I am not impressed by Akiba or any other more genuine philosopher. The professional philosopher writes for professors; the individual, on the other hand, is his own philosopher. Everyone who is able has the right to forgive his own faults and claim from men that which he believes should be claimed."

At about the time the above appeared, Ady approached Jenő Rákosi with a request for a meeting. Rákosi's reply was cold, probably because he doubted Ady's readiness to approach Canossa in the proper spirit. But concerned by the sudden popularity of the *West* the publishers of *New Times*, Singer and Wolfner, felt Ady should be wooed into the conservative camp. Overtures were made and several of Ady's poems appeared in the conservative periodical. Then Ady contracted with Singer and Wolfner for the publication of his forthcoming book ON ELIJAH'S CHARIOT and accepted a position as regular correspondent of their journal. Several members of the "liberal wing" of the conservatives became Ady's steady companions.

It was not until the appearance of Ady's so-called Duk-Duk article that the Westerners began seriously to wonder whether the poet had deserted them "just for a riband to stick in his coat." Written in the form of a dialogue with two representatives of the *New Times*, the significant passages were the following:

"I (Ady) am not the representative, leader or even the member of any kind of secret society. I have nothing in common with the so-called Hungarian modernists and my alleged literary revolt is not a revolt. Cunning little men grab my coattails because I am tolerant and a bit impractical, but I am not to blame. There is in Melanesia a society called the Duk-Duk, a kind of primeval freemasonry in which the leader seldom learns who he is. I may be such a leader, but I feel a greater community of interest than anyone with the old Magyars, whom I resemble. My dear sirs, do you think I have irreparably hurt you and those who feel the same as you do?"

"Your men claim they must settle accounts with everyone who lived prior to your time. In fact, the Hungarian modernists are preparing for this and you must be aware of it."

"No, I am not, and I do not know anything of a revolution which allegedly rages in my name. I do not regard myself as more modern than Balassa, Csokonai, or Petőfi (outstanding Hungarian poets of the 16th, 18th and 19th centuries respectively). It is well known that modernists are solid men, the classicists of the future. I do not acknowledge anything in common with those who have neglected to learn Hungarian. I have nothing to do with those who want to alter Hungarian literature on the basis of having read some German books in cheap editions. I have nothing to do with the sickly, the impotent, and all those young men who hate me more than does Pál Gyulai (a critic), who, I happen to know, does not hate me so much after all. Neither I nor my contemporaries can evaluate who I am and what I signify. But it is my right to announce that I hate all the nobodies who swagger in my name and under my sign more than in general people are wont to hate me!"

The guiding geniuses behind the *West* and, in fact, all the liberal elements reacted with the wounded cry of the betrayed. Ady wrote to his brother, "Because of the *New Times* article the whole world has slammed the door in my face (I hope only for a few weeks more, although I do not know if I can stand it that long). I have received and am receiving frightful letters. I cannot sleep or work."

Among these "frightful letters" was one from his friend and maecenas, Lajos Hatvany:

"No one, no matter how blind he may be, can fail to see that your article is directed in the most cruel manner against those who with the greatest sincerity and selflessness have written good things about you ... It shall be as you want it; I shall never again in my life write a line about you. I am canceling the lecture which I was to deliver on your poetry before the Society of Social Sciences. Unfortunately I can no longer withdraw two articles which I wrote in praise of you. In all these papers I treat you as a revolutionary, which is obviously against your wish. I hope that Ferenc Herczeg will write reviews for you which will not grate on your conservative attitudes. Your will be done ... I am sorry you jumped into the trap for Herczeg, who I hope will see that you become a member of the Petőfi Society (citadel of those prominent writers countenanced by the Government for their "correct" political attitude)... The result will be that men with less talent than yourself will have power over you... The tone and the *croquis*-like character of your article is not worthy of you. It is an unworthy appearance before a new reading public... Privately I shall remain your friend and an admirer of your poetry, but publicly we shall have nothing to do with each other..."

Despite the hurt tone of the letter, the curious hold which Ady had on his followers is illustrated by a passage from one of Hatvany's later works:

"In truth, I should have made up with Ady: I should have begged his forgiveness because *he* had offended *me*. I feel that I neglected my duty in having failed to do so... I acted as if I did not know that the wickedness of a poet is to be preferred over the false virtue of a philistine. Ady's wickedness was superior because he cast away all that was conventional; he stood far removed from everyone else and he was close only to himself, that is, not to his social self but to his true human self, which is total humanity."

Shortly after the publication of the Duk-Duk article an invitation to join the Petőfi Society came from Ferenc Herczeg. Ady declined, and at the same time he severed his ties with the *New Times*. The following weeks he spent in writing letters to injured friends. The anger of the Social Democrats he attempted to allay by writing *Ark of the Covenant*, one of his finest proletarian poems. The Duk-Duk affair finally quieted down. A 1909 issue of the *West* was dedicated to Ady, who remained a hero to the entire liberal camp.

The circumstances in which Ady found himself have occurred time and again in the history of rebellions, and Thoreau had posted a bitter warning: "I believe that what so saddens the reformer is not his sympathy with his fellows in distress, but, though he be the holiest son of God, is his private ail. Let this be righted... and he will forsake his generous companions without an apology." Although many literary rebels have been tempted and have paused to listen to the words of seeming conciliation, not all have turned back. In yielding to no more than a momentary indecision, Ady established a standard which on future occasions was to play a hidden but significant role in the courageous deportment of Hungarian writers.

The battle between liberals and traditionalists over Ady was to be repeated after his death in the form of a struggle prolonged to the present day between anti-communists and pro-communists for the possession of his soul. The struggle is sharpening the outlines of his uniqueness. He fits into the communist mold only for those who ignore the overwhelming bulk of his poetry. He fits into the Western mold more readily, but the mold becomes uncomfortable unless a part of his poetry is regarded as window dressing.

Ady passed through the Duk-Duk affair without altering his course. Nevertheless, the mood, or the reaction to it, had its effect and he passed many days at Érmindszent, where the life of the village he had left behind flooded his poetry with new life and strength. The Calvinism that had permeated his early youth reemerged as an agonized search to meet God. At the same time his first proletarian and revolutionary poems appeared. The Bible became his constant source of reading, and during the course of the following years he became almost superstitiously attached to his personal copy. On one occasion he left his beloved book in a tavern and spent two panic-stricken days trying to retrieve it.

Ady's search for God took place within the frame of Calvinism in the sense that he never abandoned the Calvinist Church or felt a compulsion to abandon it as may well have been the case had he belonged to the Catholic Church. He prowled, to use Franz Kafka's parable, about the foot of Mount Sinai without ever finding the faith to ascend it. However, he retained to the end the faith that there was a scalable mount which could be harmonized with the one scaled by Moses even as harmonizing tradition apparently combined two physical mountains into a single Sinai.

Beneath Mount Sion, the first of his cycles devoted to religious experience, testifies to the inner contradictions that accompanied, or rather impelled, him on his quest to meet God. The title poem is a confession that the Mount is inaccessible to one who approaches it with the burden of metaphysical contradictions. In *Adam, Where Art Thou?, The Lord's Arrival,* and *Prayer After War* Ady sees a personal and loving God who reveals himself in the midst of strife. In *Love Me, God* and *The Great Whale* he reverts to a God of myth-making and postulates an impersonal ground of being. The first of these two poems represents the God of the myth world as an overwhelming stabilizing principle, "the primal Beast", who like Lord Swine Head allows no freedom for individual endeavor. In the second, God is a mighty Whale on whose slippery back the empirical forms of life dance helplessly about. *Scourge Me, Lord* represents God as the image of a great father who punishes his son for his sins, especially the sin, as elaborated by Freud, of taking women belonging to the father. This theme is intriguingly developed in *The Nocturnal God,* one of the best examples of the manner in which Ady was prone to juxtapose mysticism and carnality. In the *Trumpet of God* the divinity is a clarigation, an awakening of the revolutionary powers latent in those who have suffered oppression and injustice through the millenia. *The Cheerless God,* the final poem of the cycle, conceives God as an inscrutable and impersonal force able neither to bless nor punish, love nor hate; this God is comparable, in the inner world of man, to the blind performer who tears at the keys of the black piano. Amid all these inner contradictions, the poet is aware that he sits on the unfavored left hand of God and that the right hand is reserved for those of simple faith.

In the following religious cycle, *All Right, God*, written during the height of his attempt to seek a reconciliation with Hungarian conservatism, the poet attained a spirit of piety in face of the old Mount Sion which he was scarcely to know again. He stood in the overpowering radiance of the divine and found relief only in humility and the postures assumed by the medieval saints.

The soul that had stopped to listen to the call of Mount Sion plunged, with the remarkable poem *Cain Killed Abel*, into an act of suicide-murder whereby the Cain within the soul rose to reenact the slaying of Abel. With this symbolization of his conquest over the problem of evil posed by his inner psychic duality, Ady entered upon a new dynamic stage, evident in *The Duel* and in *The Straight Star*, in which with the symbol of a "star that fleets from void to void and never finds a goal" he indicated he had ceased to revolve about his own self.

The rising of Cain and the killing of the other self resulted in the release of boundless energies which, with the following book, THIS FUGITIVE LIFE, brought Ady toward the culminating point of his evolution as a mystic. Accompanying this development was a sense of liberation experienced as a result of a decision to resign the aspirations of the past and resume a forward movement. The resignation comes with a tender lovingness in the humanity-embracing poem *The Spring Sunset*. The same spirit permeates the love poems, *Loves of Autumn* with its haunting insect music and *Girls as Well* with the infinite resignation contained in the stanza:

> How beautiful all alien things on which
> only with eyes I dwell —
> good spirit, money, chance, success,
> and girls as well.

No longer is the resignation of the kind described in *Monk of Mammon* in which riches are given up only for the sake of desiring them all the more. Rather it is of the type characterizing a man stripping himself of impedimenta in preparation for an arduous journey. In addition to this sense of resignation a spirit of rebirth breathes through such poems as *The Sorrows of Resurrection* and *The Afternoon Moon* with its Pythagorean motif.

44

It was after the above developments that Ady perceived the complete and joyous presence of God through the ecstatic vision of *Epiphany,* in which sound, taste, and light are confused into one chaotic experience of synaesthesia. As described by Bergson in his study on the nature of mystical inspiration, ecstasy is the state wherein the mystic feels that "God is there, and the soul is God. Mystery is no more. Problems vanish, darkness is dispelled, everything is flooded with light." But an ecstatic experience is not final as Bergson goes on to state: "Though the soul becomes, in thought and feeling, absorbed in God, something of it remains outside; that something is the will, whence the soul's action, if it acted would quite naturally proceed. Its life, then is not yet divine. The soul is aware of this, hence its vague disquietude, hence the agitation in repose which is the striking feature of what we call complete mysticism: it means that the impetus has acquired the momentum to go further, that ecstasy affects indeed the ability to see and to feel, but that there is besides the will, which itself has to find its way back to God. When this agitation has grown to the extent of displacing everything else, the ecstasy has died out, the soul finds itself alone again, and sometimes desolate. Accustomed for a time to a dazzling light, it is now left blindly groping in the gloom" (Henri Bergson, *The Two Sources of Morality and Religion* published by Henry Holt and Company, Inc., 1935). And so it was with Ady, for with the following book, LOVE OF OURSELVES, he fell back completely on himself in his darkest night. One of the great but little known poems in this book is *Shake Up Your Heart,* which is a startling description of the psychological block.

With the new Léda cycle, *Between Leda's Lips,* Ady rejected the veridical nature of the golden statue he had created during the blood and gold period:

> *Why does art or sculpture seek*
> *to entice you from my soul,*
> *for among the cold and quick*
> *who can still on me bestow*
> *your incomparable warmth?*

Although she briefly grew more real, by the time the MYSTERIES OF LOVE was written in 1910 a mood of weariness reflected the growing exhaustion of his relationships with Léda. Seven years of accumulated hurts both real and imagined resulted in quarrels that grew increasingly more frequent and venemous. *The Third Floor* was written as the result of one such quarrel in which Ady took offense at Léda's captious support of an attack by Jenő Rákosi, who had compared him to a certain madman accustomed to

45

entertain himself by inviting his visitors to jump from the third floor window of his apartment. Ady's incessant and unconcealed affairs also contributed to these quarrels, but perhaps the most important reason for the growing estrangement was that he had waxed independent of Léda. In *The Woman's Due* he acknowledged her role in his poetic development, but the acknowledgment contained an open reference to her self-seeking interest:

> *I know you only guard yourself*
> *by the grim jealous watch you keep,*
> *but by your stolen march you forced*
> *death to recede.*

In a short autobiography that appeared in the *West* he wrote in a similar vein: "I worked on a newspaper and wrote articles; obviously I would have perished or begun a sensible life had someone not come for me. This someone was a woman, who came because one of my poems had reached her. She took me by the hand and did not let me go until we reached Paris. There she forced on me her will that she might burgeon through me if she could."

Ady toyed with the idea of a complete break. The conflicting pulls which in his public life had led to the Duk-Duk affair began to exercise divergent influences in his private life. Although his mother threatened to disown him unless he severed relations with Léda, she later received Léda in Érmindszent (see *A Walk Around My Birthplace*) and grew fond of the lady who had contributed so much to making her son a great poet. However, when her younger son married happily into a propertied family, she wanted her elder son also to settle down to a quiet life. The younger brother lent himself to the mother's cause, pointing out that Léda, "the slowly withering woman", was no longer a help but a hindrance.

Ady hesitated, and it was months later, in the beginning of 1911, that he decided to go to Paris once more. The quarrels broke out with renewed fury. A certain Raymond appeared with increasing frequency in Léda's home. After a few weeks Ady left for Budapest only to return almost immediately to Paris, for the seventh and last time. From Paris he accompanied Léda to Florence, Pisa, and Rome, and in the Eternal City the fury of their quarrels reached a new height. Ady's friend and cicerone in Rome wrote the following account of the poet's mood: "He opened his soul and forced me to look in. What I saw was appalling. A passion that had been enkindled long ago and had fateful consequences for his life and poetry was dying out. He was still playing with it, puffing it, and inciting it, but only to let it die out again. This was a frightening game intended to cause himself and others suffering. Frequently the game was blood-chilling and inexplicable. In the warm nights as we walked home along the Via del Tritone his tongue heavy with alcohol expressed with remarkable clarity the thoughts of his illuminated brain, and I thought I heard in my soul the screeching of his perverse and Poe-like demons. The life that was behind him! The oceans of passion he had waded!"

The Chastity Belt, which is in many ways the most striking poem Ady wrote during the period, is the ultimate epitomization of his frequent avowal that life is kept in a state of purity by the intensity of desire. Like Gotama, he saw desire as a central problem of human life. For Ady, however, the problem was not to reduce desire to manageable proportions but to gain from it maximum drive. Although he acknowledged a necessary relation between desire and resignation, he saw this relation not as an ebb and flow but as a process by which the individual divests himself of inferior desires, leaving in isolated intensity the final desire for eternal renewal of creativity (see especially *Above All Miracles*). Few aspects of Ady's multifarious ideas are as essential to an understanding of his poetry as his concept of desire. Within the frame of such understanding a deeper meaning is taken on by what at first appears to be mere eroticism.

Sans Fear, Sans Faith, Sans Hope

Ady had dealt until the year 1913 with three major problems of evil: the debasement of ordinary mankind and the arrest of the powers of genius through immoral social and political systems; the death-in-life state of the individual resulting from his inner duality and his consequent inability to meet any situation with his whole being; and the loneliness of the individual man, especially the genius, in his inability to meet others, or be met in an encounter of love and understanding. With the approach of World War I he turned in poems of apocalyptic grandeur to a fourth problem of evil—war. Although he desired no personal part in this conflict which he abhorred and looked upon as a tragic turning point in the thousand-year-old history of his country, upon a symbolic battlefield he became a poet of war as he had once been a poet of Money, Intoxicants, Sickness, and Woman.

During this last period of his creative life, the period of LOVE OF OURSELVES, WHO SEES ME?, LEADING THE DEAD, and THE LAST BOATS, he reached new heights of power and plunged to new depths of weakness, some of his poems reflecting the pallor of a wasting genius exhausted by nervous and physical disorders. Disturbed by these weaknesses and the obvious failure of a long mock-heroic epic entitled MARGARET WANTS TO LIVE, Hatvany wrote:

"You are lacking concentration and the intensive cultivation of magnificent talent... Your poems are disconnected and capricious. When you arrived on the literary scene with new motives, your weakness did not matter. In every volume from BLOOD AND GOLD to OF ALL MYSTERIES you have four or five poems which are a unit in form, content, atmosphere, and fundamental conceptions. In the latest volume (LOVE OF OURSELVES) there are magnificent beginnings, strokes, and lines, but the total effect is a nervous and snakelike strumming. Perhaps I am wrong but this is how I feel. The fortunate genius, the Goethean genius, is new in every phase of his life. But you are still writing your BLOOD AND GOLD. Well enough. This is also a great deal. Your progress, however, is not a matter of renascence but of a narrower, more pregnant, and more suggestive activity in the great Adyworld. In short, you are not moving in the direction of artistic cultivation but are casting old motives into new poems in a more nervous and rhapsodic manner. This intense nervousness gives your lyrics that certain ode-like madness which Vörösmarty (a ninteenth century writer) had. However, he

48

was the master of his hallucinations, you are the servant of yours. The author of *The Demon Guile* was a lord, an aristocrat. It is a pity to abdicate . . ."

Ady's answer came in the form of a poem, *New Hunnish Legend*, which is one of the most telling he wrote from the autobiographical point of view. With this "legend" he not only traced, as he had done before, the source of his unique genius to the most primitive roots of his people, but he also accepted Hungarian civilization, which is sometimes regarded as a grandiose provincialism in the heart of Europe, as the direct legacy of the ancient nomad and warrior culture lying at the base of civilization in Europe and Asia. The poet who had once "outgrown his kind" passed to a creative and procreative identification with his forbears. This retransformation of his artistic life he made without sacrifice to his creative impulse for some of his greatest poems were still to come.

With changes taking place in his attitude toward the society around him, his relations with Léda were also reaching a crisis. In February of 1912 he suffered a nervous breakdown and entered the Városmajor Sanatorium in Budapest. The cure gave him the opportunity to plan and write *Letter of Dismissal*, a poem which irrevocably broke off his eight-year-old affair with Léda. It is doubtful that in the love poetry of the world there is anything to match the cruelty of this poem, a cruelty, however, which arises logically from his earlier love psalms in which Léda had found so much pleasure. Upon publication of the poem, Mr. Diósi pursued his own logic by returning his dedicated copies of Ady's books of poetry with a note "Return to Ady, the faithless snake."

As a prose motto to the poem Ady wrote the following lines, which he later removed: "Beware if you have counted a great deal on a woman because she will be unable to forgive you even after her death. While your male superiority commands you to fly from her, she broods, a characteristic of her symbolic and incomplete essence. In revenge she will try to find some opportune and representative robbers to relieve you of your pride. Worship the one woman who lives within your vain and godly self so that your flight will not be disturbed by feminine wranglings. (A poem from an as yet unnumbered chapter of a new Holy Script which I shall write)."

The "representative robbers" is evidence that a long-suffering mistress had taken revenge. The horrendous nature of the retaliatory poem is underscored by the fact that it was published in a widely read journal.

The *Letter of Dismissal* not only brought to end an old love but also signaled an army of women that the poet had turned from an old frustration and was ready for the new impulses of a creative love. Ady wrote: "Man is always on the trail of some woman ... If he brokenly recounts the past, he pursues the shadows of old flames." His rich, dark brown hair was streaked with only a few lines of gray; his large brown eyes gleamed from a creole face. His fame, or notoriety, was at its height. Amorous letters, which made up two-thirds of the hundreds of letters he received, came pouring in, and contrary to his past practice he began to pay close attention to them. The younger and more innocent the writer appeared to be the more he was inclined to reply.

He became acquainted in the sanatorium with a young woman whom he called Ada, "melting your name and mine", and addressed several of the poems in the *Prayer for Deception* cycle to her. But upon visiting her home he discovered to his consternation she was married and the mother of two children. Shocked by her lack of morals, he abruptly left her.

With the end of his cure Ady moved into quarters in Pest, and phantom concubines began to move in and out of his bachelor apartment and his verse. One of these phantoms was a tantalizing, dark-skinned young student, beautiful as a gypsy princess, whom he desired because "she was the blackest girl I had ever seen." A night with her brought him a mild heart attack. When his brother arrived in answer to urgent summons, he found a terribly worried girl applying cold compresses to her incapacitated lover. With the arrival of help she slipped on her red coat and whisked away into the night. Ady carried on some further experimentations with the young nymphomaniacs of Pest whom he celebrated in *Of Youthful Arms*, but finally he swept them from his life with a poem on the female pikes, those insatiably voracious fish of the seas.

A doctor who frequently attended Ady had this comment to make on the health of his famous patient: "It is not true that Ady was paralytic or that he died of alcoholism. To my knowledge he suffered from a diseased aorta during the last ten years of his life. It was this aorta which ruptured and caused him to bleed to death. What caused the diseased condition of his aorta? Syphilis? Yes, and alcohol as well. But it was also caused by his many passions, sufferings, angers, and joys. I examined him often over a period of many years, and I was always puzzled by the laborious effort of his heart, an effort that was excessive and inexplicable."

Within a half year after his release from Városmajor Ady was again in a poor nervous condition. At the insistence of some of his friends he visited the famous Freudian professor Sándor Ferenczi. He called with trepidation but left jubilant because it was the doctor's expressed opinion he was not in need of psychoanalytic treatment. Ferenczi privately told several of Ady's friends that the poet was obviously very sick but that it was his belief a doctor should not meddle with the mind of a genius lest art suffer. In lieu of psychoanalysis

Ferenczi suggested Ady be placed in the Maria-Grün sanatorium of Kraft-Ebbing in Gratz.

Despite deviations from the regimen at the sanatorium, his health began to improve in a remarkably short time, and he soon fell in love with a young woman named Mylitta, one of the patients at the sanatorium with whom he carried on flirtations. Like Ada she was a wife and mother; nevertheless, he pursued the affair seriously for a number of months and addressed to her a cycle of poems entitled *Red Autumn Flowers* that matches, and in an instance or two (especially *Your Fiery Throne*) surpasses, his best Léda creations. Like Léda, she is a dual person—Babylonian goddess and the woman.

Before the Mylitta affair had ended a letter arrived from Léda: "With an infinite, inexpressible, and deathly desire I want to see you for a few minutes. I don't even know why, for I have nothing to say, I only want to see you for a minute or two and then go on. Perhaps it would help me go more calmly . . ." Léda asked for a meeting at the railroad station in Vienna, where the Budapest-Paris express paused for a few minutes. The poet, who was traveling on "unseemly paths of youth", failed to reply.

The Mylitta affair and others were followed in November 1913 by Ady's meeting with Zsófia Dénes, a young widow of intellectual attainments, who like Léda was a Catholic convert of Jewish origin. A quick decision to marry was never realized because Zsófia's mother objected violently to the poet on the grounds of his sickness. The marriage plans were abandoned without acrimony, and the two remained fast friends until the poet's death. The only "letter of dismissal" she received was the beautiful *Hellas Sent You.* Zsófia Dénes confessed in a sensitively written biography of Ady that subconsciously she used her mother's opposition as a shield to protect herself from the hurts that would have awaited her as Ady's wife.

Among the intriguing pages of Zsófia Dénes's book is an account of a visit she made with Ady, at his insistence, to an insane asylum where he enjoyed the greatest of popularity among the inmates, whom he frequently visited. Ady was deeply gratified by the personal and literary acceptance he had won there. Some twenty copies of his poems lay about on the tables in the reading room; the inmates declaimed his verses and played Béla Reinitz's wierd musical renditions on the piano; they addressed him as "master" and regarded him as the final critic of the verses they had composed.

Before the end of the Zsófia Dénes affair, tantalizing letters had been arriving from Bertuka Boncza. She was a member of a gentry family; her father, after acquiring a moderate fortune on the stock market, built a castle at Csucsa in Transylvania and was a prominent figure in official circles. At first Bertuka wrote in the role of a little relative, addressing the poet as "my dear big brother Endre" and signing herself as "your little sister." She even discovered a common ancestry for their maternal lines. This mode of approach, which was different from the usual letters addressed to the "respected master" or "my worshipful poet", aroused Ady's curiosity. Although he replied only infrequently at first, the letters kept coming; finally in the spring of 1913 the mode of address changed to "beloved Endre" and the tenor of the contents to the unsisterly "I love you infinitely and place at your feet the genuine warmth of my little essence which awoke to life only yesterday. Perhaps you are not indifferent to my distant and white surrender. Lock me in your soul. Be good to me..."

Bertuka returned to Transylvania in 1912 after finishing her Swiss schooling. She wrote Ady more and more often but the two did not meet until the spring of 1914 when Ady accepted an invitation to visit Csucsa. He entrained after a night of carousing in Nagyvárad among old friends. Somewhat drunk, he missed his station and retraced his way arriving far beyond the promised hour, tired, wrinkled, and unkempt. Despite the inauspicious beginning the visit went off well enough. Shortly afterwards Ady wrote to Hatvany: "Call it a senile turn of mind, but I am madly in love with a girl who is scarcely twenty years old. She thinks, and undoubtedly believes, she loves me. The girl, strange to say, is not Jewish but of a prominent half-magnate Transylvanian family. However, she offers everything which has bound me to the people of Shem—the style of a Jókai novel (much to my anger), romance, a tyrant father, intricacies, and so forth. Perhaps there will be an elopement, or heaven knows what, unless she soon comes to her senses or her father unexpectedly gives his consent."

Bertuka's father was a follower of Stephen Tisza, the stern unyielding statesman who in the age-old Hungarian duality typified the ideals of oligarchy as Ady did of Western liberalism. Thus it was not unnatural that the father should object to Ady. He approached four or five of Ady's friends to ask whether they would let the poet marry a daughter of theirs. Although they spoke highly of Ady, all acknowledged they would not wish to become his father-in-law. When Ady heard of this he remarked, "Of course, I wouldn't give my twenty-year-old daughter to a man like me."

But Ady had overpowering reasons for marriage. Revealingly he wrote to his brother, "This affair has brought me a great deal of suffering, but even more it has brought me freedom from myself, a place of concealment, and a new narcotic." Marriage beckoned as a refuge from viscious habits and became all the more necessary because of the war into which Hungary was drawn. Declared unfit for military service, the poet was perforce restricted to the confines of the country.

War-time censorship restricted his publication possibilities, and war-time nationalism exposed him to irrational revilement. They were married during the spring of 1915 in a civil marriage, which at Ady's insistence was subsequently confirmed with rites in a Calvinist church. Marriage brought Ady the refuge he felt he needed. It brought Bertuka the happiness of being married to Hungary's greatest literary figure. But in conversation with a former suitor who asked her whether she was happy she replied, "By day, yes ...."

Thus Ady, the revolutionary, withdrew into a castle, the traditional and symbolic stronghold of conservative forces in Hungary. This move completed his withdrawal into the gray of Magyar antiquity, but it remains to his credit that he did not find this incompatible with his revolutionary ideals.

With the change symbolized by his externally new mode of life his style of writing also underwent a change. The short poem and line gave way to a longer construction and more tortuous syntax. The plastic picture that had made almost every one of his earlier poems the simulacrum of a dream gave way to a style he had imbibed from the Hungarian translations of the Bible and from the eighteenth century *kuruc* folksongs (one of which is widely known through the use Berlioz made of the melody in the Rákóczi March). His followers found it increasingly difficult to appreciate an Ady whose manner of writing had so radically changed.

Ady wrote a series of poems to his wife, most of which are contained in the final cycle of LEADING THE DEAD. After his pet name for her they are known as the Csinszka poems. One of the best of these is *On the Kalota*, written following a visit paid by the two to a Transylvanian village where their supposedly mutual relatives lived. This poem in which life bursts from every line begs comparison with *A Walk Around my Birthplace*, the Léda poem in which death lurks behind every word.

With the exception of two brief stays in Budapest Ady spent the war years at Csucsa and Érmindszent. The former was busy with the military activities of the Central Powers; the latter was isolated and received only tidings of bloody and far-off battles. *Recollections of a Summer Night*, one of his finest poems, reflects the village superstitions to which he had always been so susceptible but which seized him to an exceptional degree at this time. According to his brother, all the calamitous signs described in the poem actually were observed at one time or another around the Ady house in Érmindszent. *Tower of Night* is another haunting expression of the war as experienced from the village scene.

As the war progressed the poet's health worsened and in March 1916 he again entered the Városmajor Sanatorium in Budapest for a brief cure. He quickly improved and in his wife's absence he engaged in an affair with a seventeen-year-old girl at the sanatorium. This prompted him to announce to his brother his intention to seek a divorce, claiming that with the return of his health and good sense he could no longer understand how he had managed to endure marriage for a whole year. But the love affair was as ephemeral as the recrudescence of his good health, and he remained in his refuge at Csucsa.

The war brought Ady many serious problems. Declared unfit for military service, he was nonetheless granted exemption only for two or three month periods and was repeatedly called up for reexaminations. He made no attempt to conceal his lack of desire, even his fear, to be inducted into the army. Although he made no personal moves to save himself from service (on one occasion he said, "If they don't even want to keep me as a relic, then let them take me") he permitted his wife and friends to intercede with the authorities on his behalf. It would be easy under the circumstances to charge Ady with cowardice and indeed the charge was frequently made. To one such charge Ady answered: "They would make a coward of me, and they say I would be a cowardly soldier. They are wrong. I never was a coward and I could scuff whosoever fell by right into my hands. Let those sing of war for whom it is a light, distant, sympathetic, or a business matter. They say it is difficult at Doberdo (a battlefield in Italy), but I believe it is better at Doberdo than at home. The war has "cleared" everything beautifully, almost everyone is sullied." The truth of the matter was that Ady did not believe in that particular war and could not bring himself to participate in it. Whether he was right or wrong in his attitude, his courage was unquestionable.

The course chosen by Count Michael Károlyi, who as the war progressed appeared more and more as the leader of the war opposition, was different from Ady's. Although exempt from military service for reasons of age and health, he joined the army. In his *Memoirs* (published by Jonathan Cape, London, 1956) he wrote: "I admired the moral courage of the militant anti-militant, of the conscientious objector who suffers imprisonment or is shot for his convictions. As a politician, however, my role was not to sacrifice myself but to save my country from disaster. By giving an individual example of active resistance to war, could I have exercised a stronger influence on events? I do not know. Morally it might have been finer to act on conviction, and braver to appear a coward; but at the time I was not prepared to accept all the consequences involved in anti-militarism."

As a counterbalance to Ady the conservatives headed by Jenő Rákosi built up a poet by the name of Géza Gyóni, who wrote poems which buttressed the war effort. In an act of deliberate provocation Rákosi had a young boy write to Ady and request his opinion about Gyóni. Despite the warnings of his wife, Ady fell into the trap and wrote the young *agent provocateur* the following letter: "My dear young friend, Géza Gyóni never was a poet and never will be. Not even a world war can make him one. With the sense of a journalist in his uncomfortably comfortable surroundings he appropriated for his use true poetic forms and nuances. Naturally, he exploited me above all, but fortunately he is not a good exploiter. He is no more than an editor of war reviews. Let him live, poor man, and when he returns home, let him make a living of this terrible war, which has taken so many lives and ruined so many of us." The trap sprang and Ady was placed in the unenviable position of having attempted to use a child to detract a patriotic poet.

On October 23, 1918 Károlyi and the Hungarian "radicals" set up a National Council to rule Hungary. This was followed a week later by the assassination of Stephen Tisza, Hungary's war-time leader. Ady received the news with the pathetic cry, "This is frightful. You shall see it is the end of us." The agitations of the times had their repercussions on his health, and he suffered a mild stroke which left him with defective speech. On a sleepless night he destroyed his beloved Bible and on the torn cover wrote, "Eli, Eli, Sabaktani, October, 1918." The following morning he greeted his brother with the words, "I had a dreadful night. I tore up my Bible. This is all that remains. Guard it for me." On November 16, the day on which the Hungarian Republic was proclaimed with Károlyi as president, a delegation from the National Council called at his home and greeted him as the "poet of the Revolution." He began to reply but broke into an unintelligible stammer.

Ady never fully emerged from the blackest night into which he had plunged with LOVE OF OURSELVES. He never attained the calm identification of the human will with the divine will in the sense of a final home. The restless winds of genius that screech along the Danube and the unhappiness of a microcosmos that has seldom been able to find its equilibrium in the turbulences of Europe could not evolve a calm mystic who in the real world might feel that his union with God was absolute. However, he gave ultimate expression to his contemplative and visionary life in *Above All Miracles*. In twenty-five short lines, this poem carries the human soul through the suspenseful paradox between the real and the unreal, the complete and the incomplete, life and death to an unending movement of eternal motion and infinite resignation. Beyond this the poem defies analysis as it surges, in an endless quest marked by stations of loss and finding, above all miracles. Few poems in the literature of the world strain the known bounds of human experience to a greater degree. Its creation may have taken place, as the poet hinted to Zsófia Dénes, under the influence of morphine.

LEADING THE DEAD, in which the above poem appeared, is in many respects Ady's most profound book. Written during the War and published after the lifting of war-time censorship, it contains *The Lost Horseman*, one of his greatest "political poems", combining plastic symbolism and biblical apocalypse into a stark and gray creation of prehistoric and prophetic grandeur.

The duality of the human soul continued to preoccupy Ady. But now curiously influenced by the War he identified the dead on the battlefields with the Abels of his own soul. This theme is stated with symbolic sureness in the title poem, *Leading the Dead*, and brought to perfection, in the vein of Ady's later style, in *Of Yesterday's Yesterday* with its curiously beautiful lines,

> ...*yesterday's circles and holy*
> *dead diagrams, stifled in murderous passageways.*

These lines with their haunting meaning and mystery form the central idea of the book. *Above All Miracles* is the perfect antistrophe.

The poems in LEADING THE DEAD represent only about one half of Ady's war-time production. At Hatvany's insistence the remainder was omitted as unsuited to present the poet in the best light. These were finally published posthumously in 1923 under the title THE LAST BOATS. Ady's friends selected the poem by this name as the title of the book in the belief that this stark utterance was the final spiritual stage reached by Ady. This interpretation by Ady's contemporaries is no more binding on Ady's future readers, of course, than the view expressed by some of them that the poet's creative powers had lapsed to ruin in the final stage of his life. From the perspective of a half century it is evident that Ady is still to be realized. His poetry is the vision of a future that rises and whitens with time. His is that rarest kind of creativity which does not form a landmark of achievement but into which time and men grow. He stretches the soul and vision of men who foresee the Pyrennes, the Carpathians, and the Altai as one Mont Blanc.

Nevertheless, *The Last Boats* was Ady's penultimate creation. His only known publication after that date was *Salutation to the Victors* (a *morituri salutamus* of historical Hungary beginning with the lines, "do not step too rudely on/do not tramp too rudely on/our poor and lovely heart/that is about to bleed.") On January 27, 1919 Ady submitted his personal life to the dark God. He had reaffirmed and redefined the mission of a nation as it is given few men to do. He had explored the mission of man and found the way of redemption through the surge that arises from the Cain, Satan, and Gog of the dynamic human soul.

56

NEW VERSES

(1906)

These verses all belong to Leda,
who cherished and willed them. I
was wont to destroy my verses in
the growing fevers of my waning
life, in deep storms, in fires of Hell.
These few verses I pardoned. I al-
lowed them to come to life and now
I hand them over to Leda.

Psalms for Leda

OUR CHILD

The likeness of our sombre selves
will never spring from our sad love,
and others will receive our child,
Messiah of the blessed ones,
rejoicer in both you and me.

The unpremeditated hours,
the new and modern gods will come.
Then it shall be, then it shall be
that tuberoses will unfold
and kiss-born wonders wing the air.

Others shall be as we shall be —
flower of the sun, a soulful bride;
flame of the sun, a thirsty youth.
A tuberose envelops them
and blessed is their ecstasy.

Blessed be he, this you and I,
for whom we wept, and now is theirs,
whom our own fever cast away,
whom you and I did not possess,
whom they receive from us — our child.

Let him be blessed who will arrive,
whom flame and flower of the sun
created for new word and song,
this dreamer of strange dreams, this child,
who from the tomb of sorrow came.

THE WHITE-ROBED WOMAN

A mouldering castle steeped in spells,
abandoned, haughty is my soul.
(Behold these dark enormous eyes
that do not glow, that do not glow.)

The echoes roll in hollow halls,
and from the walled and sombre height
two large black windows gloom the gorge.
(Behold how weary are these eyes.)

Eternal is the mantling mist,
the cryptal balm and unlaid ghosts
ashiver in the shadowy vault,
and an accursed army moans.

(But now and then at witching hour
how glow these large and sombre eyes.)
A white-robed woman walks the halls
and laughs into the windowed night.

BECAUSE YOU LOVE ME

Your eyes are mirrors
of blessed marvels,
for they have seen me;
you are the mistress,
the cunning woman
of the caress.
A thousand times blessed
are you as woman,
for you have seen me
and looked at me.
Because you love me
I also love you,
because you love me
you are the woman,
you are the fair.

HER LADYSHIP OF TEARS

I sense the sombre presence of
her ladyship of tears;
her restless rosy fingers thrust
into my heart like spears.
Her roseate and murderous nails
a deathly fragrance cast;
and on my heart the sad teardrops
are falling, falling fast.

Her lips draw near, her curls of hair
into my face now dart;
the total woman lays me waste
here, here within my heart.
She takes revenge on life and digs
a mine beneath the past;
and on my heart the sad teardrops
are falling, falling fast.

Let die the sinner led by fate
to blind himself to fears
and scrutinize the deathless sphinx,
her ladyship of tears.
Let her remain a mystery,
always in novel cast;
upon my heart the sad teardrops
are falling, falling fast.

THE FRAGMENT FLAMES

The fragment flames of a caress
before us flare.
The night is cool. We run.
Crying we run
but reach not there.

We often stop. We embrace.
We ache and dread.
You deny me. My lips are blood.
Your lips are blood.
We do not wed.

The death-flame of a full caress
would soothe our sorrow.
How calls that death caress, that flame.
But sadly we say,
"Tomorrow. Tomorrow."

LET DIE THE BLAZE

Let die the blaze —
these sombre and senescent eyes
will never cease to gaze.

Drive me away,
but these unwavering dog-like eyes
your every step waylay.

Though love again
may kindle blazes in your blood,
it is in vain, in vain.

Monsters. Beware.
These sombre and senescent eyes
deny you leave. They stare.

IN VAIN YOU SHADOW ME

I shall defile you, yes, defile you
on the serenest, snowiest night —
in vain you shadow me snow white.

You shall rise up when I conjure you
as in a wisp of snowy stole
I wrest you from my very soul.

In vain you flutter cold and fearful —
with ink your whiteness I shall flood,
with tears and pus and bile and blood.

In vain your tremblings — I shall mar you
with patches of mistrust and blame,
prickled by poisoned nettles' flame.

And while you flutter pale and loving,
at your stray shadow I shall scoff.
I give one puff. Dismissed. Be off.

THE SAVAGE STEEP

We stand upon a savage steep,
two waifs alone beside the deep,
and cling in motionless embrace.
We do not moan or cry or speak.
One sway — we topple from the peak.

The bloodied hooks of mouth and lip
suspend us while they intergrip.
Our lips are tremulous and blue,
and while you kiss we do not speak.
One sound — we topple from the peak.

THE FIERY SORE

I am a feverish fiery sore
tormented by the light and dew;
and I have come because I crave
for further pain — I ache for you.

This longing hurts, these kisses hurt,
but let your white-hot passions glow.
You are my agony and my
Gehenna. How I ache for woe.

Racked by desire, stained by a caress,
for pain I hunger more and more.
Oh, torture me, the famished one,
and with a kiss, sear, sear this sore.

THE WHITE SILENCE

I draw you near me, but I fail.
This is the white silence, the white veil
that sulks nowhere but here so vast.
Pierce this marrowless silence with screams,
else we are lost as whiteness gleams
on tears and kisses of the past.
Scream as I claw your velvet skin,
bite as your head comes bobbing in.
Too smooth I find your fragrant hair,
disheveled let it lash and tear.
Too white I find your bloodless throat
that with my nails I would garrote.
Seize a dagger, for life now fronts
a brinkless void. There is no bliss
or joy or pain or tear or kiss.
Oh God, all came to end at once.
I claw, I bite, and I asperse.
Return, I beg, a screaming curse.
This silence slays, this veil of white.
Drive or be driven out of sight.
Here is the white satanic veil,
our world will soon be hushed and pale.

THE OTHER TWO

Beguiled to thinking that we waited,
now we caress and now we rest.
Our lips are wan, our eyes are wet,
our flame abated.

In gardens red with burning mallow
a mad red flame burned in our hearts.
Here we avoid each other's eyes
and all is sallow.

We kiss, each other reassuring,
but every night weeps into day.
We chill and throngs of kisses keep
vainly alluring.

A boy and girl, two artifices,
approach us from red garden haunts.
The flame leaps up; we turn again
to burning kisses.

THE HACKNEY COACH

My queen, the air has burst in flame,
and look, our coach begins to swing.
Today we mingle with the folk,
you are the queen and I the king.
Beneath the lightning-gilded trees,
see how the radiant coaches stream,
see how they surge upstreet and down,
how for a glimpse of us they gleam.
Tonight we lavish wealth and boons;
my queen vouchsafe a lowered veil.
(The hackney coach jolts, jolts along
and we two tremble cold and pale.)

My queen, we perish from desire.
Never before has a mortal pair
so striven for the peaks of life,
and one was never more threadbare.
Our soul is flame, desire, and sun;
and yet a beggar's life we live;
we have an uncollected claim
on all the splendors life can give.
I am a king, you are a queen,
but will our throne forever fail?
(The hackney coach jolts, jolts along
and we two tremble cold and pale.)

LEDA ABOARD SHIP

Hurrah, the ship of pleasure blows
and bears my Leda toward me.
My lady now I see, I see
upon a richly flowered rug
and in her hair a blood red rose.
I crave her hug, she craves my hug.
Hurrah, it's been so long.

Oh God, my senses swirl and sway.
Oh God, you soon are at my side,
and then two thirsty souls collide;
I whisper questions in your ear;
my head upon your breast I lay.
Oh God, don't come, I tremble, fear.
Oh God, it's been so long.

PRAYER TO BAAL

O mighty Baal, the hour of mercy strikes,
and from our galley we send up a cry.
Behold, behold us as we hellward fly.
Or rather her, for what am I? A clod.
A pain-racked soul, a contumacious god,
a fallen Titan. But here is my mate.
Merciless Baal, your goodness I await.
Sombre is she, her soul a blasted star,
mournful of eye, ambitious without par,
Dido, arraigning even when caressed.
Moody with love but fresh for every quest,
made for the purple robe, female unique.
O mighty Baal, let your soul's mercy speak.
From somewhere on your throne of Money-All
let your bright, barbarous eyes upon us fall.
I could strive, I could struggle through the strife.
I can live humbly though it cost my soul,
but look at her, this queen whom I extol.
Pillows of silk alone soak up her tears,
and flags of silk alone fly on her ship.
O pour on us a flood of golden rain.
Pour, pour! O father of the bloody gold.
O look on us — how beggared and how cold.
If you but looked, your gold barbaric heart
would tighten in your breast. Your tears would flow
and on our deck, as in the dark we soar,
the gold would pour, the shower of gold would pour.

THE LAKE LAUGHED

We soared toward night
upon a lake,
an alien lapped,
a swaying lapped,
a fearful lapped,
deep water lake.
Wrapped in the gown
of former woes
we floated on,
waiting for night.

Our boatman's arm
was quivering.
Winds blasted us
from snowy peaks.
The lake blared forth,
resounded, called,
roared, sighed and moaned.
It laughed, it laughed.
We soared, we sailed.
(Let us undo,
I softly said,
all of our woes.
This is a grave
with amorous arms,
with secrets deep.
It gives embrace
that lasts for aye
and lulls for aye,
and no one feels
its circling arms.
Come, let us leap.)
She looked at me
and sadly eyed,
longingly eyed
the distant shore.
We soared, we sailed.
To go, to go,
to live, to live,
amid our woes
to suffer pain
but still to be.

And after us
the lake laughed wild,
the alien lapped,
the amorous lapped,
the soft armed lake.
It laughed, it laughed,
and ever since
on all our ways
at every dusk
we hear it laugh.

I AWAIT ANOTHER

I drive them kneeling before you —
my desires, these famished hordes,
these wild, nomad, haughty hordes
of the blood.

I envy, pity, and loathe you,
my favored beggar-woman,
my queenly beggar-woman
of desire.

Could I but crave for someone else.
Could I await another —
a new woman, someone, another,
anyone.

MY LEDA'S HEART

A troop of witches pelted me
in the grove of sombre marvels.
I did not fear, I never feared.
But my fair leman fled affrighted,
my lovely leman, youthful smile.

The witches sighed, the witches laughed,
and through the mournful mist of midnight
a hail of hearts was falling on me
in the grove of sombre marvels,
and I concealed my pelted face.

The witches pelted me with hearts
in the grove of sombre marvels.
I did not fear, I never feared.
I stood alone within the gloom
while from the mist their hearts were falling,
their frozen, small, and sneering hearts.

And then the troop of witches fled.
In tears, in white, in deepest silence
a light-encircled woman walked
in the grove of sombre marvels.
I raised my lowered eyes to hers.

She reached into her radiant gown.
In the grove of sombre marvels
she hurled her heart against my face,
where I still feel it stinging, throbbing,
that poor and warm and sickly heart.

LEDA GOES TO PARIS

There is one who is my all,
who forsakes me, who foregoes me.
Paris, Paris, stand before her;
if you can then send her back.

Stand before her, let her know
that I am your son, my Paris,
from your purlieus banished, driven,
far away, but still your son.

Say that she was sent by you,
in your place to give me solace;
tell her not to take the little
love for life that still is mine.

How I want to live, to live.
More to marvel. Paris, Paris,
send this message to your daughter —
if she leaves me I shall die.

THE LAST SMILE

oh, I lived an ugly life,
oh, I lived an ugly life;
I shall be a comely corpse,
I shall be a comely corpse.

fair will be my satyr face,
fair will be my satyr face;
on my lips a smile will play,
on my lips a smile will play.

in my large and glassy eyes,
in my large and glassy eyes
someone is reflected there,
someone is reflected there.

and my frigid smiling lips,
and my frigid smiling lips
thank you for your every kiss,
thank you for your every kiss.

OLD FAUN'S MESSAGE

The world is sombre mummery.
An Apollo in the mask of a faun,
I send for you, Leda, and wait.

It is spring by the Danube, a time
when I always cough up blood.
Life is fair here, a sheer dream.

Now in my quest of Pan,
a seafarer of reeling galleons,
I stand before the rigid Certain.

My soul is tattered and shabby;
a breath of wind would waft
my body to Hades — and, and I love you.

You will hear no new song,
I have no kisses to give,
but I need you in this spring

that you may over me lean
and tell with a kiss what you know,
"You were Apollo, my ugly faun."

FAR TO THE SOUTH

Far to the south, far to the south
the warm and strident breezes skim.
They wait for us, they wait for us
somewhere upon an ocean's brim.

There once we listened as the roar
of vast blue waters filled the air.
We shall not hear, we shall not hear
a sound more fair, a sound more fair.

A bark is standing on the blue
and sets to sea perhaps today.
If we come late, if we come late
it never will take us away.

The warm and strident breezes skim
on waters vexed by azure light.
Far to the south, far to the south,
our bark fades vacantly from sight.

THE HAWK NUPTIALS

We sail into the autumn gloom,
shrieking, pursuing and pursued,
two hawks with languid, drooping wings.

The summer has new birds of prey.
New hawk wings clatter in the air,
and kiss encounters kiss once more.

We leave from summer, driven we leave,
and somewhere into autumn we reach
with ruffled feathers and still inflamed.

This nuptial flight will be our end.
We claw and clasp each other's flesh
and sink upon the autumn heath.

The Magyar Fallow

THE HORTOBAGY POET

He was a Hunnish large-eyed youth,
smitten by many a fair mirage,
and with his herd he struck into
the famous Magyar Hortobagy.

Mirage and twilight seized his soul
a thousand times with magic snare;
but when his heart would sprout a flower,
the herds of cattle grazed it bare.

He often thought of wondrous things,
of wine and women, death and birth;
he would have been a holy bard
on any other part of earth.

But when he gazed upon the herds
and on the breeched and dirty crowd,
straightway he buried all his songs;
he whistled or he swore aloud.

ON THE TISZA

I came from the banks of the Ganges
and dreamt by the sun-silted river;
my heart was a large bell-flower,
my strength a delicate quiver.

Drawing well, wasteland, jumble,
sty with its dungy reeking,
wild kisses, louts, and dream killers,
by the Tisza what am I seeking?

THE TETHERED SOUL

They tethered my soul upon a rope
because it frisked with coltish flame,
because I used in vain the lash,
in vain gave chase, in vain gave chase.

If you should see on Magyar mead
a bloody stallion flecked with foam,
cut loose his lariat, for he is
a soul — a sombre Magyar soul.

76

ENCOUNTER WITH GINA'S POET

Heigh ho, the night,
the wilderness, the bedlam hour.
Heigh ho, the Vaal forest,
the Magyar isolation,
the bleakness of Mont Blanc,
the comet and stark winter.
Heigh ho, I try the forest.
There come Gina and the poet.
The wild wood-singer breaks into song.
The skeleton
of the great ancient blinds me.
He leads Gina.
Heigh ho, Gina lives.
Let go her hand.
She is my woman,
mine.
The wilderness cries. Gina trembles.
Leda, I shout.
Leda. She looks at me.
The skeleton god, father of my soul,
looks and knowingly laughs.
His fingers fan out
and touch my temple.
The forest fills with firelight.
Heigh ho, Leda soars, Gina runs,
and the sombre Magyar secret
of eternal isolation murmurs in the trees.
Heigh ho, the bedlam night.
I fall at his bony feet
and the forest speaks with tongues
of fate and fear.
The Mont Blanc man
touches my temple,
my holy forebear, my kinsman.
And here ever since I feel
a holy hand,
a hand of bone
upon my temple.

THE MAGYAR FALLOW

I walk on meadows run to weed,
on fields of burdock and of mallow.
I know this rank and ancient ground —
this is the Magyar fallow.

I bow down to the sacred soil;
this virgin ground is gnawed I fear.
You skyward groping seedy weeds,
are there no flowers here?

While I look at the slumbering earth,
the twisting vines encircle me,
and scent of long dead flowers steep
my senses amorously.

Silence. I am dragged down and roofed
and lulled in burdock and in mallow.
A mocking wind goes whisking by
above the mighty fallow.

This Singing Paris

A PARISIAN DAWN

A glory shines upon my face,
and where I wander silence stirs and soars.
I waken Paris with a knock,
and on my head the morning radiance pours.

I am the conquering vigilant
who waited for the sun to burst in gold,
and in the glory of the dawn
I stand alone and proudly aureoled.

I am the servant of the sun
who ministers the midnight wake and feast.
An ancient steeple tolls. Ring out.
I am a priest — a pagan, pagan priest.

Amid the tollings of the bell
I light a lambent flame beneath the pyre,
and in my now conflagrant soul
how dance the beams, the sunbeams ever higher.

Evoe, sun-god, ancient flame.
Still fast asleep this motley forest lies,
and I alone have watched for you,
your priest and madman of the frenzied eyes.

Do I look wan? Pour rays on me.
A redder youth was Ad, my ancient sire,
when long ago he was your priest.
A thousand years I languish and expire.

I am a martyr of the East
who to the West for mitigation fled,
a scion of cursed sorcerers.
My face is sallow? Paint, O paint me red.

I hold my squalid race in spite
which got me in decline, and now I run
with sallow features toward the West
that I may worship there my lord, the sun.

Why ask how all this came about?
My blood runs thin. I worship warmth and glow.
I seek a secret, wonder-work,
and dream, but what I want I do not know.

My Magyar blood, this sluggish stream,
drinks of the West as though is were adry.
A sombre shaman of the sun,
his long ago diffused, wan ray am I.

A music lures which long ago
some wild brown maid in holy Asia sang.
A fragrance haunts — some ancestress
inspired it where a marvel flower sprang.

An ancient, slow decay soars on
before me, and I bow my head deep down.
I wait and that which I await
is neither love nor money nor renown.

What do I wait for? Nothing. Once
a woman came who sometimes kisses me;
this kiss-fed Paris never knew
kisses more sad, more like a malady.

I wait. A last convulsion comes.
It will arrive sometime when sunset nears,
and they will never waken me
with tearful kisses or with loving tears.

The sun-god's priest will pass away,
of all the strangest and the sickliest,
exhausted long before his birth,
and even in Paris loveless and unblessed.

Evoe, sun-god, ancient flame.
The fire is dead. Paris wakes with a beat.
To newer wars advances life,
the grandiose, the pompous, and the cheat.

A pagan hero I move on,
a new droll don, a modern brainsick knight,
who tears and casts from his own soul
the lovely dreams that bless his life with light.

A glory shines upon my face.
The bell is tolling, slowly I move on.
Upon the stones of Paris I,
the poorest nomad, sacrificed at dawn.

BOIS AT NIGHT

A musical, hushed, and mournful night
enshrouded Paris and my soul.
We were astray; within the great Bois
our coach was searching for the road.
As if no one was aware of us,
as if no one was awaiting us,
with a sleepy roll we jogged along;
from far off came a muffled din,
the lanterns beckoned through the trees,
my soul was in a mournful mood.
The coachman whistled a tune.

We seemed to sink into deep night,
into wonder-world, infinity,
into a secret disc, a secret time,
into a new life and a new present,
while holy shadows wheeled before us.
Heigh ho, coachman, to that white house.
There, there, heigh ho, let us fly.
Drive, drive into the past, into youth.
There it is. I see it. O thunderous life,
we turned on the great Babel road. I wept.
The coachman whistled a tune.

BESIDE THE SEINE

The other lives beside the Seine,
we breathe one breath, one breath,
a twofold form with a double life
in single death.

Beside the Danube
a demon army jibes and screams,
and by the Seine a hundred holy loves
envelop me in dreams.

When Paris laughs,
the other gleams a mirrored glee,
but here the midnight minions screech
and bear me on a rapturous spree.

There I am noble, fair, and great,
my songs are foretaste of a kiss,
and Saint Cecilia leans from heaven
in dreaming bliss.

Beside the Danube
I seek for joy in every whore,
I dream with wine
and hurl my goblet to the floor.

But there the twang of twilight lulls me,
and life I kiss as though it were
an orchid
in my Leda's hair.

On Virgin Summits

SIGH AT DAWN

O world of splendor,
bathed in dawning.
The lazy pleasures
of rested bodies.
Mysterious, radiant,
soft, thousand-nested,
exquisite city.
O song of morning
with spheric music.
O life majestic,
I want to hold you.
How many pleasures,
and all for others.
How many riches,
and all for others.
How many forces,
and all for others.
How many women,
and all for others.
How many blisses,
and all for others.
How many ambitions,
and all for others.
How many marvels,
how many beauties,
how many holies,
and all for others.

HEARTS FAR APART

Somewhere a sombre sigh expires,
and in my soul it sleeps;
somewhere a peal of laughter rings,
my heart no longer weeps.
Somewhere the world is very fair,
a girl invites my eye;
somewhere the curse is very great
because I cannot cry.

Somewhere, I know, there is a heart,
shattered and saturnine,
slain by desires and ecstasies
the very same as mine.
They listen to each other's tick,
night spreads a winding-sheet,
and in one moment of vast night
they both will cease to beat.

THE CURSE OF THE KISS

It was conceived in a chaotic coitus
one great and sacred night.
Since then the act is eternal,
and every little motion debouches in a kiss.
The coitus-kiss is our world,
in the beginning the idea,
and chaste little bunches of cerebella
chime in the chummage of a kiss.
The most searing conceives
the loveliest, greatest Word
and streaks triumphantly
into the eternal and the void.
The indifferent conceives
grayness and a copy of the old.
Today there is no wildcoitus
or Messiah.
The world perhaps is sound
and we the sick and the stunted
conceived in a cold kiss
and held in glacial inanimation of the soul.
The kiss is sacred and life is sacred,
the eternal end of coitus.
The kiss is a curse and life is a curse
if the kiss is without rapture.
In the ugly connection of the impassive coitus
and tepid night
the curse swells around us.
Life becomes limp and old
and we, mating drones,
sombre, shabby, and sick,
neither firm nor free
to kiss with unslaked fire.
If thirsty kisses were shed
by none but thirsty lips on lips
our earth would become an Olympus
of living gods.

ON THE FENS

This is the world of fens, a gray
and infertile world of eternal fog
filled with ogres.
I wait among fen dwellers
for radiant morning.
Crepuscular fog envelops me,
but the morning will arrive.

Everything turns gray
among ogres and in swirling fog.
Now and then the levin strikes in me,
and I hurl red sparks at the ogres.
Now and then I protrude
my proud large head
from the grayness to show I am.

I am a man of light who hides in fog.
I am the losing will.
I am the miracle of the fen dwellers
who was born for light but remains behind
waiting for the morning,
waiting for the dawn.

A dawn will come, a miracle.
Volcanoes will rise on the fen
and a host of rays
streak across the world.
The terror will rise in a tower of flame.
The foul will become a river of fire,
and the sombre losing will,
a triumphant will.

I shall ascend volcano peaks
with a proud, blood-red flag
and scream above the barriers
calling down ruin.
I shall release the sea of sin
and extirpate root and reed
that the sea may roll from end to end
to cleanse the earth
and the old losing will which yearns for a dam
fill up its strength.

But the peaks
meet a smile from someone below
covered by gold-red sea kelp,
daughter of a devil
with murderous eyes, breath of fire,
and seafoam shoulders.
I cast my flag aside,
run, and fall before her
desiring to sear and be seared.
The enchained power of the great fen
swells a hundredfold in me,
and I fall on her with a strangling love.
The gold-red sea covers me
overwhelmed as I kill and die.

A WOMAN'S LAP

Whenever my sombre satyr-head
upon a woman's lap may fall,
I can recall.

Within a hot and carnal clime
as a large woman once I strayed
and dreaming played.

In space of time far-off and deep
I was a woman — shapely, round,
and lovely found.

And gaunt young men behind me came,
desirous, smooth, with sickly pall,
I can recall.

SCION OF MIDAS

I walk in fields of whispering reeds,
striking about me with my royal mace,
and in their mocking deep the reedlands roar
wherever I walk with my royal mace.

I know this secret tongue, this reedy talk.
The stalks are whispering as I shout afar —
O reedland, look, your mighty king has come,
the scion of King Midas has arrived.
Although you laugh, you light and fluttering reeds,
you shall pay homage to the new King Midas,
you shall pay homage to me, I am sure.
Because my sire is blessed and throne is blessed,
my sire I worship and my throne I guard
here in the windy fields of whispering reeds.
O reedland, do you hear? How fair this world.

I bless you, reedland, and I bless you, life,
for all your beauties brightening for the blind,
for all your calmness seeking for the storm,
for all your truths that trumpet on deaf ears.
I bless whatever you may give, O life,
your mighty cowards who outdo the brave,
and mighty Midas, ass-eared sire of mine.

O royal sire, how fair it is to live
with ass's ears and my ancestral mace
in lyric rapture, frenzied drunken toil.
O royal sire, how worthy is this life
in deep and windy fields of whispering reeds.
I bless you gratefully, disdainfully
for every little minute I enjoyed.
And let the reedland round about me laugh;
scions of Midas shall be rulers here.
Laugh if you will. I have my faith in faith.

Resplendent is the dawn which shall arrive
with flourish and in triumph, I am sure,
fair are the melodies which shall resound,
and worthy all the frenzied loving of
the amorous woman who shall come for me,
fair the desires, the dreams, the deeds, the kiss
which shall elope hereafter into life,
and I am blessed within this drunken mail.

Of unsung songs that never will be sung,
of unkissed girls who never will be kissed,
of towering deeds that only live in dreams,
of fair tomorrow, of the unarrived,
I am the king, I am the haughty hero,
who scorns the dismal mummy of Today,
who dreams about the sacred, mystic Morrow
and who descended from the ass-eared Midas.

THE CHASMS MOAN

Its snowy summit views the sun —
this sacred mount of song, my soul,
hollowed by wicked chasms below.

Young women, visions, shattered lures,
anguish and scars pitted the deep —
the chasms and the monsters increased.

High, high on the peak a virgin hush —
demons of thought on demons follow,
and down below the monsters bellow.

Startled, the nimble demons tread
their holy dance atop my soul —
from below, below the chasms moan.

One moment and the mountain moves —
the dancers on the peak are swept
headlong into nothingness.

THE YELLOW FLAME

My dreams have been enkindled by
the yellow flame. I smoulder, burn.
O dip me in a tide of gold,
give me, give me a refuge place.

Wild music hunts and harries me,
music of clinking, golden coins.
O let this sound grow mute before
the magic wand, the golden wand.

Let come that soft and muffled night
when songs are stilled and flames are quenched;
I long to sleep on a bed of gold
in surfeit, indolence, and sloth.

THE SAGA DIED

Icequake of sagas — then the saga lived,
and I awaited someone in the spring.
Icequake of sagas. A longing in me cried
and swept ashore a scented saga,
and swept ashore a wraith of woman.
From where? I only knew they were so fair.
Recent the saga, shaman wan the wraith.
I always loved the wraith and saga;
these fairest two I long entreated
upon a spell-struck night of throbbing spring,
entreated wraith and saga into life.
Icequake of sagas — then the saga lived.

Icequake of sagas — then the saga died
before the night expired. I saw in fright
the living saga and its living wraith.
This saga is not my own saga.
As for this woman wan as shaman?
She is everyone's woman, not my own.
Alien the wonders of my thievish soul,
alien the wraith, alien the saga.
The saga is antique — I entreated
a painted wraith upon a vernal night
when last my longings overflowed the plain.
Icequake of sagas — then the saga died.

LORD SWINE HEAD

The Lord Swine Head will murder me,
murder if I give in, I know.
He grinned his teeth and stiffly sat
upon the gold, the gold aglow,
murder if I give in, I know.

I stroked his bristled frame, the foul;
he shook beneath my flattering hand.
"See who I am" (I softly said).
I took my skull and I trepanned,
but with a laugh my brain he scanned.

(A seeker after wild desires,
or so he thinks). And then I kneeled
upon the thunderous shores of life.
We were alone and vespers pealed.
"Your gold, your gold you now must yield.

"The moments flee and I may fall,
I cannot wait a moment more.
Mysterious words are tempting me
to a remote, suggestive shore,
I cannot wait a moment more.

"A mail of bristle shields your heart,
my vitals burn with chancrous flame.
Devoured by fiery teeth of life,
my heart is still the blessed aim.
I must proceed. Your gold I claim.

"The seas are waiting for my yacht,
pavilions by the thousand wait.
A distant balsam, distant sun,
an alien maid and rapturous fate,
for me they wait, for me they wait.

"All life is gasping in my soul,
by all things new I am obsessed.
A divine disorder are my dreams,
while yours have never known unrest.
Come then, rip up your golden breast."

The blindly sombre night sank down.
I whimpered. The waves rolled and rolled
an endless message from the sea,
"We still await. Do you have gold?"
The endless message rolled and rolled.

We clashed. The shoreline shimmered, quaked.
I tried to rip his folds of fat.
I tore and tugged but all in vain.
He clinked his gold and laughed thereat.
There I remained and sat and sat.

A thousand nights on thousand nights
my blood is shed, forever shed.
And voices tempt me from afar,
but we fight on half live half dead,
I myself and the Lord Swine Head.

NEVER SEE ME

Invest me not in robes of gold,
I do not want the diamond crown;
but also keep the cap and bells,
I do not want the motley gown.

In land of gray where I am king
my secret throne shines but for me;
perceive and gild and rubricate,
and then I shall no longer be.

THE RED CHARIOT

The sea, this ashen drunk, has swallowed
a molten lava stream.
Earth shakes. We wait in anguished fever
amid the sombre scintillation.
The palmy shoreline reels,
wild cactuses lean on each other
and hosts of jasmine weep.

See, in the distant iridescence
of pulsing purple shades,
where firmament and flood are mingled,
a pinioned, rose-ensanguined chariot
upon the water breaks.
The mighty crimson pinions flutter.
It stops, it rests, it waits.

Whence comes this shape? Will it come hither?
Is this despair or hope?
How red the inconcinnous pinions.
What does it augur, blood or dawning,
this flame, this crimson glow?
We wait. The great red chariot pauses,
pauses in misty mauve.

ON NEW WATERS

Fear not, my ship, Tomorrow's hero guides you.
Your steersman is drunken, so the laugh derides you.
Fly on, my ship.
Fear not, my ship, Tomorrow's hero guides you.

Sail on, sail on, and sailing never falter;
to vast and virgin seas your passage alter.
Fly on, my ship.
Sail on, sail on, and sailing never falter.

New, new horizons ever wave before you;
the moments new and perilous life assure you.
Fly on, my ship.
New, new horizons ever wave before you.

I want not dreamt-of dreams; I want new oceans,
new secrets, new afflictions, new emotions.
Fly on, my ship.
I want not dreamt-of dreams; I want new oceans.

The bards of faded gray will not inspire me.
Let tavern-stench or Holy Spirit fire me.
Fly on, my ship.
The bards of faded gray will not inspire me.

Notes on NEW VERSES

1. **Her Ladyship of Tears.** Appeared in ONCE MORE (1903).
2. **The Hortobagy Poet.** The Hortobágy is a plains area near the east Hungarian city of Debrecen, colorful and "undeveloped" like the wild West of the United States. The mirage is a natural phenomenon of the region.
3. **On the Tisza.** The Tisza is regarded by Magyars as "the Hungarian river." In pre-World War I Hungary it rose and emptied within the frontiers of the kingdom, and even today the inhabitants along its 800-mile course are almost all Hungarian speakers.
4. **Encounter with Gina's Poet.** The Encounter is Ady's acknowledgment of his spiritual relationship to the nineteenth century poet János Vajda, in whose poetry are pre-figured a number of Ady's themes. The most striking specific example of Ady's debt is **The Straight Star** (see page 292), which brings to perfection a similar poem by Vajda entitled **The Comet.**
5. **Hearts Far Apart.** Appeared in ONCE MORE (1903).
6. **The Curse of the Kiss.** Appeared in ONCE MORE (1903).
7. **On the Fens.** Appeared in ONCE MORE (1903).

BLOOD AND GOLD

(1907)

Kinsman of Death

THE GHOST GOT INTO PARIS

The ghost got into Paris yesterday
gliding as autumn down Rue Saint Michel,
beneath the noonday Dog and hush of trees
she met me with her spell.

I had been sauntering slowly toward the Seine;
small, twiggy songs within my spirit burned —
purple and pensive, strange and smoky-hued.
I knew for death they yearned.

Then autumn whispered something from behind.
The road of Saint Michel began to shake.
Whish, whish — the jesting leaves arose in swirls
along the gusty wake.

One moment — summer had not even blenched,
and autumn fled away in mocking ease.
She came, but that she came, alone I knew
beneath the moan of trees.

A FAMILIAR BOY

He visits often at my house,
the little boy, asmile and dead,
who I once was.

Moody and ill, a lonely cub,
he hovers about and fingers soft
my shabby bed.

I fix and fix my aging face
on him in wonder, and his tears
slide on my eyes.

I waken like a weeping child
upon a fitful night of spells
as once of old.

THE HOTEL LODGER

Old bachelor, happy bachelor, ho,
never smitten by fireside cares,
lodges cheaply and alone
in a row of small hotels,
old bachelor, happy bachelor, ho,
barren, prudent, filled with rue.

Old bachelor, happy bachelor, ho.
Some fair day I shall collapse —
but no casus, a waiter here
or in Buda will report,
"Old bachelor, happy bachelor, ho.
Room thirty-six on the third floor."

(Paris)

KINSMAN OF DEATH

I am the kinsman of death;
I love the love that leaves the heart;
I love to embrace and kiss
those who depart.

I love the roses that droop and die,
the withering women whom love dismays,
the mournful, the radiant
autumnal days.

I love the ghostly, beckoning call
of gloomy hours that stay the breath,
the playful image of great
and holy death.

I love whoever journeys forth,
whoever wakes or weeps withdrawn,
and frosty mists on the field
at chilly dawn.

I love the weary who are resigned,
the tearless sobs, and the hermitage,
retreat of the poet, of the sick,
and of the sage.

I love whoever is deceived,
the crippled, the lost, the deprived of mirth,
the futile, the failed, the infidel,
and all the earth.

I am the kinsman of death;
I love the love that leaves the heart;
I love to embrace and kiss
those who depart.

SHIPS IN MIST

Red sails upon the azure sea,
pleasure bedecked, gay wanderers,
trim sailing ships, where do you fly?
Lords, lords — mysterious mournful joys,
hush ecstasies.

Red sails, heigh ho, where are you bound?
The mutes are standing on the bridge.
They signal, clap their hands, and steer
pet sailors of the happy seas,
the merry death.

Red sails that fly the merry mutes,
heigh ho, may I not leave with you
and soar away into the void?
All that is deathly, blind and fair
I love so much.

Red sails upon the azure sea,
let the mute pilot speed me on
and yellow fogs envelop me.
Let sound the ships engulfed in mist,
the mournful joys.

MY SONS' FATE

I fasten fetters on my heart
and shackle strophes on my songs,
I seek and shun the storm.

For loathsome fetters I implore,
my reasoning mind I hate and bless
but think of it when I should forget.

I fain would take French leave of myself,
for beauty always madly I try
but like a coward die in desire.

My songs, dreams and phantasies,
your father is death, the good and true,
but you are slain by your mother — rule.

THE PLANE TREE'S DREAM

The sister of the sun a green-eyed girle
whom phantom cavaliers adore
looked down at me a moonlit night and charmed
me with her lore.

I felt my spreading feet grow woody cold
as both into the soil were grown;
a plane tree on the silvery field I stand
here all alone.

My sad and scraggy trunk darts up on high,
my foliage proudly shows;
the leaves are striking at the glooming clouds,
gone are my woes.

Here I await the sister of the sun
in fields with darkness overspread;
and from my crown the sombre leaves descend,
ashake and red.

ON AUTUMN NIGHTS

Have you ever heard?
In autumn when the fog swirls
a something moans in the night.

A something goes thump,
a someone has amassed his woes,
a someone walks on rotten planks.

A man long dead
who saw no stars while he lived
now longs to look about a bit.

THREE AUTUMN TEARS

On autumn noons
          autumn noons
                    autumn noons
I cannot smile
on girles.

On autumn moons
          autumn moons
                    autumn moons
I cannot scan
the skyes.

On autumn noons
          autumn moons
                    autumn noons
I only shed
a tear.

MY COFFIN STEED

The dream-urchin comes at midnight,
myopic, close of mouth, afrown;
he beats a coffin like a drum
and dances madly on his hands.
With raucous laugh he cries, "Sit down."

Another and another comes,
like demon-shuttles round they speed.
Their eyes are always fast on me
and this on which I sit and ride,
my black, mysterious coffin steed.

In my left hand a bloody rein,
and in my right a whip I hold.
I drive my steed — gee up, gee up.
The urchin army laughs and swirls,
for hours on end my heart is cold.

While flames of sulphur pierce the dark,
upon their heads the urchins stand,
and, listen, these relentless lads
in comic, gay or horrid wise
give new and ever new command.

"Laugh till the coming of the dawn
and gallop on that magic horse."
Among bloodthirsty dream-urchins
I laugh and follow all the night
upon this coffin steed my course.

THE BLACK PIANO

The screwy strings — they whinny, whine, and croon.
Be off unless you have a fifth.
This is the black whorehouse piano.
The stone-blind tickler tears the ivory keys.
It is the melody of life he beats.
This is the black whorehouse piano.

My roaring brain and swollen, tearful eyes,
the writhing wake of my desires,
all this, all this the black piano.
From the depth of my lit-up crazy heart
the blood is pouring to the music's beat.
This is the black whorehouse piano.

The Magyar Messiahs

MATTHIAS' DEMENTED SCHOLAR

"Scholar, compose a Magyar song,
great Dante also lived on earth."
The scholar laughed and laughed.

The song in Latin meter soared,
but not in Magyar, never once.
The scholar scanned and scanned.

A Petrarch sang within his soul,
a newer Magyar song was born,
the scholar dreamed and dreamed.

But now and then in secret night
he wrote and tore up Magyar lines.
The scholar sobbed and sobbed.

THE MAGYAR MESSIAHS

More bitter is our weeping,
different the griefs that try us.
A thousand times Messiahs
are the Magyar Messiahs.

A thousand times they perish,
unblest their crucifixion,
for vain was their affliction,
oh, vain was their affliction.

SAINT MARGARET'S LEGEND

Saint Margaret's Isle confessed to me,
one hush and storied night, this tale —
the king had promised Margaret,
his snow-white daughter, to the veil.

She was a dream-maid, a sigh suppressed;
one angry word would blanch her face
while in the courtyard rumbling rode
a shaggy and barbaric race.

She awaited someone from the West —
no wild-bewhiskered, noisy boor,
a gentle, bardlike tender youth,
a tearful strolling troubadour.

She waited long, her heart grew sick.
The clang of arms she heard in fright
as hunnish horsemen would arrive,
but he came not — the phantom knight.

He never to the Danube roamed,
this soft-songed youth with softer smile;
and she became a bride of Christ
and died upon Saint Margaret's Isle.

CITY OF CLOUDS

I saw the black genie
at Hortobagy, high, high
before a thousand turreted city of clouds,
a wild sentinel against the sky.

A sombre seer and gentle God
who fixes the sun's flare
with sad and arrogant eyes. He is like me,
the father of my fathers, I swear.

"My father in the golden sky!"
He is tranced. "Wait!" I call aloud.
I plead, but he soars onward
in black of dreams, a magic cloud.

The city of clouds shook.
"It will fall to rags within an hour!"
He stared down and boldly stepped
from topless tower on tower.

I AM NOT A MAGYAR?

The ancient Orient dreamed him
as I am —
heroic, sombre, proudly extreme,
ruthless, but one who bleeds
pale at a thought.
The ancient Orient dreamed him
bold and youthful,
a noble, eternally big child;
sun-spirited, thirsty, melancholy,
a restless warrior;
the pain-fraught tested masterpiece
of a true unhappy god,
the child of the sun, a Magyar.
(And for the drowsy and dirty,
for the mongrel and gaudy,
for the half-alive and frothy-mouthed,
for the magyarasters and fog-eaters,
for the Hungarians come from Schwabs,
I am not a Magyar?)

112

The Demon Guile

WIDOW BACHELORS' DANCE

Saint George's eve, the flittermice
are screeching shrill and fidgeting;
in ancient halls and mouldy towers
the widow bachelors dance and sing.

These lads are lunatic and white.
Toward the holy moon they glance,
they chant a Mary full of grace
and hop into a country dance.

Chimera woman's spellbound crew.
Where they advance the real is slain,
and priests pursue them with a cross,
pot-bellied burghers with a cane.

Saint George's day, the dance is done.
.Each widow bachelor turns and goes
into a midnight yawning grave
where bloom the woman and a rose.

And far away the noises swoop.
Swift-sinewed spies bear off the news —
"Heigh ho, amid the honored ruins
tonight the widow bachelors booze."

Each one tears off a blooming rose.
One sighs — dawn comes with rosy tips;
one seeks a Leda — stares obsessed
and dies with pale, kiss-puckered lips.

At light the folk collect in vain.
Of song and dance and grave no clew —
a few wall spots of tear and blood,
a page of frenzied verse or two.

GOOD PRINCE SILENCE

My teeth are chattering. I whistle shrill
as down the moonlit trail I wind.
And at my back ten fathom high
the Good Prince Silence
stalks. Woe if I should look behind.

O woe to me should I grow mute
or at the moon look gapingly.
One wail of grief, one grinding crunch —
the Good Prince Silence
would take one stride and trample me.

BY DARK WATERS

By Babylonian shores I sit somewhere,
and I have sat beside the shores of care.

I have beheld a throng of little woes,
and I have seen love's long and sickly throes.

The years of crisis have possessed my soul,
and in my dreams I often played the droll.

Sometimes I thought my eyes had been unsealed
and now and then I saw the Lord revealed.

My harp I hung on bending willow trees,
my harp I lifted for my burden's ease.

My soul and body knew the burning knout
of sickness, women, wine, the Lord, and doubt.

I was a warrior and a troubadour,
my back has often bowed upon this shore.

How much I freely gave to every claim
until a weary resignation came.

I sit with slapping waves and chilling air
by gloomy Babylonian shores somewhere.

WHO COME FROM FAR AWAY

We are the men who are always late,
we are the men who come from far away.
Our walk is always weary and sad,
we are the men who are always late.

We do not even know how to die in peace.
When the face of distant death appears,
our souls splash into a tam tam of flame.
We do not even know how to die in peace.

We are the men who are always late.
We are never on time with our success,
our dreams, our haven, or our embrace.
We are the men who are always late.

SUMMER AFTERNOONS

The pointilism of a purple sky
and girls who steal to hideaways,
upon these summer afternoons
how queerly strange our spindrift daze.

We walk in mistfall of the senses
about the avenues, headless and high,
while black and unforgiving lines
are sketched upon the summer sky.

This moment of shadow and motion
white arms, white chimneys, and white spires
stretch toward the loving heavens
as though in quest of distant desires.

Upon an unanchored island of time
they are poised in flame and out of breath,
the Sky and City. And both hearts beat
in a barbaric rhythm of death.

We stare far off in longing and fear.
Our eyes are moist and laughing we cry
for an ineffable someone we only sense,
our cold and distant mistress the sky.

And from above somewhere, somewhere
they steal a spying glance below,
and on our streets we laughing weep,
while there the smiling watchers know.

THE PAINTED STEPPES

The tailed one tempted me upon the steppes.
He packed a swinging, singing sack of rime
and tripped on me in time, time, time.

The treasures rained before my burning feet,
and on the spot among the prickly thorn
I saw a hundred thousand roses born.

I sing and gather up the cool, plump gold.
I laugh, my lazy revery grows and grows,
for look, I walk upon the steppes of rose.

The caustic and the thorn have scorched my soles.
I sing, and from a thousand wounds I bleed —
O life that in the grove of rose I lead.

THE DEMON GUILE

In purple robes he left the Orient
upon the ancient dawn of rime;
astride a mount, in winey humor,
with songs and instruments he came
and sat beside me — Demon Guile.

The rakish rogue, my ear he jingles.
We drink and drink, I hear his lays.
Long rows of dawn in reeling russet
whisk by, and with a drunken jest
they rap against the window pane.

The sordid and degrading present —
this perished pleasure of the East —
is dancing with the mist-limned future
over the winey table-top
while Demon Guile is wrestling me.

I drowse within my threadbare jacket;
empurpled is the Demon Guile.
A crucifix, two candles, dimness.
This is a tourney, grim and vast,
and on the table — gushing wine.

This Demon Guile has struggled with me
since ancient days of Babylon;
a wanton forebear may have roamed there,
and ever since he is my sire,
my boon companion, caesar, god.

Wastrel Apollo, sneering-featured,
his mantle slips, his courser stirs;
the ball swings on, the tourney rages,
and on the table dark with blood
the brimming goblets lurk and lurk.

"Excellent sir, gracious companion.
O grant me leave, my head has sunk.
I have enjoyed too much of goodness,
too much of sin and night and bed,
O master, I have known enough."

He laughs as with a moan I offer
my heart and lyre with broken strings;
thunderous life is pacing, rolling
beneath the sacred window of
our winey, bloody, songful inn.

"Enter, my lord, the list with others;
there is no joy in joy for me.
Both fame and drinking are a headache.
My arrogant and horny claws
have worn away in wicked dreams.

"My homeland is the home of Magyars,
barren, exhausted. Then what serves
your mighty, rapturous inspiration?
What boot the bouts of wine and blood,
what boots a man his Magyar birth?

"My lord, I am a vagrant vassal,
a jaded and colossal fool.
Why should I drink until I falter?
I have no money; faith and strength
have fled, and death approaches soon.

"I have a mother — holy woman;
I have a Leda — may she be blessed —,
a dream or two like bolts of lightning,
a friend or two, and in my soul
abomination's mighty fen.

"And I may have a few new poems,
a great luxuriant song or two.
But look, I am about to falter
beneath the wine, beneath the board
and yield within this ancient duel.

"My lord, dismiss your sombre vassal,
nothing remains except the curse,
the ancient curse, the certain ruin.
Give up your spell, do not incite.
My lord, what is this drinking worth?

"I have great nausea, abhorrence,
a sickly spine and broken back.
I make to you my last obeisance
and hurl my goblet to the floor.
I give myself into your hand."

I watch him vault into the saddle.
He taps my shoulder, laughs aloud;
a drunken dawn and heathen lyric,
and whirling winds of witchery
whisk him off on his magic mount.

Farther and farther West he courses
toward tourneys new and infidel.
With crucifix and shattered goblet
I — cold body, grinning and stiff —
beneath the table stretch out dead.

THE YEARNED-FOR NAUSEA

Only once, only once
could I but stack a heap of gold
before the wicked, lovely, strange.
Only once, only once
could I but have my fill of love.

Only once, only once
could I be struck by nausea,
the celebrated, blest, and great.
Only once, only once
could I but take farewell of love.

Only once, only once.
And I would let the proud gold fall
before their dainty, simpering feet.
Only once, only once
I would have full account of love.

THE SPRING SHANTY

Shantied upon the grassy throne of spring,
I sit, old heap of hankering bones;
unstill, with eyes fixed far away I burn
a fever.

The shanty walls of spring are spun of dreams,
the floor is past, the roof desire,
and on the heath a soft derisive bed
is laid.

Commotion is the daughter of the spring
who winks at me from every nook,
while on the winds the old and dungy songs
are piped.

This is the always promised bridal day
which we will never have fulfilled,
and as we die the latest spring will sigh,
"Tomorrow."

But in the shanty of this spring I wait
where longing is of yesterday
and someone left for good or never will
arrive.

THE SLEEPING KISS-SERAGLIO

This side of death but life beyond,
where only man can ever go,
only the morbid male can go,
in mist and darkness sleeps and sleeps
the kiss-seraglio.

In countless chambers countless women,
fair, lovely women panting lie,
large, burning women panting lie;
like an alarum-bell you feel
your heart is beating high.

From door to door you steal and find
a bed and woman in disarray,
bed and flame-woman in disarray,
kiss-labyrinth and countless women
and everywhere a nay.

There shall you always run about,
trembling, unkissed, and unembraced,
acold, unkissed, and unembraced,
while on your sable locks the frost
of autumn ferns are traced.

WOMEN ON THE SHORE

Countless women lined the shore
holding flowers, waving kerchiefs,
some were sobbing, some were calling,
and I whooped aboard the deck.

Twilight came and wrapped in mist
countless women lined the shore.
But I saw receding kerchiefs,
and I saw deflorate flowers.

Twilight deepened, darkness fell
like the past and like Erinyes.
Countless women lined the shore,
and I wept aboard the deck.

Lost in night the fading women,
waving kerchiefs, holding flowers.
Like a fable sang the quire,
"Countless women lined the shore."

Money, Our Lord

BENEATH LIFE'S TREE

From below I behold your tangled spread
and your scarlet marvels hung overhead,
oh, life,
you vile, vile, vile.

No one has craved you more than I;
no one can love you more and sigh,
oh, life,
in vain, vain, vain.

Of all your marvels give me one;
obey just once the word of your son.
Oh, life,
I yearn, yearn, yearn.

With my blood I call and lure and wait;
with my blood I worship and I hate.
Oh, life,
I gaze, gaze, gaze.

And I shall remain here in the dust,
I know it, here below and crushed,
oh, life,
till death, death, death.

FAT CITY

The golden slopes and golden domes
of Fat City
I flee
blood splattering the dusty road.
My home was Fat City,
and my wretched body stings
where they whipped me for I fell one day
into sin of sadness.
I flee.
They send curses after the sombre rebel
and only now and then a little gold
for meager pleasure, wine, and girls.
O golden slopes and golden domes,
the eternal flush of Fat City,
whenever I feel my pockets burn,
I weep for you in joy.

LAZARUS BEFORE THE PALACE

I

Midnight and someone carouses;
the palace sends a noise.
Someone is counting money,
music of music,
what sweet, what melodious joys!

The silken paper rustle
ascends to a stately hymn;
the puppy-coins are jingling,
the gold is clinking.
My eyes with tears overbrim.

I prop the resplendent palace.
Listen to the majestic psalmody.
It storms, resounds, arises,
as if all pleasures
within these strains might be.

Whose is this money?
I weep and rave.
Let wither the hands,
the wicked, happy hands
of the contemptible knave.

II

Within a gaudy dwelling,
in joy and fever swelling,
there gathered the wealthy,
and sang the wealthy,
within a gaudy dwelling.

Upon the street's dark corner,
listen, what a wild forewarner.
A psalm. Lazarus is singing;
he watches the house while singing
upon the street's dark corner.

As shades of midnight darken
to the wild singing harken.
Pallor befalls the wealthy,
numbness befalls the wealthy,
as shades of midnight darken.

And silence. The song is ended.
Applause and laughter ascended,
noisy applause from the wealthy,
mock laughter from the wealthy,
and silence. The song is ended.

III

In autumn and in gloom appears
old Lazarus from the Bible page,
and the wealthy greet him with timid fears.

Lazarus listens, watches, lours.
Together with him come unseen
a host of numb and ancient powers.

The wheeze of his husky chest is dry,
and he would like to laugh aloud,
but weeping crooks his mouth awry.

The eternal autumn-palsy is he;
and since it is custom on earth to rejoice,
he too would like to be merry and free.

Old Lazarus would like to sing
with russet satyrs in russet woods
by the tune of a doodling pipe to spring.

He enters into the pleasure-mart;
with his wheezy chest he waits for women
and something with which to ease his heart.

The frightened wealthy hasten to seduce;
they bring him must and sparkling wine,
and he sips the sweet and honeyed juice.

He sips, and in his heart arise
tingling desires for a woman or girl;
this is his endless enterprise.

And deep in his asthmatic chest,
like a distorted sigh of lust
the cough of autumn racks his breast.

At the sound of his cough and raspy breath
their face and heart grow white with fear.
It is autumn. It seems like the coming of death.

A DREAM OF RICHES

Sun drenched after passing dark,
samaras of russet gold descend
on one
who sleeps by dawning in a dank park.

His eyes are bright and gold
as he scatters handfuls of leaves
and sings,
"Hallelujah, lovely pieces of gold."

The sun smiles in envy and warms
the happy man. The park is still.
The air
is shimering with golden swarms.

JUDAS AND JESUS

Upon basalt of Golgotha
I gash my heart-beat's anguished plea.
O Christ, my poet, holy Form,
I bartered Thee.

Thy dreamings all were dreams of mine,
I was Thy semblance and Thy soul.
I placed a crown upon Thy head;
my love was whole.

I bartered Thee, my sovereign,
because for life I hold regard,
because I also dream great dreams,
I am a bard.

I hear no more Thy psalmic lips;
Thy kingdom I forsake to Thee.
A woman longs for money, silk,
and waits for me.

And am I vile? Life too is vile.
Where is the magic in the Word?
Why all this craving and distress
by money spurred?

I cast the written rock down deep;
earth shakes for centuries on end.
And later sinful, sombre eyes
will comprehend.

ONLY ONE MOMENT

One moment and I am kissed by life;
my body is a caldron of flames.
Avenues, houses, women, dreams,
and hearts are aglow — everything burns
in an immortal blaze.

One moment and devil urchins come
to damp the flame beneath their tails.
Now follow doubt, extinction, frost,
mud — and perhaps there comes to mind
a wrinkled pair of pants.

One moment and stupid mishap sits
with icy buttock astride our chest.
We hear a raucous laugh — flat purse,
my troubled man, my nobody,
go easy with yourself.

One moment and all within us dies;
the fairy prince yields up the ghost.
Our joy dies, and sadly we weep —
O God, could we but have ten times
longer than one moment.

ALPS AND RIVIERA

The storm whelps rip our snowy forelocks,
our icecaps never sleep in calm,
beneath our feet a springtide smiles,
the blooming cactus, aloe, palm.

We are the alpine outer limits,
victim of foppish winds and shrews.
Below, a sea of sacred light
and mad cacophony of blues.

We spike our heads in pride of anguish
against the cold of night and day,
beneath our feet the merry lords,
the finely perfumed, are at play.

We defend them; we outer limits
with jagged, frozen armoring
stand on this watch so others may
bask in the suns and suns of spring.

The season down below will perish
if we collapse upon the shore,
the palms will perish, and the smile
of simpering lords will shine no more.

If like a frightful, great example
our thunderheads would loom and frown!
If one fair day, O mountain mates,
we should decide to thunder down!

THE USURER'S GARDEN

This was Athen's fairest spring,
unsurpassed in splendor.
Chiron was the Grecian youths'
money lender.

Harder curses never fell
on a pompous dwelling.
Nowhere were the flowers more
sweetly smelling.

Life is fair — the garden rang,
with a holy ringing.
Lads of Athens never heard
fairer singing.

By this money far and wide
languid night was haunted.
Fragrance rose and Chiron's ground
rang and vaunted.

Curses fell and fragrance soared;
many a youth who foundered.
Haughty flowers their laughter on
heaven squandered.

BLOOD AND GOLD

It sounds alike upon my ears —
the gasp of lust, the groan of ache,
the squirt of blood or gold ashake.

I know and vouch that this is all,
and all things else I worthless hold,
but blood and gold, yea, blood and gold.

And all things die, and all things pass,
rank and song and fame and wage,
but gold and blood forever rage.

Nations decline and rise again,
but blessed like me are all the bold
who keep the gospel — blood and gold.

FLIGHT FROM WORRY

The coal black devil,
(gee up, my magic steed)
we flee from worry,
the coal black devil.

On a black stallion
(gee up, my magic steed)
I galloped hither
on a black stallion.

No dreams attend me
(gee up, my magic steed)
here by the Danube,
no dreams attend me.

Pagans begot me,
(gee up, my magic steed)
worry pursues me,
pagans begot me.

Do not bedazzle,
(gee up, my magic steed)
bright Western heaven,
do not bedazzle.

The guldens beckon,
(gee up, my magic steed)
Turan is calling,
the guldens beckon.

The plains of Asia
(gee up, my magic steed)
still claim obedience,
the plains of Asia.

There we were heroes,
(gee up, my magic steed)
here we are cowards,
there we were heroes.

We were unfettered
(gee up, my magic steed)
by money worry
we were unfettered.

The coal black devil
(gee up, my magic steed)
hotly pursues us,
the coal black devil.

MONEY AND CARNIVAL

I live and gaze upon
the carnival of life;
a bold and beggared few
thus weep and pray with me —
"O carnival of life,
innumerable cheers,
O rushing happy hours,
deflowering of girls,
hot coals of rapturous joy,
beauty, the unveiled Muse,
you blessed, powerful,
vile god — money, money —
O pity us, Amen."

THE MUTE GRIFFINS

They pass across the sky at noon,
the summer noon,
through seas ablaze with searing light —
the golden barbed and golden scaled
lions of flight.

The birds of story, treasure griffins,
unglossal griffins,
are gazers of the solar zone
who proudly bear a vulture head
of diamond stone.

These birds are voiceless, proudly mute,
despairing mute,
and if they make a sound they sway
and fall to earth a shadowy brown,
a sparrow gray.

And there they pass the sky at noon,
the summer noon,
in black of pride through seas of light —
the golden barbed and golden scaled
lions of flight.

THAISES' SPRING FESTIVAL

Blue dawn. Black night
runs into its nest.
Spring.
Hillward I lead
a crowd of girls
with summer song and pipe and string.

Kerchiefed caravan,
slakeless gardens of love,
darlings of night.
Here is the new Pan.
Follow, follow,
sad Thaises, devotees of delight.

New Pan.
The Danube blares,
the thickets hum.
New girls,
nymphs of night,
the darling girls of Buda come.

Let the seductive city rest.
This is the hour of vernal spells.
Sing of virgin love and bliss.
Poor darlings.
This one day
not even Thais sells her kiss.

I hold the stalks of sacred spring
to painted lips.
Money is not the master here.
Lavish your kisses on flowers.
Sing
and hasten for the dusk is near.

Brown dusk. Black night
runs from its nest.
The city calls
and money moves.
The spell is fled,
scatter into your nested walls.

MONK OF MAMMON

By gloomy banks of Babylon I sit,
my harp suspended on a sacred sallow.
The waters lap and winds of life are shrill.
My father, Mammon, hear these fawning prayers
trembling from your little servant's lips.

The harpstrings quake and cry, I sit enslaved;
I am your snow chaste priest, I want for nothing
for over you my longings hold no sway.
My father, Mammon, soothe my sorrowing chasteness
and say that it was you who willed my fate.

Hum that my lot is good, my rags no curse.
Hum that I am your bonze and saintly brother,
that I am spurned by life, by money spurned,
but you find pleasure in your little servant,
the chaste and sombre whom no treasures serve.

By gloomy banks of Babylon I sit
and beg to stay a chaste and monkly orphan,
and beg that money from my face be hid,
and beg I freeze to saintly, icy sculpture,
and that of you this harp should freely sing.

Leda's Golden Statue

ON DEAD SEAS

Her flaming head is circled by
a black and scarlet aureole,
and, look, the lady I call Leda
has stroked once more into my soul.

Into dead seas of darkened youth
with slitting, silent strokes she fades,
two sleek and silvered arms of woman,
two blessed and saintly rowing blades.

Life sits before a mighty feast,
and sunrays roister in the skies;
upon dead seas the sombre shallop
now darts, now darkles, and now flies.

By peace and by a deathly age
the shallop and my soul are spanned;
my soul and dreams are deadly waters
from where the shallop cannot land.

With flowers she once wandered here,
the shallop's silent, sombre guide;
but then the splashing seas were mirthful,
and from the deep, death never cried.

She strokes and strokes encircled by
a black and scarlet aureole.
I know it is her fate to founder
and sink at last into my soul.

ABSALOM'S HAPPY DISGRACE

My spiraled hair,
my bright hair, my brown hair
flutters in the wind.
A youthful god,
lord of strength —
on a black steed
the cowardly curs
I charge, I charge.
O God, my snorting stallion
leaps from beneath me.
My bright hair, my brown hair
snarls on a snow white arm.
A bugle blows.
Somewhere my army flees,
beaten and humbled.
Lost is the proud,
grandly conceived,
glorious battle.
(O evening wind,
gently fan
the disgraced leader's
tingling body
in Leda's pompous arms.)

THE ABANDONED CROSS

I die, let me depart;
like Christ I go, behind me leaving
a hot, charred cross upon your heart.

I kiss your fleshy frame,
your breasts, your soft and saintly shoulders —
and, lo, the cross leaps into flame.

GIVE ME YOUR EYES

Give me your eyes
to spade in this senescent face
and see my own resplendent grace.

Give me your eyes,
your vision that forever builds,
forever grieves, forever gilds.

Give me your eyes,
their killing, burning, aching stare
that pictures me unstained and fair.

Give me your eyes.
By loving you, myself I love;
I envy you those eyes above.

COME, LEDA, WE EMBRACE

Your eyes are sad and wicked,
a deep Gehenna nest;
may salty tears eat out my eyes
if ever there they rest.

Your lips are bloodless gluttons,
a caterpillar swarm;
may my own lips be apoplexed
if for your kiss they warm.

Your lap is soft and tempting,
a downy pillow case
of sin and sorcerous somnolence —
come, Leda, we embrace.

LEDA IN THE GARDEN

In a dark garden on a scarlet swing
I see you toss and sway,
and listless flowers with their grieving cups
are weeping at our kiss.

Dreaming I watch while two scarlet clouds
are straying in the skies,
tossing a languorous kiss on kiss
to perish in desire.

Two scarlet clouds, we sail. Our flame
in licking hunger leaps;
and here below the sated poppies droop
in pity for us two.

SUMMONS TO SACRED JUNE

My aged lips are dank and numb,
above me flares the summer noon,
and Leda clings upon my mouth.
Have mercy on me, sacred June.

Smite me with sunstrokes of desire
and let my mouth be young and wild,
the fresh and scented strawberry
mouth of a girl still undefiled.

Let me once sprinkle with these lips
my Leda's graying autumn eyes.
Our soul will burst with summer's flame,
with blissful troops the Hour will rise.

My mouth would root in Leda's heart
a fair narcissus-flowered grove,
and I would lie in midst of it
like an adventure-seeking Jove.

Small hotelroom. Twilight. Ocean shore.
She is gone and comes again no more.
She is gone and comes again no more.

She has left a flower in her place,
on the shabby couch which I embrace,
on the shabby couch which I embrace.

Like a fleeting kiss the perfumes soar.
Far below, the waves rejoice and roar.
Far below, the waves rejoice and roar.

Far, far off a pharos is aglow.
Come, my love, the ocean chants below.
Come, my love, the ocean chants below.

Listening to the savage salt-sea cry,
dreaming on the shabby couch I lie,
dreaming on the shabby couch I lie.

Here she yielded, lay, and kissed me last —
quiring ocean waves and quiring past,
quiring ocean waves and quiring past.

THE BLACK MOON

(Sail, sail, black moon.
Brown clouds burst into crimson hue
when fell this ugly vagrant youth.

Thunder from far.
And there I lie half way to death.
I ran full speed, I cried, I fell.

Women? Life? Wine?
I fell upon a yellow sward.
How good to lie forevermore.

Sail, sail, black moon.
Hush, hush, tonight the dead wake up.
Hush, hush, they hum and hum and hum.)

Chorus of Shades

Charm order of the charmed and childless kiss,
maelstroms, desires, and mighty bouts of wine,
deep lore in fate and lack of feat —

such was the man,
hallelujah, hallelujah,
born by the Er, the land of reeds.

Chorus of Women

Slumber, slumber,
slumber, fondling,
songful sorrowing,
tender sorrowing,
amorous sorrowing,
ugly youth,
dark brown youth,
slumber, slumber.

Chorus of Shades

Lo, from the East he came, child of the Sun.
Dancing, seductive stars allured him West.
His journey done, now let him sleep.

141

The hands of women,
hallelujah, hallelujah,
sowed his sombre path with grief.

One Woman

Shoo, shoo, dark shades.
Bury, black moon.
With my brown hair
I cover up
the fallen one.
His blighted soul
I lit with fire.
In his sick veins
I poured a venom.
In his bright eyes
I stole a tear.
In his brown fate
I sent a flame.
In his queer heart
I twist a dagger.

(Sail, sail, black moon.
Hush, hush, below the dead wake up.
Hush, hush, they hum and hum and hum.

Fresh dawn awakes
and vainly sheds a kiss on me —
in feverish sweat I sleep and sleep.

Dim shades of women
keep on my sleepless sleep an eye,
wheeling and waiting to alight.

And on my heart —
this night of never ending spells —
a haughty woman stands erect.)

MARY AND VERONICA

From Mary to Veronica
the male embraces span.
Veronica, my lady, Leda,
I want to dream again.

To dream of babies' arms
and of the warmest kiss of all;
before the cross, before my death
now Mary I recall.

A kiss gave me her living breath,
and on my body I employ
the rack of life. But what is life?
A woman's, woman's joy.

Who gave me birth, taught me to kiss?
Upon this death, my dawning other,
lull me, my Leda; let me dream
you are my mother, mother.

LEDA'S GOLDEN STATUE

Never with play could you beguile;
in golden casting you would smile
before my bed.

Green beryl would your eyes compose,
each of your breasts wild opal-rose,
topaz your lips.

Your golden life would never leave;
your essence fair could not deceive,
woman perverse.

Whereso your fleshy self would be,
your golden self would pant for me
forevermore.

When life would hurt me overmuch,
your thighs would cool with blessed touch
my burning brow.

MARUN THE WISE

The simple song about Marun
began with "once upon a time."
Marun the Wise knew all the tales
in the Euphrates' fabled clime.

The young and amorous desert sheikh
the lovesick and immaculate maid,
all ornamental courts of love
their tribute to Marun relayed.

But Bajla, carnal woman, came,
turned round and looked into his eyes.
With "once upon a time" they end,
the stories of Marun the Wise.

Toward Tomorrow

CHARIOT OF SONG

My fitful coursers, whoop, halloo.
The lash will draw your haunches' blood.
I am the young Apollo now,
and who can overtake
the fiery chariot of the sun?

Gee up, my fallow — youthful sin,
gee up, my sable — shadowy dream.
Beyond the bounds of sallow death,
beyond this grayish life
we break, my wild and fitful steeds.

Let not my wheels be flecked by mud.
Let not your hooves be fouled by dirt.
Never across our swaying path
of fame — halloo my steeds —
will aged, faint-armed coachmen swerve.

Behind us little jolting carts
are hurling curses — let them hurl.
By then where do we ride, my steeds,
by then where does he soar —
the young Apollo of new songs?

WHERE ARGYILUS SLEEPS

I am as I shall be. I sleep
within the future's flowery womb.
My radiant Argyilus face
slumbers within the dawning soul
of teenish girls and beardless boys.

I hate these merry little chits.
They are the future who perceives
and yet conceals my slumbering
Argyilus face. They know I am.
Must it be secret while I live?

I long to seize and strangle them
until they lay the future bare
with childish screams and rasping cries —
"Fool grownups, here he walks and lives,
Argyilus, king of mighty dreams."

I AM THEIR NURSE

I am a nurse, a buxom Magyar mammal;
rime-swaddled infants, countless and frail,
roost upon my breast, roost my babes.

Suckle my many blood-rich words
and learn from where this power flows;
so grow the little ones, so they grow.

And when my bulging dugs have dried,
my tiny riming saints, you will,
is it not true, anoint me king?

And I at last — dry nurse, old lion —
will marvel at the men in arms
who grew on the victuals of my heart.

AM SEGULAH

The ghost of Christ and Heine's devil face
have danced before us from afar,
and swept by hailing curses, laughter, light,
the wearers of the patch are running
seared on the forehead with a yellow star.

The chosen race. On their horizon rise
the gallows of the shapeless hills.
The stigmatized, dispersed, and yellow patched.
I go with you, O sombre devils,
you holy keepers of the fiery kilns.

Although a thousand times our blood be strange,
you still are mine, you still are mine.
Your honied women with the tongues of fire
and friendly youth with hearts of love
transfused into my veins the holy wine.

Although you cast me off a hundred times,
I shall return wherever you are.
Eternal signs and roamers of the sky,
leaven of time, I go with you,
wearing a streaming stigma and a star.

This great and sorrowful life belongs to us.
Let us speed on toward the Good
on beds of sickness or beneath the cross.
My pack hounds of the yellow patch,
I run with you and bless you if I could.

THE GREAT HAND

Do you behold, my sombre brethren,
prepared and hopeful for the fray,
a hand has scrawled across the heavens,
"My fellow-beings, come this way."

The great and jestful hand has moved,
and generations scan the sky;
before they make the awkward letters out
an era will have hurried by.

We dance on strings beneath the hand,
and since we read the sky for signs
how many a work of greatness proudly dies,
how many an ancient fame declines.

The hand, the jestful hand, has paused:
Is there a Peter down below?
And when we almost read the writ, it wipes
the slate and scrawls another row.

TOWARD TOMORROW

"Stop!" Into the night cries out
yesterday with motley crew.
"Stop!" And I move on, move on.

"Stop!" I strike toward the copse,
toward hell and moon and clouds,
all alone, all, all alone.

Toward tomorrow I proceed.
Father, mother, priest, and bard,
I desire no more of you.

Ghosts and shadows of the past,
kin in brain as well as blood,
horrid yesterday, remain.

Toward the boundless gloom I stride.
"Stop!" But no, tomorrow waits,
waits for me and I rush on.

FROM ER TO OCEAN

The Er is a droll and dreamy ditch
with muddy water, sedge, and cane;
the Kraszna, Szamos, Tisza, and Danube
bear to the ocean its waves.

Though crushed below the Scythian heights,
and barred by thousand burrowing moles,
and clutched by curses of the blood,
to the ocean I shall flow.

I will this sombre, reckless deed,
I will this wonder of the world,
to flow into the sacred ocean
when starting from the Er.

Notes on BLOOD AND GOLD

1. **The Hotel Lodger.** See the Introduction, page 33.

2. **On Autumn Nights.** Set to music by Béla Bartók.

3. **Three Autumn Tears.** Set to music by Béla Bartók.

4. **Matthias' Demented Scholar.** Matthias Corvinus was king of Hungary from 1458 to 1490. His reign was marked by the rapid development of Hungary into a centralized national state and the spread of Renaissance culture. In the annals of early European history he stands for great power, administrative efficiency, military strength, and great culture. Surrounded by Italian humanists, he maintained a resplendent Renaissance court, the earliest non-Italian court of its kind. Although a serious and highly reputable literature in the Hungarian language began to flourish by the latter half of the sixteenth century, Latin was both an official and a literary language from the time the country was founded in the tenth century until the nineteenth century. In the "demented scholar" Ady recreates a "living witness" of the Corvin era.

5. **Saint Margaret's Island.** Saint Margaret (1242-1271) was the daughter of Béla IV, king of Hungary during the Mongolian invasion and the subsequent reconstruction period. Margaret preferred a monastic to a court life. Rejecting three royal suitors, she took her final mo-

nastic vows at the age of nineteen years and lived a life of poverty in a convent on the Danubian island now named after her.

6. **City of Clouds.** For "Hortobágy" see Note 2 in Notes on NEW VERSES, page 96.

7. **I Am Not a Magyar?** Schwabs is the name given to magyarized Germans. The literary standard bearers of the conservatives during Ady's lifetime were for the most part writers of German origin.

8. **Alone with the Sea.** Set to music by Béla Bartók.

9. **The Black Moon.** For the "Ér" see Note 12 below.

10. **Marun the Wise.** Marun is a fictitious name of the kind Ady used on a number of occasions when treating Near Eastern themes, thus recreating the "lost" mythology of the Magyars, who had spent a part of their history in southwest Asia after leaving their original Finno-Ugric homeland in central Russia.

11. **Where Argyilus Sleeps.** Argyilus is a fabulous prince or lucky third son who marries the princess in Hungarian folktales.

12. **From Er to Ocean.** The Ér, a tiny stream that flows by Ady's native village, is tied to the Black Sea by the river system of Kraszna, Szamos, Tisza, and Danube.

ON ELIJAH'S CHARIOT

(1908)

ON ELIJAH'S CHARIOT

The Lord bears off Elijah-like
those whom he greatly loves and tries.
He gives them swift and fiery souls,
the flaming chariots of the skies.

Elijah's men toward heaven rush
and pause on caps of endless snow.
On summits of Himalaya
with clattering wheels the chariots go.

By winds of fate they are impelled —
outcasts between the earth and sky,
as toward a wicked, chilling grace
the chariots of Elijah fly.

Their brains are ice, their souls are fire;
earth laughs as on their path they sway.
With cold and glinting diamond dust
the sun in pity strews their way.

Beneath Mount Sion

ADAM, WHERE ART THOU?

The misty brown of mourning flees,
in vast white radiance comes the Lord
to subjugate mine enemies.

Although his face he still conceals,
the lingering sun of his large eye
now frequently upon me steals.

If now and then I vanquish foes,
the Lord it is who strides before,
with naked sword ahead he goes.

I hear his footfall in my soul;
at his sad "Adam, where art thou?"
my heart rings out an answering toll.

I now have found him in my heart,
found him to hold him fast embraced
and never in death to be apart.

ON GOD'S LEFT

Somehow or other God exists
bottom to every thought we have.
For him we always toll the bell,
but, oh, on his left hand I sit.

Our God is the compassionate;
for long he stays unseen and mute,
but now and then he tolls the heart
with bell-tongues of a hundredweight.

God does not come toward us, of course,
to give us aid in our distress;
God is the self, the anguished mind,
the plan, the kiss — God is all.

God is a great and powerful lord;
he is the darkness and the light,
a tyrant whom the centuries
have squatted deep into our soul.

God is the simple and naive.
He wearies of the very good,
he wearies of the restless men,
the frequent dreamers of great dreams.

God does not love me — I have searched
too long for him, and even before
coming across him in my quest
I dickered with the Lord of Hosts.

Somehow or other God exists
bottom to every thought we have.
For him we always toll the bell,
but, oh, on his left hand I sit.

THE WOODLAND CROSS

A snowy cross within the woods
upon a vast and wintry night,
an image marbled from the past.
We rode there in our tinkling sleigh
upon a vast and wintry night.

My father was a joyful man
who sang when on the cross he gazed.
I was the son of such a sire,
who wearied of the graven wood
and sang when on the cross he gazed.

Two stiffnecked Magyar Calvinists,
like flight of time we flew along,
father and son — a yes and no.
We sang as in the sleigh we sat,
like flight of time we flew along.

And twenty years have passed since then;
my sleigh is flying in the night.
No more, as once, am I remiss,
I lift my hat and bow my head;
my sleigh is flying in the night.

THE LORD'S ARRIVAL

When they forsook me here
and with my soul I stumbling trod,
unlooked for and unspeakingly
I was embraced of God.

With mute embrace he came,
not with a trumpet call of fright.
He came not in the blaze of noon
but in tumultuous night.

These eyes that were so vain
are blind. My youth has ceased to be,
but him, the radiant, I behold
for all eternity.

160

PRAYER AFTER WAR

My Lord, it is from war I come,
all things surcease, surcease.
Set me at peace with myself and Thee,
in truth, Thou art the Peace.

An aching tumor is my heart,
and nothing soothes my pain.
Upon my heart set Thou a kiss
that somewhat it may wane.

My sombre eyes are closed toward all
that is on earth to see,
and they have nothing to behold
save Thee, my Lord, save Thee.

My speeding legs one time knee-deep
waded in bloody lees.
But now, behold, I have no legs,
just knees, my Lord, just knees.

I do not kiss, I do not war,
my lips are sere and dry.
These arms are shriveled stumps — my Lord,
measure me with Thine eye.

Look down at me Thou too, my Lord;
all things surcease, surcease.
Set me at peace with myself and Thee;
in truth, Thou art the Peace.

Divinely bearded and unkempt
in rags he flit and puffed cold air,
my long ago forgotten Lord.
Upon a dank and blinded dawn
beneath Mount Sion it was somewhere.

He wore a flowing, bell-shaped frock
with scarlet scripture patched and sewn.
Shabby and sombre was the Lord.
He flapped and beat upon the fog.
I heard a bell-like Advent tone.

I held a lantern in my hand,
within my soul was faith again,
and in my mind departed youth.
I recognized the smell of God,
for I was seeking someone then.

He paused for me beneath the mount,
the stones leaped into blazing fire.
He tolled the bell and soothed me
and soaked my face with gentle tears —
merciful was the ancient sire.

I kissed his wrinkled, ancient hand,
and with a racking wail I thought —
"What is your name, my kind old Lord
to whom I said so many prayers?"
But for his name in vain I sought.

"I have returned to you in death
from life where I was damned to hell.
Must I recall a childhood prayer?"
He looked at me with sorrowful eyes
and tolled the bell and tolled the bell.

"If I but knew your lofty name."
He paused. I heard a dirgelike air,
and psalmic heels withdrew uphill.
And weepingly I sit and moan
beneath Mount Sion lost somewhere.

LOVE ME, GOD

My God in glebe and grass and stone,
let us no more give hurt for hurt,
I often walk the burial grounds.

I cite and call you often to mind.
You are now the most real Are-Not,
by old Magyar name, the primal Beast.

Love me if you know how to love.
Love me, for I am held in spite,
and there is good in being loved.

Love me, and softly give embrace.
Ha, we live within a knavish world,
and my salvation depends on bread.

I would like to be a reinless lord,
but lot and life are measured out,
so must one live, so must one eat.

So must one kiss, and so survive,
so must one forge his mighty plans —
to ask, but always give and give.

THE GREAT WHALE

O God of ours, you awful whale,
for countless worlds what fate shall be?
On your prodigious back we dance.
Move not, your spine is slippery.

Slimy the back on which you hold
our soul and universal space.
A trembling heart and feeble legs
are all that I before you place.

In turn remove the fears that have
like winds into my marrow roared.
Reveal that neither Jew you are
nor Gentile, but a frightful Lord.

Take me up midway on your back
that my weak legs may find repose,
that easier my heart may beat,
and sleep at times my eyes may close.

Or cast me off for once and all,
dance not, hang still, sport not for aye.
I bear no more. Your lifeless stars
now light my face with tranquil ray.

THE JOYFUL GOD

You have mistaken him for death
although he is death's lord,
and you are in his presence when
you dare to tease and banter death.

If you speak out, "All hail to life,"
death's lord emits a light;
the joyful God shines down on you
if you speak out, "All hail to life."

MY DREAM IS GOD

My pack is the ponderous none,
my path is the nihil, the nought,
my fate is to go and go,
my dream is God.

I want to encounter my dream
with great, unreasoning faith,
to pray as before and cry,
"My God, my God."

The war of defiance is done,
I fill with a godly desire —
when dying, man likes to make
his peace with God.

SCOURGE ME, LORD

You tyrannized, abased, and hurt me, Lord.
Your many scourges whistled in the wind.
You best know why.
Your little servant must have greatly sinned.

I was not guiltless; I stole your songs,
I kissed your women, gulped your wine at urge.
I merit this —
the tear-soaked, acid-sharp, and salty scourge.

You spun a scourge for me from every sin;
my drops of sickly blood would often fall.
But your kiss scourge
is the most agonizing one of all.

My Lord, withhold this scorpion for the last
that I may worthy punishment receive,
but scourge her too
for whom this stung and wicked heart I leave.

THE NOCTURNAL GOD

My God is playing games with me,
the trump of old he now repays —
he slips away when morning grays
the room he kept with me all night.

And now and then I know an hour
when I behold his form complete,
but never by day's light and heat —
he stays but always stays at night.

He is the woman who will show
her person to adoring eyes
but flees before they scrutinize.
He stays but fitful is the night.

My God, my playful, jestful God,
who are you but a shadowy veil?
I fain would walk your radiant trail —
you stay but only stay at night.

When the oppressed, the nobodies,
come uttering moans and bearing arms,
God comes₁ and untold powers and joys
that died within the spirit's womb
come uttering moans and bearing arms.

To those who murder life and joy
no grace or mercy will be shown.
God waits for several thousand years,
but then, woe to the murderers
no grace or mercy will be shown.

For God is living sense of truth.
This he commands — everyone live.
This he commands — everyone cheer.
This he commands — murderers die.
This he commands — everyone live.

God will arrive, this primal life,
and then his trumpet will resound —
"Lo, ye unborn, ye dead, ye quick,
today I render justice here."
And then his trumpet will resound.

And those who lived on others' tears
will die a ghastly, gruesome death.
Tyrants in grave, in life, in groin,
this plague besmitten carrion flock,
will die a ghastly, gruesome death.

GOD THE CHEERLESS

God is the all but cannot bless,
God is the all but cannot chasten,
God is fulfilment of all time,
and yet he cannot see into our hearts.

Mightier than Jehovah's mighty self,
God is the father of a cold amen.
God is only a smile, a will,
a frozen semblance of a frozen sun.

Incessantly he spins the infinite
as if he wearied of a paltry toy.
He freezes here a world or two,
and five or six he flings into the fire.

God does not warn, reward, or vindicate,
and he conveys us to no sky or grave.
Though God and mankind are the same,
he is the must and will be and amen.

If maddened by a dreadful agony
we mangle flesh and bone of our own selves,
God is amused — he does not love,
he does not goad us to a greater rage.

God is the mighty watercourse of life
which neither dams nor sluggish banks contain.
It rumbles, blares, resounds, and moans,
ceaselessly crushes, rolls, and seethes.

God is the mover of the mighty course
that is without beginning or an end.
He is the cheerless and the all,
the one unalterable, awful God.

The Hungarian Winterland

SONG OF THE HUNGARIAN JACOBIN

Red inspissate spurts from our fingertips
when we palpate you,
poor anaesthetized hungary.
Do you exist? — and we?
who would raise a ziggurat to the zenith
but cozened of orb and vision
wait for the riff raff
of babel to waken?
When will we fuze a thousand mycelian desires
into one enormous will?
for magyar, slav and roman sorrows
are issue of a single sorrow.
We shared one anguish and humiliation
a millenium.
When shall we meet invincible,
screaming on the barricade of ideas?
The voices of our rivers are one,
murmuring, gentle, and deathly.
What hell in the land of the arpads
unless you are lord or dastard.
When shall we coalesce
and call out in one voice,
we the rabble and homeless,
the magyars and non-magyars?
How long will they be rulers
and we the sheepish millions?
Will our people always be penned?
We have no faith or bread,
but all belongs to us tomorrow
in this land of the sombre disinherited
if we will and if we dare.

ALONE WE THREE

Alone we three are on the field,
a peasant curse and God and I.
We all shall perish, well I know;
I give but one unsparing cry.

I do not tremble for myself;
Satan already owns my hide.
But by the field, the peasant curse,
and God with watchful care I bide.

Here summer, autumn, winter, spring
have reassured our hopes in vain.
No miracles can come to pass
unless we three remain, remain.

THE HUNGARIAN WINTERLAND

Whenever on wintry nights I sweep
upon my train in arching course
above the snowy Magyar plains,
the farm huts are asleep.

How bleak the fields, how white they gleam.
While keen and fitful gusts of wind
are whispering lullabies above,
what do the farm huts dream?

Or do they dream like long ago?
I am now homeward bound for Yule,
an aged stripling, but my soul
is there beneath the snow.

And as across the plains we fly
I think that both of us are dead,
as dreamlessly we dream away,
the farm huts well as I.

MOHACS

If God is, may he have no mercy
upon this people callous to the lash,
faint-hearted singers of a gypsy dirge.
Scourge him, scourge, scourge.

If God is, may he have no pity,
because I was born a Hungarian.
Let not his dove arrive with leafy tip.
Whip me, whip, whip.

If God is, may he always drive us
between the lowest world and brightest heaven.
Let him not grant a moment's rest to sigh,
or we die, die.

THE COUNTRY HOUSE

White walls, blond beams,
a silent, sombre rustic roof.
When you and I are in cabal
we do not spoof.

In shriving night
our deepest secrets we must weep.
And if we stare into the dark,
black shadows creep.

How much we shrive
on nights when sleep remains far off.
Pst! moaning snow ice trickles down
the tinny trough.

LAKE OF DEATH

We wheel above the Lake of Death —
fair, bold, and haughty birds;
and lazy, loathsome, hungry fish
with serpent heads emerge.
This reeking lake, this sombre curse
they give the name of Hungary.

And all is vain, we all are drawn
into the lake below.
In vain our love, our bursts of flame,
our goodness, brain, and soul,
for we will never win or own
this Lake of Death, this Hungary.

Between Leda's Lips

YOUR INCOMPARABLE WARMTH

Why does art or sculpture seek
to entice you from my soul,
for among the cold and quick
who can still on me bestow
your incomparable warmth?

With my every kiss I die
on your lips to be reborn.
Let sirocco women come —
vainly do they waft their sweet
and emaciating warmth.

Vainly would the quick and dead
try to cool you — yours alone
is the warmth that will not die.
Who can still on me bestow
your incomparable warmth?

BETWEEN LEDA'S LIPS

I want to steal between your lips,
but, lo, you open up your eyes.
My boon companions spy the stealth —
upon the night a full moon lies.

How long, my Leda, must we play
this winking, guileful hide-and-seek?
I know they are upon my trail,
I must not moan or cry or speak.

Within your large green, sorrowful eyes
my fellows reel with winey breath;
they ogle, gloat, and lie in wait —
the three are Rapture, God, and Death.

They may wheel on my heart at will.
My Leda, kiss, kiss me to nought
that they shall have arrived in vain
should I between your lips be caught.

KISS TILL FAINT

This is the land of Kiss till Faint,
which folklore sings in dreadful plaint.
With satyr form and forest beard
somewhere in sombre mountain deeps
like a big young girl it lies and sleeps.

It palpitates beneath the moon,
and moaning mountains fall in swoon.
Worshiping white and radiant holms,
they lie where sacred wells arise,
and choke on kisses, blood, and sighs.

And woe to him who roams this place
and meets a woman's warm embrace.
His hunger never will have fill.
His lips and heart will wear away,
but kiss till faint he shall for aye.

At eve and dawn in endless length,
though having neither woman nor strength,
he lies and pants on violet hills;
and with a woman or without
he kisses till death comes about.

THE LOVERS' MOON

There is no moonlight,
only a moon
for this immaculate night
on sky and earth
flow dark and fateful tides.

Legendary
we ride on swiftening currents,
this is the night
the moon is dark
at the knell of a kiss like ours.

This night
dies a suicide at dawn,
we speed, embrace,
and die ourselves
if we should see the moon.

THE OTHER WOMAN

The seigniories I claim as mine,
and I remain a sexton slave
under the cruel command to live
a woman gave.

When will the other woman come
and sunder twain her living spell
with a command that I should bid
this life farewell?

DELILAH AND RUTH

In hundred forms a hundred ways
I see you as Delilah and as Ruth,
I see you as everyone.

I see you as the fair and good,
the golden gorgeous and the loathsome foul,
I see you as everyone.

I see you sharp and evil eyed,
immaculately white and stained with blood,
I see you as everyone.

I see you as the part and whole,
the honeycomb, the kiss, the curd, the salt,
I see you as everyone.

I see you as the queen of flies,
an ugly carcass, angel, glorious truth,
I see you as everyone.

I see you as the quick and dead,
the feast, the wake, the blessing, and the ball,
I see you as everyone.

In hundred forms a hundred ways
I see you as Delilah and as Ruth,
I see you as everyone.

THE WOMAN'S DUE

From passions of the purple past
a marbled obelisk remains,
your sombre figure marks the stone
upon my grave.

I know you only guard yourself
by the grim, jealous watch you keep,
but by your stolen march you forced,
death to recede.

Pompous you stand in shaded light;
and when the searchers come like ghouls,
you will proclaim the greatness of
the woman's due.

You will proclaim it was your wish,
that you effected all events,
that you are mightier than I
and even death.

ABOARD A DEATH TRAIN

O trains that wail me to
and from her,
fare unwell
as you fly into the noose of night.

O winking lamps, you draw
me deathward,
and we meet
on the death cry of a wedding feast.

THE BLACK STAIRS

Click-clack, as if a woman nears,
stealing from darkened flight to flight.
My heart stops, and I wait for strange
adventures in the autumn night.

Click-clack, my heart begins to beat.
I listen — in deep ecstasy,
in muted tempo, secret rhythm
someone is coming, coming to me.

Click-clack, and now the autumn dark
is strumming with the muffled hum
of a sepulchral night — again
no one has come, no one has come.

BESIDE YOUR SOUL

Where shoots of tendrils lie in curls
I want to kiss
pale temples, two blinded eyes,
the two fair valleys of your head.

I want to sleep beside your soul,
steal in your head,
stay undespoiled while I invent
or find some new and hungering thrill.

Inside death's drying-house I lie,
heavy in thought;
my tissues may have dried away,
but even bodiless I crave.

Before I leave I want to kiss
with virgin mouth
the two fair valleys of your head,
I want to sleep beside your soul.

MY BRIDE

Our past is ruin and decay.
You were at the spear tip
of destroying angel hosts.
For this I love you.

Return not with the fire caress,
my mistress bride of old,
the spark and ash of every kiss,
the heart of living.

Our soul is ruin and decay.
Did we not wish for this?
A cerecloth covers up our fate.
For this I love you.

The Street Song

STAR OF STARS

Never will the red star fall —
sun, moon, and Venus streak from sight,
but the red star lords in the eastern sky.

The falling star is never red
but rose, lilac, blue, white or green —
caprices of the celestial sphere.

Falling star, fall, fall to death
with a thousand tumbles, thousand woes,
dawn can emerge with one star alone.

Red star, shine refulgent and rule.
Since first men looked toward the sky,
the red star has kept their hope alive.

GRANDSON OF DOZSA

I am grandson of George Dozsa,
people's griever, sombre, noble farmer.
Ho you magnates, step in parley
with my scythemen, for the summer hisses.

Summer hisses, scythes are sharpened.
Ho you silken magnates, fists of evil,
what if Dozsa's vagrant followers
seethe upon you with appalling fury.

If the people come, ho magnates,
whither from marauding castle litters
shall you flee? What if the portal
shuts and clatters?

Flower of Death

My Lord God, send me in your grace
before I die
some kind of strange and curious love,
some kind of strange and curious love.

Let him who sees become stark mad
at my embrace,
the science of an evil kiss,
the science of an evil kiss.

A scherzo burst of mighty sex
seize on the dolts
and bring that night of evil on,
and bring that night of evil on.

And though accursed I am absolved
because I lived
the truth of life, the kiss, the key,
the truth of life, the kiss, the key.

This life, debris of a perished love,
I long to shame
with a new concept of the kiss,
with a new concept of the kiss.

FLOWER OF DEATH

On the dark way to my last kiss
with a team of sable moths I wing.
My mistress is the flower of death —
she is the strangest flower I know,
an aster blooming in the spring.

O flower of death, whenever the first
May moon upon the heaven beams,
I lay me on your swaying bed.
See to, see to, O flower of death,
that every little petal gleams.

Now lay your chaliced body bare
beneath the wonder-stricken moon,
and while we to each other cleave,
let all the garden bushes ring
with an impassioned wedding tune.

Let all the little flowers whisper,
"This was the kisses' Lazarus.
Though born a mighty lord of love,
he never won a worthy kiss,
and now his last he kisses thus."

Let glow your hair, your eyes, your mouth,
your godly breasts, your hips, your arms,
your velvet-satin legs, your all.
Sweeten for me, O flower of death,
this love, the last to work her charms.

And then my team of sable moths
with their empty coach will fly away.
Flee then you too, O flower of death.
I do not want you to perceive
what death and I, when alone, shall say.

WHOM I KISS

Those whom I kiss grow yellow, smother —
I do not even dare to kiss
my mother.

O woe to those whose dreamings hover
about me as a faithful friend
and lover.

O woe to those who seek to love me,
to be sincere of heart is far
above me.

Those whom I kiss grow yellow, smother —
I do not even dare to kiss
my mother.

HOTEL AT TWELVE

At twelve o'clock in my hotel
I hear the songs of mighty Sex,
the springy songs of Mister N
and of Miss X.

The mothlike pairs have found their mates
beneath the gaslamps on the streets,
and in my bed I lurk and wait
between white sheets.

I eavesdrop through the lonely night
and listen to the tireless lovers.
I pity them that dawn must spy
upon the covers.

Dawn comes and I am still alert.
They sleep upon an unsexed sea.
Will they awake and turn to love?
And what of me?

IN THE FONTAINEBLEAU

The sombre showers of yellow acacia blooms
descend in streams.
In the ruinous forest of the Bonapartes
with sparkling eyes I trace a maze of dreams.

Near by I hear the smothered sounds of lips;
the heated noise
of strong embraces strikes upon my ear;
here too are joys, here too another's joys.

Here too is love, here too delight abounds
and pants for air.
And yet the kisses and the acacia blooms
within this forest are not more lasting or fair.

A Parisian couple here made their marriage bed.
They laughed in play.
They laughed as they kissed and did not even see
how fell the yellow acacias where they lay.

O lovers wise, you know how to kiss. Kiss on
in handsome ease.
This is the true kiss — in the Bonapartes'
ruinous forest of yellow acacia trees.

ON MOUNT ATHOS

Two friars carry up the wine;
the board will groan today.
Brothers, now let us take our fill
hallelujah, hallelujah,
of rapture and of grace.

How strange tonight the autumn sky.
This wine is blood of Christ.
The little stars are cherubim.
Hallelujah, hallelujah,
how bright is Mary's shrine.

The crucifix is dancing there;
our song resounds on high.
Harken, how low the organ moans.
Hallelujah, hallelujah,
how bright is Mary's shrine.

The Lord it is, the Lord who wills
his servants' dark desires
should burst out freely now and then
hallelujah, hallelujah,
into the shining night.

Behold that Mary made of stone —
a smile bestirs her lip.
A scarlet toga is our frock,
hallelujah, hallelujah,
and in us is God's mirth.

How bright aglow the ancient church,
how fair the steeple's shape
as though it were the gleaming white,
hallelujah, hallelujah,
form of an undraped maid.

Tomorrow comes the confiteor,
devotion, curse, and rite.
Today raise high the wine-filled cup,
hallelujah, hallelujah,
the brothers sacrifice.

AFTER A MAY SHOWER

Far off the mountain stood in mist,
the meadow vapored, the brook flowed strong.
And straight within my weary veins
upon a soaked and spongy field,
my blood burst into scarlet song,
my blood burst into scarlet song.

The grass, it seemed, in growing scraped,
the light caroused, the sun rode high,
the leaves burst forth, the earth grew green,
the heaven danced, the earth danced,
and all things kissed beneath the sky,
and all things kissed beneath the sky.

I close my blinking urban eyes,
to all these kisses unconcealed;
trembling and restless I invoke
the Lord with hushed and solemn voice,
"Thy blessings on this much-kissed field,
Thy blessings on this much-kissed field."

A troop of women here and there
is hoeing where soon life will be.
(Oh still, oh still, it's good to live.)
How young and strong these women are,
their legs are naked to the knee,
their legs are naked to the knee.

With King Frost

THE PEASANT SUMMER

In the lordly tread of my autumn days,
behold, I see a comer —
a handsome peasant, an ancient peasant,
the summer, the lazy summer.

Blessed is he who is his son,
blessed again and again.
Blessed is he whom summer loves,
the strong and sturdy men.

Blessed who always begins anew,
blessed whom life detains,
blessed is he who mows with cheer,
blessed a peasant remains.

Summer is the kindliest sire;
he gives of the strong and pleasant.
I doff my lordly hat before
summer, the ancient peasant.

Summer does not dream, but mows
and sings and does not run;
he reaps with strong and certain strength,
happy beneath the sun.

Behold, the lordly autumn's child,
a sickly footman am I;
summer behind me, winter before,
and in spring-time I shall die.

And summer tramples me and speaks
with neither haste nor worry,
"He also was a child of mine,
but he was in a hurry."

A RASORIAL SONG

big bellied clouds and wind songs
the tassel of light shadow on fields
anguish in the heart sacred spring
mirrored people and villages
man from the past
the hen in a spaded field
scratch up a worm

spring returns
once more enticing and inciting
and autumn again
over and over
desire is born a-dying
man runs from winter into death
and into a hencoop the hen

STEEDS OF DEATH

Upon a highway white with moonlight
whenever the herdsmen of the sky
are rounding up their scattered cattle,
the shoeless steeds of death come trotting,
trotting toward us ever nigh.

Noiseless and murderous are the chargers,
which ghostly horsemen sit astride,
moody and melancholy horsemen.
The moon is awed and hides in panic
when down the silvery road they ride.

From where they come, who could but tell us?
When all the world is fast asleep,
they slack the stirrup and stop in silence;
always a ghostly, empty saddle,
and always one free mount they keep.

The one for whom the riders halted
turns deathly pale and mounts his steed;
and in the search for other riders
they gallop through the misty midnight
and on the moonlit highway speed.

WITH KING FROST

The dwarf of spirit live in winter,
their sovereign is the mighty Frost,
a tyrant king, a frozen king,
whose beard is meters, meters long
and mercy is so short.

O little, frosty, mighty King
who has no eyes but has a heart,
a heart so small and profitless
of sleet and ice and hail and snow,
O grant me leave, King Frost.

I came here from the land of giants,
our emperor is the holy Warmth,
whose serf I am, O little king.
O grant me leave, you have a heart,
although it is so small.

HYMN TO NIHILITY

Midnight is radiant,
dawn is black lust,
God is unrighteous,
the devil is just.

June is an ice-pit
December is heat,
grief a red poppy,
glory brown deceit.

Snowflakes are beetles,
white like pitch tar,
the actual a dream,
and the subjunctives are.

Death is an orgy,
life a little inn,
vice is a virtue,
and virtue a sin.

Salt is a sweet,
honey bitter ruth,
today is a falsehood,
tomorrow the truth.

Nothing exists that is,
the common is odd,
the devil is our kinsman,
our enemy — God.

WHITE LOTUS FLOWERS

Deep from my oozy, sinful soul
rises a strange and bubbling spume,
like tears of brides who weep by night,
when lo, upon the surface scum
white lotus flowers burst in bloom.

And birds of legend, golden-winged,
on foamy waters splash and fret.
I feel my soul is flowering forth,
that I am childlike, big, and blessed;
I burn, desire, believe, forget.

My fenny soul is crystalline,
like fabled lands where children dwell,
where castles swing upon web feet,
and all is white as virgin snow,
enchantments of a fairy spell.

White dreams and thoughts, white lotus flowers
spread far about; the froth obscene
becomes a molten silver lake.
Aflame with heat I learn to know
my life is holy, dear, and clean.

The lotus flowers curtsy low
before the summer moon above;
and in the twilight of my soul
there bathe the moments, high designs,
graces, and women bright with love.

But gusts of wind whirl down the street;
once more I see the dreary hours.
The frozen fen begins to creak.
They were, but swiftly are no more,
my empty soul's white lotus flowers.

The Constrained Hercules

MY NEW BOOK

As here they are envolumed, dead,
in print, I do not even know
if from my lips these songs have sped.

To whomsoever they belong,
they are so strange and so remote —
the curse and psalm, complaint and song.

They are bemocked, and they misgive,
these satans of my sombre soul,
those who their lives but halfway live.

I know how splendid it would be,
if it had been but someone else
who lived and wept this agony.

But it was I, O woe, O woe,
who bore these wild new gloomy songs,
which I atoned for long ago.

Notes to ON ELIJAH'S CHARIOT

    1. **Song of the Hungarian Jacobin.** Árpáds—The Hungarian royal dynasty from the time of the conquest (896 A. D.) to the fourteenth century.

    2. **The Hungarian Winterland.** Ady made a special point of visiting his parents' home every Christmas season up to the time of his marriage in 1915. The farm huts are **tanyas** or isolated settlements which are characteristic of the great Hungarian plain. Having developed as summer houses for peasants during the period of the Turkish invasions, they remained as regular habitations when the Turks were expelled and cattle breeding increasingly gave way to agriculture. Because of the difficulty of providing educational, medical, or social services within the area, the **tanya** population was left almost entirely to its own devices. This area was the most backward in the Hungarian kingdom, although the population was almost entirely Magyar.

    3. **Star of Stars.** See the Introduction, page 42-43 for comments applicable to this poem.

    4. **Grandson of Dozsa.** Dózsa, rimes with closure without the final **r**, was the leader of a bloody peasant rebellion in the year 1514. See the Introduction, page 21.

LONGING FOR LOVE

(1909)

LONGING FOR LOVE

Neither the issue nor the sire,
neither fulfilment nor desire
am I for anyone,
am I for anyone.

I am as all men, the sunless sea,
the alien thule, mystery,
a fleeing wisp of light,
a fleeing wisp of light.

But I must look for friends and brothers;
I want to show myself to others
that seeing they will see,
that seeing they will see.

For this my lyric masochism;
I long to close the gaping schism,
and thus belong somewhere,
and thus belong somewhere.

Thomas Esze's Gossip

GRANDSON OF OND

Upon a bout of wine and blood
I summoned shadows of the dead
and met with Ond, barbaric chief.

Upon a Cossack horse he sat,
arrogant on a plundered horse,
and at the sight my blood ran cold.

I would give him my love in vain,
for nothing binds us and we are
unlike in vision, spine, and thought.

Different my steed, my blood, my dream.
I come of him and yet how strange
my kind, my father, and my king.

A patch of grief like this is sewn
on no one in the whole wide world
but Magyars who outgrow their kind.

THE PRINCESSES DUL

By the Sea of Azov a story spread
the King was a senile, stubborn fool,
but never were there maidens more fair
than the hundred princesses Dul.

At headlong speed on a summer's eve
a hundred handsome warriors came,
who stared into the Azov sea
and a forest full of game.

They were goodly, lofty Magyar youths
who scanned the stretch of waves and trees,
when mum, they sent a sign somewhere
and dreamt of white chemise.

By the Azov this was the great cabal.
With peril the times were overawed.
In summer men's desires are hot,
for she is a mighty bawd.

In summer men live countless years,
and their souls roll swiftly on before.
To take the princesses Dul the hook
was cast upon the shore.

A hundred sinewy warriors vowed
that horses might perish and arrows snap,
but in flush of passion they would spring
a certain castle trap.

Upon a shaded slope they struck
a youthful and seductive tune,
while they awaited the maidens' descent,
the kiss, the victor's boon.

By the Sea of Azov they lay in wait
as the heat collected and grew dense.
By tent doors old and shaggy chiefs
awaited in suspense.

And then the princesses Dul arrived,
led forward each by a savage groom.
The bulging hearts of the ancient bloods
silently burst in bloom.

And on these hearts before the tents
a far-off tragedy seemed too light,
as darkly on the princesses Dul
descended the wedding night.

Two Saintly Sailboats

To my lady Leda, whom I would
leave in vain and who would leave
me in vain, for she shall always be
the Woman.

BEFORE THE CATHEDRAL

Eve, autumn eve.
Milan. Before the spires
a something sank on us
and wracked our hearts with wounds.

We bled and hurt.
We kissed each other's eyes
and asked with bleeding lips,
"Whose curse, whose curse is this?"

The spires, mute spires,
stretched skyward in the autumn fog
and mocked and laughed to scorn
a sinful, sombre, lofty love.

YOUR DAUGHTER

The calyces of elfin gold
at midnight by her bedside glitter,
and rows of princes stand on guard
but never touch her coverlet,
so I conceive your daughter.

Before her cedar trees salaam,
behind her mother-curses flutter.
She leaves behind for centuries
the fragrance of her virgin flesh.
a nemesis your daughter.

She casts a spell on every youth,
the undesiring she could fetter,
her very breath an act of love,
her very glance a genesis,
a woman is your daughter.

She makes the veins of man and earth
hiss like a hot Gehenna gutter.
A trembling world turns pale and white
when incandesced by her white skin,
and brightly laughs your daughter.

Although death followed on my crime,
tonight the world could not burn hotter.
I think of you with eyes shut fast
and reach out two accursed arms,
I would embrace your daughter.

THE AUTUMN ISLE

The graying grass, the fretted boughs,
the autumn flowers
I saw today upon an isle,
the graying grass, the fretted boughs,
the autumn flowers
within my ashen autumn heart.

I neither envy nor accuse.
Six years have fled,
six aching autumns frayed our hearts,
and still there was our happiness,
the fleeting spell,
elusive intervals of spring.

But can we not essay once more,
once more throughout,
the antique saga of the isle?
The graying grass, the fretted boughs,
the autumn flowers
I shame to see within my heart.

TWO SAINTLY SAILBOATS

On crags we lie, two castaways,
our bodies are so fair —
fleet nomads of the stretching seas,
two sails that stormed the deep.

The waves have dashed our robust planks,
but sound are sail and mast.
Suppose the specter of old winds
should of a sudden spring?

Ours is the right to live again,
never to be afraid
or query for how long we leave.
Slip back into the sea.

Though battered may we boldly fly
beneath ill-omened night,
and saintly winds godspeed our ships
that damaged on the kiss.

THE COLD MOON

The moon is cold in vain. Once
an hour of frenzy struck,
and sacred fevers burnt the night
in which unguided time
corralled a fair and wretched pair —
one unit of manifold time,
mad, merciful, luxuriant time,
which drove my woman and me together
and which is without end since then.

The skies are studded with burning sores,
on earth an aguish mantle rustles,
behind us a mantle rustles,
the flowing mantle of our sorrow,
our fawn-colored and royal cover,
streaked with red and sombre love.
But from the front we gleam uncovered,
and our free breasts give forth a light.

Now neither near nor far exists
for my woman and her bachelor youth.
We glide along, we cling together
while the cool moon envelops us.
We hold each other and tremble
as though we never had dissolved in two.

I have always loved this woman.
I was always in her mouth and heart,
and she was both my mouth and heart
when drunkenly I often wandered
lost and damned in nights at Varad,
when I had already buried my throne
and clumsy fate had shattered me,
and I was less than nothing.

It happened as often as
my dear and driven woman came.
It happened whenever in adoration
our twofold self embraced
and again grew one.
And this was not even love
but a rewelding here on earth
within this arrant and divisive time.

In this vagrant time, this vagrant woman
you shall see me again if you will.
This one street of time, this tyrant,
will again assault our twofold one.
My woman is growing gray in vain,
and I am wearing away, but all in vain
because you still shall envy us.

The cold moon is our star.
A colder star you will never find.
But gray hairs and unfinished songs
love us, burningly love us,
though no one fathoms this never known love.
Our sombre mantle stretches and laughs,
but our uncovered front gleams in the night,
and tumbling and fainting again and again
together forever we cling.

A WALK AROUND MY BIRTHPLACE

This is the Benedict, do you see it?
a gentle mound of melancholy spells,
old cloister site, on every Benedict eve
you see a misty tower gleam and leave
among the gonglike ghosts of sunken bells.

This is the Er, our dreamy little stream
that meets the Kraszna of which you have read.
Today the banks are dry and caked and sick.
Would you, my lady, wish to have me pick
a few dead flowers from this morbid bed?

This is the ghostly Koto, vanished town,
sacked by a Turkish horde or sunk somehow.
A land of legend and of haunting sign.
I wanted you to walk this soft decline.
Let us return into our village now.

This is the village and this is my place,
from here I came and this is still my nurse.
They call it Mindszent after every saint,
but all in vain because it bears the taint
of every strangling wickedness and curse.

This on the other hand is your strange host
in whom the soot of long dead embers hide.
Above our heads a whistling wind of fate.
Fly free from me and scream your curse and hate
or see me with the boasting eyes of pride.

The Ancient Chamberlain

A NORTHERN MAN

I am engulfed by light and speech
whenever in the South I bide.
The light is easy, speech is glib;
a deep, cool, blind, and yawning trench
between each word spreads far and wide.

I am a man of the bleakest north,
on stormy paths of thought I blaze.
Each letter of my speech is hell;
I seek for deaf and hollow death;
my tongue is slow and loath to praise.

The South — a land of gibberish folk
where like a fleet and darting bird
the verb elopes from every lip.
More firmly rooted in the North,
more deep, more noble is the word.

Woe, woe, I look about and gape;
I watch and silently I strive.
Why should I prate in foolish joy?
Why should I clamor noisily
because I find myself alive?

I hold both light and speech as false
as my own life in fullest power,
as false as were the lives of those
who spoke this painful, mighty truth
long time ago in their brief hour.

Mine is the North. Frost and fate
can never from my lips depart.
Whenever I speak there speaks a man
for whom his lot, his life, his days
ache to the very roots of his heart.

THE EMPEROR EZVORAS

Here lies the emperor Ezvoras;
he loved his idols and his gods;
he loved his cup, his concubines,
his men-at-arms, the martial cry.
He loved the soil, he loved the seed,
but died in gloom
for he begot no young increase.

An ancient priest squat by the bed
as Ezvoras lay near to death;
and softly, sadly from afar
the beauties of the harem sobbed.
"O woe! perhaps his last he breathes,
and now he dies
having begot no young increase."

A hundred footmen scoured the land
and brought a hundred handsome lads,
kingly in frame, ruddy in soul
engrafted from a peasant rose.
A charm was chanted by the priest
on lads and him
who begot no young increase.

It came to pass when he was dead
(and, lo, beside this grave) there wept
a hundred women, and their unborn,
a hundred lordlings, sprang to life.
The emperor slept a happy sleep —
he died a sire
though he begot no young increase.

FINGERS IN THE SEINE

Paris plunges
its fingers into the deep,
their distorted length is a frightful
scarlet, pewter, green, soot, and yellow.
The Seine sobs.

Mysterious fingers
slide into the soul,
and we shudder in our deepest self.
The fingers are frightfully long and we cry
into unanswering night.

I stop on a bridge,
beneath me sobs the tormented Seine,
within me the frightful fingers plunge
their distorted length
and claw as in the bed below.

THE ANCIENT CHAMBERLAIN

There is a knock upon my heart,
upon its red and stately door,
and many visitors arrive
in frequent file.

An ancient, threadbare chamberlain
comes trudging with a beck and bow.
His master journeyed forth from here
long, long ago.

"He was a good and gracious lord;
sadly he went, he was compelled.
I dwell alone and even I
await him not."

THE INSANE NIGHT

a window beetles on the north
the rattling window of my room.
below, the roar of rock and sea
and on my bed a pounding heart
what insane music are these two.

i see the gloom of distant mountains,
the snowy loom of bloodstain mountains.
the seafields are a foam of green.
my room is white. i go and go.
this is a night of colors insane.

the mountains where i lower my eyes
are stirring up the blessed flowers
and fragrance rises on the winds.
today the world is only fragrance
and what a fugue of insane fragrance.

the moon has swallowed a snake of fire
a snake of flame a snake of fire
the moon that old and phthisic mount.
the clouds are boils of burning red
and scarlet mad the world today.

i go and go for this is Death
i know and know that this is Death.
i dress and open wide the door
and there it stands to bar the way
oh night of dying oh night insane.

(monaco)

DEATH OF CATULLUS

When poor Catullus was denied
even to tell his pains and fears,
another whispered gallant words
in Lesbia's attractive ears.

When all his songs were stricken dumb
and poor Catullus gasping lay,
an upstart youth with songs more new
allured one half the town away.

When they had strewn upon the corpse
the flowers that summertime allows,
about the garden in wonderwise
a thousand blooms burst on the boughs.

When the true friend of him who died
was weary and could cry no more,
a strong and princely babe was born
to the patrician dame next door.

And when fair Lesbia wept and cursed,
the sight was nothing to detest;
she tore her clothes that one perchance
may see her white and lovely breast.

AGAINRISING

The againrising of winter,
the far, far strum of a lonely insect
in an autumn arbor,
and wind and cloud above the quavering wold.

In good cheer of solitude
I shove the meddling doubts aside
and raise an amber cup toward winter,
the sacred future.

Few will find a second self in death's
crypto-double,
and few will be the resurrected
when the ancient horn hosannas.

But in this winter
I sense my oldest ground of being
my brooding from a once before,
my weeping from a once before.

THE SUNDAY AFTERNOONS

I have met
the ones I still regret
the autumn sunday afternoons
my cold and long dead brides
the sombre girls of small towns.
I have met
again the autumn sunday afternoons.

My strength
into arms you held at length
I carried in stealth and weary dreams.
The dark tower tolled
and I carried Babel desires
into arms at length,
and so many unfinished youthful dreams.

The deaf as stone
stared as I trudged alone
every hour a long hundred years.
Maids walked the streets
and ladies in my heart,
around me the deaf alone
and every hour a long hundred years.

I have met
the ones I still regret
the autumn sunday afternoons
my cold and long dead brides
the sombre girls of small towns.
I have met
again the autumn sunday afternoons.

We Fought Unfoiled

To the **West** and to all of us who
have striven because our souls de-
sired strife and the beauties of
strife.

1908
December 25

Christmas has met me,
pagan with the yellow face.
Christmas has met me
in the village of my childhood
and thought of turning me
and gently converting me.

December 26

Better
to fall back
and in sickness seek
for the Christ of the past.

Better
to leave this brooding
and sit as of old
before Christ in the church.

Better
here in the village
to speak with a cry —
hah, you still live, O God.

December 27

This is Christmas no more,
and no concern
of man or God
how I shall live
or die.
Peace unto God,
peace unto man,
peace unto death,
peace unto everyone,
but unto me
let war remain.

Beneath a row of chilly palms
I read a script, a mighty script
written on blue with biting pen
by wicked winds, by fasting winds.

Millions of letters, waves of white,
the restless and the undulant,
upon the foaming water move
and spell out who and what I am.

A dark defiance holds my soul,
an uninvited, strange belief.
I read with laughter and with sobs
the scribble-scrabble of the sea.

Am I no more to have a will?
Is this a message from my fate?
Is this my correspondence from
the sea, this mighty paper waste?

But here is my reply — I live,
though wan and hurt, the best I may;
and over fate and sea and all
a lord I always shall remain.

(San Remo)

SNOW IN FIRE

The fire is winking to its death,
I cannot gather simples,
but I shall learn what joy it is
to shiver.

The caves of snow are blowing cold
upon my whitened temples,
and I am laughing warmly while
I shiver.

I shall give heat without a fire,
a heat that no one tramples;
come learn from me what joy it is
to shiver.

WHO TAKES MY PLACE

And can it be, and can it be
that summer days with heat aswoon
and nights with tumbling meteors
will find me on the deathly shores?

The wine-press with the oozing grape
in pompous harvest-time will flow,
and then beneath the autumn gloam
intoxicant I shall not roam.

Somewhere a woman's warm salon
will beckon in the wintry cold,
but soft divan and flaming scent
for me no longer will be meant.

And springtide shall again return
with flowers, splendor, dewy joys,
and heralds of the spring alight
to find me parted from their sight.

And can it be, and can it be?
Why truly all these once were mine.
Did I not crave them, their praises sing?
Was I not all and everything?

And never yet and never yet
has one with so much longing craved,
wept for and dreamt of and pursued
each night a phantom faery brood.

Let him forever be accursed
who is about to take my place,
let poison on his palate drip,
and blindness hold his eyes in grip.

In deafness let him walk about,
and let his quivering pulse-beat fail;
and when he wins a woman's grace
deny him strength to give embrace.

THE RAINBOW'S DEATH

Never such a lovely rainbow,
like a hoop it held the sky.
Never was a hoop so hallowed,
so embracing and so spacious.
But, behold, the night drew nigh.

Peasant, beast, and bird were weary
to admire and gape aloft.
Eye and fist with shameful feeling
here beneath a shoddy rainbow
on the open field grew soft.

Mockingly the old sun twinkled,
in his dying light revealed.
It amused him that a rainbow
could create this strange amazement
on the sober, dungy field.

Still the rainbow waited longer;
as it fell more fair it grew,
sadly on the meadows gazing
till at last those skyey sisters,
passing clouds, imbibed its hue.

With a smile the sun sank under,
and the world now breathed free —
not befitting toilsome meadows
is so mighty and so frenzied,
so divine a comedy.

Altar of Hagar

THE FLOWER HANDS

the etiolated flower of her hands
floats into my brown hair,
faints, fans out
and trembles at last.

passion petals and passion
perfume of hands
I sense,
white petals of a purring girl.

the wretched years and haunts.
they flutter,
the sister roses of her hands,
chaste and hot.

where is the old
longing for petals not laurels?
I shake off your aniline hands,
white and insane.

the old and screeching winds
of autumn blow
the petals into the suck of mud —
now take away the buds of your hands.

ALTAR OF HAGAR

With artless meals, white turtle-doves,
with nibbling lambs, marrow, and gore,
to Hagar I had sacrificed
already at the age of four.

The fires on Hagar's altar burn;
I gaze in silence, priestlike, numb.
I have awaited thirty years
for my beloved one to come.

I know not whether I am clean;
I know not what I will or why,
but woman is the altar-place,
without a woman I must die.

I felt this sinful love arise
one time upon a sorrel lea.
Rosie, the little neighbor girl,
was playing hide-and-seek with me.

Of Hagar I knew nought, and yet
my blood would cry and sing so strange.
I have read Spencer and Kant since then,
but they could never bring a change.

I spit on them and kiss them, Them —
nihilities and worlds in one.
I bring them from the fair of life
the dearest fairings gold has won.

I never touched the skin of some —
Serena, Trudy, Dora, May,
Irma, and many others; still
proudly I held their hearts in sway.

When I would have to buy a kiss,
my eyes and heart fast shut I drew;
no one has gained more sombre strength
from so many a perdu.

I love as though I were a god.
When I embrace and lie in bliss,
Genevieve and Phryne are my kin;
not gender, but myself I kiss.

But I have loved them one and all,
the Mary and the Magdalene.
I love these slayers of my sex
and, too, the comic kissing scene.

The little confirmation girls,
with doltish look and white array,
in Paris I would often watch
as like the sick they went their way.

They are the future's fountainhead
for whom I mean this wreath to be.
They are the girls of holy Hagar,
the women of futurity.

I love them soon as they are born,
the babe, the girl, the old, the hale.
I love whoever is a woman;
I am the true and moody male.

And gladly I shall cast into
the fire of Hagar all I own;
when beggared, I shall wait for night
and gracious death without a moan.

Then I shall see my coffined women,
my blood and dreams within the fire,
and in the holy light a corpse
will throw his kisses on the pyre.

THE KISS BATTLEFIELD

Upon kiss battlefield at night
the fallen lie in swarms.
Swiftly with whir of wings approach
unbodied knights-at-arms.

Death-white their faces, woebegone,
in cloaks of flame revealed,
they gather all the men who fell
upon kiss battlefield.

In violet mountain-deeps they dwell
where kisses are like dew,
and kiss-flayed bodies of the dead
awake to life anew.

All that we see as black and rough
they see as white and smooth.
They live untainted, fair, and good
in sempiternal youth.

There we forget our wounds and sores,
the world of body fades;
the virgin heroes never seek
to touch the snowy maids.

Love is unlabored and benign,
funny and free from guile.
He who desires picks out his love
and eyes her with a smile.

And with a playful look the maid
on whom the youth has smiled
receives an angel in her womb
and she is blessed with child.

When here upon kiss battlefield
death-blows upon one smite,
in violet mountain deeps a maid
sighs and brings forth a knight.

And on kiss battlefield the dead
lie not for long in swarms
as every night there come for them
unbodied knights-at-arms.

A GIRL SETS OUT

A girl sets out for me,
and I hasten to meet her.
All hail, child of the immaculate dawn,
silken slave-girl of my long twilight.
The world is music as I prepare for love,
and a girl who never saw me kneels.
Blessed is your girlhood,
strange child with eyes like haloes.
She comes now swinging her young body,
and my eyes cling with jealous joy
to those carriers of bliss, her hips.
Here is a girl, and I teach her to love.
Tomorrow night I meet someone.
Tomorrow night I forget the past.
Tomorrow night the world is a fable,
and I shall tell a story of my body.
I desire so much
to love this girl who has set out for me
that I sweat drops of balsam
and my knees melt to the ground.
I shall love someone.
O tell her to come quickly
that tomorrow like a grateful dog
another woman may lick my hand.

THE SNOW-CASTLE MOUNTAINS

Beneath the snow-castle mountains,
beneath the shaman-white mountains,
within a moonlit forest
an amorous cascade is falling.
With deep and unbridged waters
a mountain cascade is falling.

Beneath the snow-castle mountains
the moon is bright and from the foliage
a hundred goblins glide into fountains.
And there they rendezvous at midnight
a troop of maidens, a troop of lovers.
On either bank a fiery troop hovers.

Beneath the snow-castle mountains
the youthful troops are seeking bridges,
and to the fringe of plangent fountains
from my bed the words of women
bear me at midnight deeply sleeping
to freeze where mountain streams are leaping.

Beneath the snow-castle mountains,
above the green and gleaming fountains,
I am a bridge, a frozen footbridge.
With burning feet across my body
a hundred snow-white maidens are running,
to their amorous, restless lovers running.

Beneath the snow-castle mountains
at midnight by the singing fountains
the fables of a kiss are quiring.
Within a forest, dense dream thickets,
lovers are moaning, lovers are fawning
until arrival of the dawning.

Beneath the snow-castle mountains,
beneath the shaman-white mountains,
the back of the bridge will weaken.
The midnight bridge will shatter
and with its troop of amorous maidens
into the icy waters clatter.

Beneath the snow-castle mountains
still sing the green and gleaming fountains;
at midnight on the swaying footbridge
a hundred girls in nude are running.
The amorous cascade is still falling,
the sombre cascade is still falling.

233

Whites of the Future

ARK OF THE COVENANT

Ark of the covenant, my heart, I send
and bid a militant good day.
My kinsmen, many rumbling millions,
although you may deny me, still, oh, still
I must belong to you.

Our bond of union came from destiny
and not from virtue, worth, or sin,
and not from want and even less from greed.
Oh helot people and helot poet,
we have already met.

Within us great, exalted powers wait
to be awakened into life;
a lovely nation lies concealed in us
like a big stag within a curtained grove
where hounds are on the watch.

If you refuse to count me as your kin,
the wrinkled lines will furrow up
the sombre regions of my brow and soul,
but in full youth I always stand before
my raving Judases.

I do not want to wear a martyr's crown.
I only want my fate fulfilled —
to give you lovingly from my own self,
this laughed at nought which you did not desire,
my revolutionary soul.

I must be yours, and it is all the same
whether you want or want me not.
One is our sun upon the glorious sky,
but, oh, at times the racks of evil may
conceal me from the light.

THE HOLY CROWS

Black crows, black crows, vagabonds,
free on fields of dung and grub,
muck-fowl of the bird salons,
black crows, black crows, holy birds

When in startled flight you wind,
black net wailing on the breeze,
drown the censure from behind
sailing with an ill intent.

Like a laughter is your caw;
when your tattered feathers fall
do not moan the loss and flaw,
other crows and fields will come.

You are holy, holy birds
who will always higher soar
followed by the jealous words
of the painted bird salon.

Yours the envious odium,
yours the happy future life,
come unto me, come, come, come,
black crows, black crows, holy birds.

WHITES OF THE FUTURE

White Babel
that remains behind me,
white kiss, instrument, sorrow, chance,
large white bird of death,
now sing.

Now sing for I am healed,
now sing for I depart,
and I see life as never before
without tears,
and I am happy.

I was hypocritical and evil,
but life
is a holy land giving much to all
who guard their heart.
I die.

I die without green bile
seeing all in white and nothing
that is not white and shining.
Simple and unstained by colors
I depart.

I reached for wild peaks
and found
a color emptiness
of rainbows, dreams, and the never.
Leave me.

One merit I have. I saw deep
and loved those who suffered,
the whites of the future,
unsullied working masses,
now sing.

THE REBUS OF REBELLION

Who centers man
into a single sad, unseeing eye,
whose chemistry has dyed with red
the rebus of rebellion on the sky,
sweat of the human brow.

You are the sign
of God's own power and creation's deep.
The men of sweat are single tears
wherewith the eternal cries itself to sleep,
stain of the men who make.

Blessed Village Mist

To my mother

THE YELLOW ROSE

On a hill of gossipers
flooded by the southern sun
hark I listen, hark I listen
to the chatter of the flowers.

Dark and bilious violets,
laughter-loving, raucous pinks,
scintillant and snowy whites
utter stridently their tenets.

Philosophic lazuli,
wrathful, dark-green hollyhocks,
and sarcasm-dripping reds
may commit a lapsus linguae.

Only one is listening,
he is near a fathom high —
one autumnal, yellow rose,
whose large head is proudly drooping.

Of the petals' misery,
of the petals' pensive thoughts
he is the accursed bearer,
mournful, large of head, and comely.

242

All Right, Lord

To those sombre persons who un-
believingly seek for God with sombre
and believing passion but without
hope.

ON DEATH'S PORCH

Ishten, my Lord, I have left behind the carnivals and games,
the paper sailboats, and upon death's porch I stand.

I sit humbled, but were someone to say of me 'knock down
that swellhead', I would sigh 'so be it'.

Whoever despises me does right; whoever punishes makes
me holy. Ishten, my Lord, your porch has healed me.

I have never known such self-love as now upon death's porch.
I have come to love my past. Boldly I step up and in.

Cursed and scourged as I was, I cannot be all bad; and death
will be no worse a lord than life.

Ishten, who are Death, you know how I sought to find myself
in the blood-suck of battle. I did not want to do bad.

SHOWER OF HUMILITY

The sun shot arrowy beams at me.
I found no mitigation, Lord,
and lo, there drizzled from Thy clouds
the shower of humility.

Behold, I bow my head and hide.
I rue my arrogance, O Lord;
if self-esteem in me remain,
I rip out both my heart and pride.

Show me an enemy of mine,
a scurvy someone, O my Lord,
and I will kiss his filthy tracks
that worthy worship may be Thine.

On little streams before me flow
Thine interrupted favors, Lord;
and in my soul the humble rains
are splashing kindly to and fro.

I want all things before Thee placed,
before Thy holy whim, O Lord;
each moment I desire nought
but utterly to be abased.

244

PRAYER BEFORE COMMUNION

Give me the cold faith to believe,
O Lord,
I may search with Hungarian eyes,
freely look about and parade
beneath free skies.

Give me the cold faith to believe,
O Lord,
I need not drink the cup to the lees,
a swallow of your wine will do
for my soul's ease.

Give me the cold faith to believe,
O Lord,
I can endure another day, and then
no more, no more, no more,
amen, amen.

THE WAY OF THE ANTICHRIST

My fertile sins like palms of hell
with skyward-groping richness climb,
and yet as though it were a babe
I tender with a quiet smile
my substance all in all to time.

In newer men and newer times
a nobler aim and fate reside.
The earth will gulp my sinful flesh,
the future swallow up my word,
and time will make me sanctified.

But for the future and the past
now damned and sinful I must be.
Grandchildren, laughing, blithe, and sound,
you future man-inheritors,
look back on me forgivingly.

A shadow on the dial of time
are all my days with sorrow rife,
a station every sin of mine
whereby the new and modern man
will brightly blaze his path of life.

A bitter path but noble still,
this is the way of Antichrist,
who wears away till he is black,
for others' sake, for dreadful need,
for a white future sacrificed.

THE REJOICING PSALM OF A PENITENT

I know He sent me to the peaks,
and yet a tearful climber I have been,
my sadness is an ugly sin.

He summoned me for cheerful songs,
and yet I furnished Him with wicked strife,
Jehovah of Jehovahs, Life.

I had forgotten man is blest,
washed by white waters of eternal law,
wonder of wonders, awesome awe.

Blest are all they who come to life,
for everyone is both a son and sire,
and cursed is every life decrier.

Blest is all life in like degree,
the seed producing and the germless rot,
he sins whoever loves it not.

All is begettal, the barren too,
the genius, hero, beasts of herd and flock,
ulcers, and syphilitic pock.

Only rejoice we may, rejoice,
never despond; all things we must outvie,
but may not cry, may never cry.

Jehovah of Jehovahs, Life,
my woes with peals of laughter I lament,
forgive this sinful penitent.

GENTLE EVENING PRAYER

My Lord, a quiet night,
a vast and peaceful night,
give to your aged child,
your bad and sickly child.

Let royal revels,
the bitter revels
of music shun me,
from far off shun me.

Let not into my heart,
into my wretched heart,
the wakeful will-o'-the-wisp,
the awful will-o'-the-wisp.

Let me sleep laughingly,
let me dream laughingly;
and prosper me in dreams,
and make me young in dreams.

A something greatly great,
a something gloriously great,
dreaming let me conceive,
in night let me concelve.

And let me pray
as schoolboys pray
with godly love,
sleep-bringing love.

And when the twilight falls,
the dark brown twilight falls,
old prayer on my lips
I whisper with my lips, "Give
a peaceful night to my parents,
and give a peaceful night to everyone.
O God, walking and lying, sleeping
and waking, I adore you as my
sweet Father. Good Father, take me
into your care. Amen."

A STALE QUESTION

We ask
our stale and troubled question
meekly
as becomes an old and timid poet.

We become, move,
and die.
A Someone governs here. You cannot see him,
but he governs.

If death, why come?
And if we come, why the care?
Why so many sombre wise men among us?
A Someone governs here.

This is the greatest reality,
a holy unarranged order.
Life is a share in an old debt we must
pay off,

a bad memory
the great Someone wants
kept
from pale and misty oblivion.

Church and prayer will not help us here.
Let man accept his fate
without redemption. Let him suffer
and go to his death.

LORD OF LORDS

My soul was lost in sinful shame;
still evenings came.
He smiled upon the wars I warred,
the Lords' great Lord.

His face was like a sunset fair,
with mercy there.
Though life so much of new had brought,
God changed in nought.

And as a schoolboy long ago
I knew him so —
for a bad heart he could exchange
one new and strange.

Each strand of gray and falling hair
is in his care.
If sinners spurn his gentle love,
he waits above.

He does not try those who transgress,
or love them less.
He calls though toward hell we track,
and we run back.

How good to know there is above
this primal love.
He even in the churchyard blooms
when faith relumes.

He washed me of my sinful mud
and flowing blood;
and on my wounds he laid the calm
of fragrant balm.

And now with quiet, easy breath
I wait for death,
my eyes his eyes, my hand his hand —
all to command.

War is was he who sent me in,
stripped me of sin.
He smiled upon the wars I warred,
The Lords' great Lord.

Ever Lengthening Days

CARTWAY AT NIGHT

How gibbous is the ghostly moon,
the steppes of night how mute and waste,
how sorrowful I feel today,
how gibbous is the ghostly moon.

And every whole is now deformed,
and every flame has split in half,
and every love has partly lapsed,
and every whole is now deformed.

I race upon a wobbly cart,
behind as if a cry of woe,
one half deep silence, one half moan,
I race upon a wobbly cart.

MY BED CALLS

I lie down. O my bed,
O my bed, yesteryear,
yesteryear what were you?
What were you? Den of dreams,
den of dreams, well of strength,
well of strength, house of love,
house of love, merriness,
merriness. What are you?
What are you? Coffin now,
coffin now. Every day,
every day closing in,
closing in. Falling down,
falling down fearfully,
fearfully waking up,
waking up fearfully,
fearfully I wake up.

Waking up, looking out,
looking out, feeling strange,
feeling strange, sensing self,
sensing self, catching sight,
catching sight, burrowing,
burrowing, peering out,
peering out, rising up,
rising up, willing it,
willing it, growing sad,
growing sad, steeling self,
steeling self, breaking down,
breaking down, feeling shame,
feeling shame. O my bed,
O my bed, coffin now,
coffin now, beckoning,
beckoning. I lie down.

SWEET SISTER NIGHT

Kiss me upon the mouth, sweet sister night,
seal my lips and waft abroad the news
your brother, the strident,
has brought with defiance his songs to a close
and for the last time sings
what little pleasure he took
in his lunatic songs.
Kiss me upon the mouth, sweet sister night.

Sombre vetoes and merry shrifts,
warbling moans and bleeding wounds,
for you I shall no longer shaft my soul
with wells of music.
Every fountain of blood is sealed
and on the grave of silence sit,
mute and cross-like,
sombre vetoes and merry shrifts.

All hail to every one and thing,
all hail to lovely words,
but Endre Ady does not speak,
but Endre Ady must not speak.
With a heart turned deadly blue
let him hide wherever he can,
let him forget what he desired.
All hail to every one and thing.

We grow mute, sweet sister night,
with a long kiss we grow mute
and look into deaf darkness
like spent instruments.
We may break the silence again
but our voice will be no mystery of torment
to ourselves and others.
We grow mute, sweet sister night.

Notes on LONGING FOR LOVE

1. **Thomas Esze's Gossip** (title page). Esze, rimes with **lesser** without the final **r**, was a peasant leader of the early eighteenth century who supported a freedom fight of the Transylvanian prince Francis Rákóczi II against Austrian rule.

2. **Grandson of Ond.** Ond is an assumed Finno-Ugric proto-form of the family name Ady (Ad from Od) based on an etymology by Ady's younger brother, who had learned in a philology course that Hungarian final **d** developed historically from Finno-Ugric **nd.** Finno-Ugric exists only as a language reconstructed by comparative linguistics. It was spoken in central Russia some four thousand years ago and is the source from which modern Hungarian, Finnish, Estonian, and various languages within the Soviet Union developed.

3. **The Princesses Dul.** Dúl is a legendary figure, the leader of a people whom the pre-Christian Magyars attacked as the warriors of early Rome had attacked the Sabines. The last stanza probably refers to a similar attack made subsequently on the Magyars by a Bulgarian people.

4. **The Cold Moon.** Várad: that is Nagyvárad, See the Introduction, pages 26-30.

5. **A Walk Around My Birthplace.** Mindszent: literally "All Saints"; Er and Kraszna, see Note 12 to BLOOD AND GOLD.

6. **The Emperor Ezvoras.** Ezvorasz is a fictitious name like Marun. See Note 10 to BLOOD AND GOLD, page 151.

7. **Againrising.** The "ancient horn" of stanza three is a translation for the "tárogató", an instrument introduced into Eastern Europe by the Arabs via Balkan trade routes. In Hungary it developed into the national instrument and was indentified with the Rákóczi freedom fight.

8. **My Bed Calls.** Set to music by Béla Bartók.

OF ALL MYSTERIES

(1910)

To Lajos Hatvany, who with his
cold love was more to me than any-
one else, more believing and good,
I dedicate this book of verse, which
may be my last.

THE DUEL

A duel was fought — the youthful All
with his mysterious spear transfixed
within my heart the heart of death,
and now my heart and God prevail.

Mysteries of God

I BELIEVE WITHOUT BELIEF

I believe without belief in God because no living man or dead
has greater need. My anguish gushes from the dungeon where
it has lain in silent death or emptiness of art. Every word is
a prayer, or a cudgel on my heart and body and soul. Every
word brings merciful thirst.

Beauty, purity, and truth. Derided words. Would I had died
when I laughed at you. Virginity, goodness, and rectitude, how
much I need you. I believe in God. I wait for Christ. I am
sick, sick. I stop and start like a sleepwalker. I seek to
awaken, and in the holy scintillation a thousand secrets
swarm before my eyes. Everything is a mystery, God also if
he exists. And I am the secret secret.

God, Christ, virtue, and all I yearn for, why I yearn is a
secret greater than myself.

IN THE TABERNACLE

"And Solomon went up thither to
the brazen altar before the Lord,
which was at the tabernacle of the
congregration, and offered a thou-
sand burnt offerings upon it."
II Chronicles 1.6

Inside the tabernacle of the Lord
for almost fifteen years I stand
with turtle doves, white horses, rams,
and fiery offerings from the shining hoard.

I shed my drops of blood like boiling rains
upon your brazen altar, God,
but neither your keen fire nor mine
has waned the least within our pounding veins.

Your holy grace in full of fortune sent
I vainly wait these fifteen years,
while on your brazen altar there
the golden treasures of my blood are spent.

The insecure of heart have never wrought
a deed within this tented shrine,
but with a thousand burnt offerings
I still have come to nought, have come to nought.

THE GOD OF CHIMERAS

Ishten,who are a Secret, you know I am not a man of today. My cause is your cause. Smite those who rise against me.

We started the hullabaloo together because our nature is a Secret. Together we forged whatever is false in our work of fever.

Ishten, we are one. When I was infatuated with chimeras, you stood by me lest I succumb to foolish wounds.

Stubbornly you incited me to strike into the thicket in Hungarian and with song lest the music die.

I was the insane arrow, which I will not let fall into the dust again.

Because this work is great and greater than the price of one life, I shall not go as a fool of others on Calvary.

Now we shall see whether you want our sword to prevail and whether what we started was worth what we wanted.

You are a Secret, an ancient Secret like me and the world, but I do not wish to be consumed for your momentary whim.

We started together. Since then storm clouds have gathered above my head. Ishten, who are a Secret, every song was your sin and mine.

When as a schoolboy I wrote psalms in church, you were my comrade, my accessory.

I felt your stormy fingers in my hair. You were my beginning, and you must now be my end.

My cause is your cause. If you will not save your believer, no one will believe in you. Ishten, Secret, draw forth your sword.

THE SHARK LOAN

I have come with the interest payment, Lord. I drove hard lest I be late.

Here is my life and here your money.

I borrowed at dreadful cost, my Lord. I have nothing because all went to pay the interest.

Life moved with a murderous sweep.

The freshness of my muscles, the fullness of my brown hair, and my strength in bed and blood

I leave to you.

It was costly, but now that you tormented me, leave me your dear money.

Shark loan, shark life.

Without will or ambition, Lord, let me remain in your power and, maimed in your kingdom,

keep paying the loan.

My Lord, let me keep returning to pay the huge interest and tax.

Only let me live, let me live.

A PRAYER FOR LAUGHTER

Ishten, I have seen your face borne by the levin through furious clouds. Often I have bathed in tears.

I have never beheld the shining face others see. Where are you and why do you shun me, holy God of laughter?

I am hungry, my Lord, for good humor. I thirst for your smile. Never have you had such a grateful and fun-loving believer.

Let my past burst into a great and glorious laughter. Let me see for once your merry face drowned in the laughter of holy tears.

THE GOD-SEEKING CRY

Ishten, your name is queer,
but my two orphan eyes have seen
so much of bedlam
that in my avalanche
of fear
I send a cry to Thee, my Lord.

I have assayed men's dreams,
but none has proved the probing test.
I search for Thee
with heart and ganglia lanced
by screams,
for, Ishten, everything is Thine.

CAIN KILLED ABEL

My Lord, Jehovah, I knew
your canon, shalt not kill,
but Cain rose up once more and slew
Abel in self slaughter.

I cannot hide or gloze
the blood upon these hands,
I did not sin when I arose
nor am I sinning now.

Our private deed was done
when you denied me strength
for two of us to live as one
before your holy face.

As in the bible myth,
the son who suffered more
destroyed himself together with
Abel, who was your child.

None can accuse the dead,
not even you, my Lord,
although from heaven above you said
my children shalt not kill.

As two we were so strange
I had to kill the one.
My Lord, accept our twofold change
with understanding love.

Mysteries of Love

I ask my long-loved and only lady
to accept from her mournful servant
these songs, which are occasionally
exultant but always plaintive, al-
ways the same, and always created
because of her.

SHACKLE OF PATIENCE

I send you word
take upon yourself
the rusty shackle of patience;
if the lock is stuck
I shall repair it.
You were my shackle,
and I was yours,
a shackle our entire life.
Our love and sun,
our lewdness and faithfulness,
our kiss, fatigue, and flame,
our many mistaken vows,
what good shackles they were,
what sturdy gyves.
We would always have been slaves
even without slavery and shackles.
But now put on this final lock,
the most loving of all,
the shackle of patience,
and wait while with little delay
I snap it closed.
Now wait
and yearn for the final bondage,
the peak of all life and joy,
patience.
I command it.
I send you word.

THE SORROWS OF RESURRECTION

Through slits of red fog-abscesses
the inconstant sun squinted at me
while I spoke,
"Arise and be free."
It was Budapest or somewhere.
I scarcely remembered the other world,
but sorrowfully I came alive.

The stones rolled,
the skull hill smoked as I stepped forth,
alive and hesitant,
from the dragon-grave of the past.
Like one whose blood runs thin
I set out in search
of new apostles.

The storms and shrieking Tatra forests
were my Thomases,
who thrust their fingers
into the wounds of my side.
I walked
through an eddying fog,
ruined and oblivious,
and left the past behind.

Again I spoke, "I do not know who I am,
whether I live or have lived,
whether I am the name
or heir to the melancholy name
of a dead man.
The night brings a fever,
the postman my mail
as though they had been long, long
in coming."

Morning came with a chill
from a stubble field
of memory.
I fingered my sores
that hurt and burned in abomination.
Where did I receive them?
Where had I been?
Was I alive there?
Is someone crying after me?
Who am I and where am I going?

I wandered forth while Slovak psalmists
sang in the pines.
Did I know psalms like these
of my own
at one time?
I listened without joining
because I had forgotten.

I heard the sounds of others
arriving from afar.
But where is far and where is near?
And where is the station
between?
It seems I have never come
and yet I am here.
Why do eyes, letters, and messages
search me out?

I do not know why other faces
seek mine,
where there are no inscriptions
for the great legends
of old struggles are leached
from my face.
I am like an ill conceived
or never begun love.

A blond girl, like a young cedar
proud in the bright sun,
appeared before me.
Gnashing my teeth
I ran away.
Are these memories or hurts?
If I existed, if she loved me,
if I were alive, I think
she could be mine.

And here I watch with wonder two women
with flowers in their hair.
It seems I was once in love
with a young pair like this.
They seem strange. For whom are they waiting?
They speak to me
and stroke me with prying eyes.
They address a strange man
standing behind me.

Something holds me like a slave,
a sleepwalker on a cliff
whom trembling I watch
as someone estranged,
and whatever I say is cold
like a storm
whistling in a cave of ice.
My former self
is lost somewhere in the snow
on a far and icy field.

A sea moans
in old anguish
merciless and estranged,
and this sea is a forest of pines.

Oceans, cities,
women, and desires flicker from far,
and Paris is their crown.
They are brighter
than the most rapturous visions.
Did I once know them
or was it someone else
who admired and loved them?

I am the resurrected
who does not feel his own life,
who speaks the hollow speech of puppets
and is himself a puppet on a stage,
a question, a ghost, a mystery.
I wait for someone to call me
and with a warm sweet mouth
whisper who I am.

Here in the lap of the Tatra is a lake,
gleaming, pure, and wild,
where I seek the centuries,
my life,
and songs that burst the grave.
I seek for my own nearness,
time that soars,
and the magic mirror
to see myself.
Life stops,
and I know that nobody
and nothing lives,
nothing is true.
A worn and bloody face gleams from the lake.
I do not know whose it is.
I am come alive, I am come alive.

YOUR EYES

I yield all that you gave,
if yieldable the prize,
but I shall always keep
your eyes.

From sockets they will watch
an azure lake and you,
and all that vision may
still view.

I yield all that you gave,
if yieldable the prize,
but I shall always keep
your eyes.

ONLY TO SEE YOU

Remove your haughty clasp for me,
like angels on old pictured walls
unfold your beauties joyfully.

Remove your haughty clasp for me,
like some young virgin in decease
lie here before me quietly.

Remove your haughty clasp for me,
you whom I do not want to kiss
my eyes are hot afire to see.

Remove your haughty clasp for me,
and I shall fall upon my knees
and bless this moment fervently.

272

A HUSHED FLIGHT

Sing softly
songs of the nomad north,
songs of the tramp winds,
haggard storms.
This June day
I departed from somewhere
sadly
and without a goodnight.
I inserted heart
and feet
in soft and stormless
summer,
and now I would recall them
too long detained.
Sing softly
songs of the nomad north,
songs of the tramp winds,
haggard storms.

THE THIRD FLOOR

My room is on the third floor up.
Who comes to love
should pause because the stairs are long,
and she is false
who comes halfway.

My darling, do not pant and strain,
the cost is paid
in more than only three flights up,
and if I run
on you by chance,

I bring along all that I have.
I shall not damn
whoever climbs but half the stairs
for lack of faith,
but stay away.

THE SPLIT SKY

Someone has just remembered me
for my eyes are full of tears,
and the finials of Paris
split the sky,
the soft carpet of the great sky.
Merry young men
emerge singing
from the throat of a dark street.
What am I thinking of?
The time is all the same.
Someone has just remembered me.
Is there a way
from the deep of this dark street
to the split sky?
Their song pursues me,
and I grope,
seeking who remembered,
seeking in my soul
someone for whom I might go on living
sombrely,
searching the sky from dark streets.
Someone has just remembered me
in sorrow,
in sorrow for him
who in dark passageways
watches and desires
the sky
and cries at the song
ragged boys
sing
as they pass into the night.
Someone has just remembered me
for my eyes are full of tears,
and the finials of Paris
split the sky.

Mysteries of Sorrow

THE BUBO BIRD

In stillness of the squinting dawn
a curious bat has streaked my room
with large blue ears and awkward wings,
the Bubo bird from specter tales.

The wings beat on the window pane.
I am alone and I must be,
but I have never felt so strange
and never saw my life like this.

Will it fly off if I arise?
Oh, nights that gray into the dawn,
oh, this my past, my lot, my life,
the Bubo bird with large blue ears.

PSALM OF NIGHT

This is how the Night sang:

If your heart were so large
it would flood or warm
the world
with an arhythmic beat
in Hungarian
or some other language
or any rhythm, flood,
or way,

I would still not give you
a warm cover and pillow,
I would still not whisper
encouragement in your ear,
I would still remain
the nigh, nigh, Night.

The Night can only be the Night,
for the dying
are always dying,
and this small life
is imperfect, dying, and weak.

I cry because you weep,
but I am the night
who blames the Dawn for tears.
I cry because you live,
I cry because you madly seek
something to cry for,
I cry because you are mine,
I cry because it must be so,
I cry and cry and cry.

This is how the Night sang.

Mysteries of Magyars

THE MARCH SUN

Sun of the March month, mighty is your power,
and yet in aeons you never seared us with
a Revolution, a Hungarian March.
Like mastodons we sate in mirrors of ice.

Let the Lord God smite the sweat of our brows,
let the Lord God smite all hours of our life
if in this daze of death we drag along.
Let the Lord God smite the kiss of our mouth,
the dream on our pillow, the charm of procreation.
Let him smite our every deed and dream,
our long bivouac on the Danube.
Let him smite our past and smite our future,
the issue of our bold and bandit nature
if we fail to trample those who bar our way,
all those who hinder a Hungarian March.
If there is a God who smites, let him smite
those who would keep the smallest bit of old.
A curse is on this land, we must destroy
all the agglomerations of our past,
all that languishes and all that betrays
and makes our land into its loyal home.
The keepers of the past are charging us.
Young month of March, gaze deep into our eyes
and let us have as much of power and warmth
and strength as we believe in this revolt.
We see revolt in every passing hour
and look with unspeakably murderous eyes
at haughty aristocrats and the newly rich,
because within this world that hurries on
our future and our life is now at stake.
The stench of rank and money stupefies.
The need of change and of the new cries out.
If priests are proudly waving frankincense,
our deadly fate is only made more clear.
We need a better word that Petőfi's word.
The radiant March has ordered everyone
to be reviewed and weighed in battle ranks.
At last this March may reach sad Hungary.

Sun of the March month, mighty is your arm,
a miracle of beauty your coming,
but grant at last that we should have a will,
but grant at last we die no ugly death.

A TEMPLE FOUNDER'S DREAM

On a black and lofty mountain peak
in honor of
unfounded sorrow
my temple would be built.
There would my people foregather.
Before an altar
and a red draped bier
in the assembly of the sorrowing
I would stand, the temple founder.
Our lamentations — organ pipes.
Our incense — dreams.
Our prayer — "forever
blessed be he
who knows not why he thirsts,
who knows not why he hurts,
and who without a crown
is still a king."
This would be the sorrowful ecclesia of
unfounded sorrow.

With dripping blood of turtle doves
I would baptize
my babes,
and gently I would wed and bury people
as though I walked among the beds
of the sleeping sick.
A thousand shades would rustle
of those who had no temple
and who for long are dead,
because my people of the tortured faith
and of the unfounded sorrow
come from long, hah, long ago.
"Ite, missa est."
Each day more fairly I would say it,
and we would weep
with more and more
bitterness, bitterness.

Mystery of Glory

To my friends, the good men of
the **West** and of any place where
they or I may have kindred souls.

SAILBOAT FOR SALE

Sailboat for sale,
with broken cables, shattered mast,
and all good qualities of bad.

Sailboat for sale,
a few repairs and it would go,
the owner wearied of his boat.

Sailboat for sale,
it had a glory in its day,
to launch it still would be no shame.

Sailboat for sale,
the spars have seen a thousand storms,
but is has touched at countless ports.

Sailboat for sail,
the worthy now may dart aboard
and toward a saint's damnation soar.

Sailboat for sale,
it wants new hands, a newer charm,
a chase by bolder, better charts.

Sailboat for sale,
whoever comes, the cost is high,
a flight to hell but worth the price.

MY TROOPS

Flaming fighters,
my youthful troops,
no matter if I die.
This land is mine,
and yours the holiest calling
if I die.
I do this well.
Come ye,
young fighters,
more sinful than I,
more loved and honored,
more mighty and strong.
You are my nation,
and all will be yours
for asking
in return for your souls
and me.
Forward, my troops.
Forward
and wave
the red banner of sin
frayed with the black edge
of my virtues,
and I shall look on you
(although this is a cliche)
with bright eyes from the grave.
Forward,
brave men,
young men.
I have nothing but you.
You are the heritage,
the reward,
my song.
My young sons,
I will be glad to die for you,
almost
while young.

MY ORPHAN ORIOLES

My wood-notes, golden orphan orioles,
vanish away. You did not know
how to blare forth a haughty trumpet,
how to ring out a happy laughter
over the sippers of your dulcet souls.

Over your arbors lies a chilling air,
upon you are the chirping swarms,
upon you are the falsely haughty,
and you will never learn, my singers,
that wood-notes wild were never sung more fair.

My wood-notes, golden orphan orioles,
vanish away. You did not know
how to blare forth a haughty trumpet,
how to ring out a happy laughter
over the sippers of your dulcet souls.

Mystery of Life-Death

To my mother and those who have
loved me even a little bit in a moth-
erly manner, have shown solicitude,
and perhaps by now have bid me
farewell.

THE STEALER OF MY FATE

The man who stole my fate
I saw
in America or in Nippon.
I cannot recall,
I saw him in a dream.
He reaped and sheaves of success
and treasures stood before him.
The man was young although like me
upon his third and thirtieth year
he trod.
He seemed to burst of strength,
and as he came from work
he took and kissed his youthful wife
hotly in the cool of dusk
while children played in the yard.

In rags,
I also was there in my rags,
an alien beggar of the selfsame face
and age.
With good humor
he offered me food,
some bread and apple wine.
They set a table in the yard.
Benumbed
I guarded the little paradise.
I did not say I could have been
the youthful master and not a beggar guest.
In stealth
I took to my heels
toward a sombre road
and ran away
forever from the stealer of my fate.

SEASON OF MIRACLES

Spring, winter, summer, autumn come and clash;
from deepest beds the rivers rise like seas,
and I am left alone by even those
who lovingly had always sought to please.

A somebody has gone insane in space,
somewhere a maddened sun will dance till numb,
a somebody has disarranged the all,
and men foretell that streaming stars will come.

Now ties of great desire are broken off,
and new unreasonable loves arise,
and on our arms the joy of long ago
like an abhorrent, sombre burden lies.

Now every knife is thirstier for blood,
and trains are crashing, piling into trains,
and men who always had a love for life
sigh out and call for death in sad refrains.

Who walks abroad among us, does these deeds?
All things are only part of one great whole,
and clouds are driven by the selfsame end
which tramples here and there within the soul.

Within one moment everything will change,
the long dead sea, the maelstrom's furious lash;
and in my fevered brain with lightning strokes
another thought, another law will flash.

Oh, oh, I am afraid, I am afraid.
What does tomorrow, oh, tomorrow hold?
Caprices of some distant, burning worlds,
what newest orders will you now unfold?

When will my fate arrive and trample me?
And all whom I hold dear, how will they die?
Oh, sorrowful and awful single world
within whose heart eternal secrets lie.

THE INVITED DEATH

Two hours,
if I will this mad mechanism of the mind will stop
and the prince of subliminal darkness enter triumphant —
the invited death.

In purple
he would come and not in segments of common oblivion,
but he wears now a mask of paperwhite in twenty grams
of sleeping powder upon my bedside table.

Two hours,
if I will this majestic lord would put on his regal dress
and with a kiss of my becalmed brow
enfold my brain.

A great sleep
will come if I wish and not the little men,
incomplete and phocoid whom I fear
in every shortened nap.

My passing
need not wait like foliage ripped
by cold and sombre winds and left to freeze
a curbside death.

Two hours,
how many a sombre beauty would meet the calm,
how many a sorrow, if I were to encounter the prince —
the invited death.

Enthroned
the gorgeous ghost sits on my table in white powder;
in two hours the brilliance of his throne will blind me,
but, God, I am afraid.

SUMMER OF TREASON

An unslaked summer sears me,
I know not where I go,
a gibbering forest quivers
and gestures,
I know not where I go.

I spoor the sunless summers,
the passions and angers of old,
the kisses, throes, and envies,
the summers,
the passions and angers of old.

A something comes this summer,
my dying powers screech,
I bend before the forests,
the deathlike,
my dying powers screech.

The summer is old and slakeless,
I know not where I go;
summoned by death defiance,
by mountains,
I know not where I go.

A something drear and wicked,
this summer wilderness;
the spoors are bleak and cruel,
a desert,
this summer wilderness.

This is the summer of treason,
for I never summered yet;
I strike with sombre scourges
of anger,
for I never summered yet.

THE STRAIGHT STAR

This surging sky,
this endless secret sea of space,
has cast on shores of our dark eyes
its gleaming stars
with a tightfisted grace.

Cold, scattered stars
that cause my dazzled eyes to spin,
where is the rarest of
your mates,
my brother and my phantom twin?

You sombre marvels of strewn light
that on recurring courses roll,
show me the star that fleets,
from void to void
and never finds a goal.

Where is the one real star
which cast away by fate
bursts timelessly
into the timeless times
upon a path that blazes straight?

Across the market of infinity
it dashes arrow straight and like a dream
it hurtles by,
and only once does it
on any one horizon gleam.

Myriads of wandering worlds and suns
come rumbling from afar,
spinning like sycophants,
and gaze
after my one straight star.

Cast out by endless time
forever it will soar
and seek the cause in space
where God can never come
behind it or before.

THE BLOODWOOD BOAT

Pensiveness, sombre bloodwood boat,
I loose you from my cove of death;
we go
and I unfurl my flag of blue.

My swift and far-off sailboat winks,
but I forsake all things of life;
we go
and may oblivion strew our way.

Of wonders all, this is most fair,
a soul high on a catafalque;
we go,
to life and to all else — farewell.

Between both life and death I stroke,
allured by storms of faraway;
we go
and settle on the pensive seas.

Pensiveness, sombre bloodwood boat,
I loose you from my cove of death;
we go
toward morrowless Tomorrow's blue.

Notes on OF ALL MYSTERIES

1. **The God of Chimeras.** Ishten (Isten) is Hungarian for God.
2. **The March Sun.** Petőfi: see Note 1 to WHO SEES ME?, page 402.
3. **The Straight Star.** See Note 4 to NEW VERSES, page 96.

THIS FUGITIVE LIFE

(1912)

The Innocent Pilate

THE INNOCENT PILATE

A forgetting, and the wry smile
of one who consecrated the orotund curse
into soft orisons
and sounded the angry sennet of mystery.
Releasing my letters in smoke
and stirring my past into the wind,
I have willed away desire.
I am bored with the buffalo pace of the future,
bored with remembrances,
penance,
vows,
and squandered kisses.
Whomever I see, I see transformed,
and I wonder at the old in myself
which they say like an ancient tale
perhaps even beyond the sea.
Graysound, graygrass, and graypassing,
field dry in the russet of autumn,
and I would shame now to be startled
at stingless death.
Perhaps this is a smile at a last tomorrow,
and I, deceived bedlamite,
look back like a god
across my cast off life.
I do not regret whatever was rapturous,
and sobreness always followed.
A wife or friend I never bent
upon my way.
I, Innocent Pilate, wash my hands
forgetting, forgiving, and unwaiting
for love, money, rebellion, belief
or for myself.

THE CHASTITY BELT

Racking disease,
the brown eternal flash
of lightning death,
lover of laments,
the cursing Job,
and leprous Lazarus,
racking endless disease,
you are life.
You are the castellan of life
who faithfully guards
the loose and wanton lady
of the marauder.
Hah, without hurt
life would be
what holy, erotic storms
of fairest youth
are to a jaded courtesan,
a nothing.
And even when I moan,
cursing the heavens,
lashing and tearing,
smitten by lightning death,
within you I sense life.
I sense you are the feeling
which I received
that I may never, never
repel the sensation of life
as long as I live.
Oh, faithful castellan
racking disease,
I thank you for your visit
with the chastity belt
of my lord.

AN ASHEN SEA

"He maketh the deep to boil like a
pot: he maketh the sea like a pot
of ointment. He maketh a path to
shine after him: one would think
the deep to be hoary." Job 41: 31-32

An ashen sea — this was my blinded hope,
to leave an antiquated sea
and hear it moan
where with my sinewy arms I struck the waves.

To make the gray unroot its silvery hair,
to hear them sorrow for the sea,
the ashen main,
this terror-stricken and enormous hag.

If once the chorus of old men should come
and ask what happened to the sea,
then you speak up
and say here swam the behemoth of God.

Upon the painters' painting ointment, waste.
Now cast your eyes upon the sea,
a little gray,
but hah, it altered not a single whit.

Like a great shaft of God here someone whirled,
and still look you upon the sea,
a painter's work
whereon are several lordly strains of fish.

My bible, oh, a mystery remain,
and if they look upon the sea,
then you shall say
that once perhaps a something will arrive.

Sometime perhaps the heavens will unclose,
and there will streak across the sea
in lightning strokes
the behemoth beloved and scourged by God.

THE NIVAL NEFILIM

The nival nefilim
of my days fall on winter silence.
But whites and pinks
rattle
and from below the snow the grass winks.

I think on't — the fever is fever,
and still I am only a wraith.
I race
young winter for unborn spring
but scarcely hold the pace.

My purling dreams
fret the purple hem of winter's eve,
and infant violets run
at my heels like cubs,
but will we arrive with the returning sun?

THE FAR-OFF WAGONS

An hour before the moon will rise
upon the cobbled highway
that shining leads into the town
they trek,
the far-off wagons trek.

The moon is up, a piper peeps,
the autumn dew is fallen,
and creaking down the moonlit road
they trek,
the far-off wagons trek.

Who turns in dream toward the moon
sleeps in a restless sleep
whenever straining from afar
they trek,
the far-off wagons trek.

They hold for town to buy and sell
as with their wobbly wheels
they creak and squeak toward the square,
they trek,
the far-off wagons trek.

The moon has turned, the dawn is come,
and in the morning twilight
electric lamps have gone to sleep,
they trek,
the far-off wagons trek.

Within the narrow streets of town
the lonely men wake up
and wait for those who come and come —
they trek,
the far-off wagons trek.

The weary moon sinks down and falls;
the amaranthine sun
climbs like a wonder in the sky,
they trek,
the far-off wagons trek.

THE AFTERNOON MOON

Squinting, it sails on Rome
with embassies of swarming swallows
and scatters a merry grin,
this summer afternoon moon.
A vast blueness and pinkness
once more bring back
that which was long ago,
while mists play on the sacred meadows
and dreamy colors on the hills.
Triumphs and ruins
hedged between the sun and moon.
Sprawling on the lap of time
the city hustles, bustles.
Oh, bright eternity,
inconstant, ancient, holy city.
Urbs, you banisher of care,
upon your sacred, protecting peak
soul and body escape
from life's hell.

I am here again.
Protect and cover me,
you deathless, beautiful, and wise.
I have lived and will live forever,
changing only my shell
like Ulysses of Greece.
I worship this teeming Rome,
embracer of all
and great even in cowardice.
Today, if I so wished,
upon the arms of sunset dreams
I might be Remus.
I look at the women of today,
at the times that were and will be.
How long I have lived here,
how all life is the same.
The moon has recognized us,
it grins but does not inflame —
squinting, it sails on Rome.

THE PEACEFUL DEPARTURE

Dry me up from the iris of eyes, sun,
who have ever seen me.
The clumsy composition of my face
leave no picture for pity.
The Nothing be my destiny,
the ear stuff
and eye stuff
Nothing.
Grant leave I go without anger
or sensible desire.
The hydroptic Nothing suck up my voice
as it sucks dreams,
the weak voice of my complaint
an echo for no one.
Grant me take leave of everyone
in flight and annihilation,
take leave from ears and eyes
unrememberable
for eternity.
Let it remain unwhispered in the night
what I long held in soul secret,
someone has departed
without his life,
someone has departed who was.
Let me forget him,
in great happiness forget him,
and drop him plummeting out of the world
and myself.
Let me not belong
or be unbelonging.
Let me look with a cold and lovely smile
on my beckoning and eternal bride.
I never belonged to myself or anyone.
My bride is the cold Nothing,
and I have no right to leave memories
or remember.
Let me plunge
as a forgotten question unanswered.
If I was not,
do not desire me to be.
And if I was,
I am forever a secret.

Woman and Death

MY SON'S CRADLE

Within a grove this aged summer day
sleep, while your father lulls you into sleep,
my little son,
upon the cradling clouds whereon you sway.

I softly fan your wee and fancied form;
the many kisses I recall from which,
my little son,
love never called you to be real and warm.

You never were and are but wisp of breath,
Never was your poor father grieved so much,
my little son;
I think he must be very near to death.

Sweet issues of desire are now fulfilled.
It is but you that now my kisses want.
my little son;
sleep, sleep, your father is so sick and chilled.

Did you perchance sometime, somewhere desire
to see your vagrant, melancholy father,
my little son?
O aged summer day, O childless sire.

Death lurks and stalks today about this place;
it seems that I within your cradle lie,
my little son,
and softly stroke your wee and fancied face.

LOVES OF AUTUMN

Autumn's Preacher

Unsurpassed is the autumn scent,
unsurpassed is the autumn song,
for the blood a somniferous chant,
and God has no better chorister
than the youthful autumn gnat
that sings, "Himhum, we go, we go."
Somewhere winter is bundling up
and stamping his mighty, frozen feet;
though summer still, the youthful minstrels,
when darkling winds are calm,
chant autumn's great and holy hymn.

Chorus of Autumn Gnats

Himhum, himhum, summer fades;
himhum, we go, we go.
A thousand diggers are delving graves,
but our song is gay.
Himhum, himhum,
life is empty humdrum,
fair like autumn twilight,
so fair that we leave
through the flowery parapet
of the balcony of life
and sink into the deep.
Himhum, himhum, we go
singing and unfearing.
To our holy music
the lame will walk again,
autumn will turn into summer
and summer's fury turn meek.
All will be open and serene
and all a harmony.
Quench the mighty flames,
make love, make love
in an embracing flood of tears
for the last time unrestrained,
himhum, we go, we go.

Autumn's Kiss

Come, you who are spent
from embraces but desire
to keep kissing until death,
you whose teeth are worn away
but still would feed on lips.
Come, every distress of love,
vexation, grief, hunger, sin,
you who know only longing,
and with a kiss I shall steal myself,
the autumn day, into your kisses.
There will be a marvellous kissing
in the mellifluous autumn nights,
which are not tiring like summer's;
the kisses will be full, like in spring,
and with the madness of youthful love
winter will step on your hearts
like spring with violets in her front,
your lips will kiss but will not live.

Chorus of Autumn Gnats

Himhum, himhum, summer fades,
himhum, we go, we go.
Quench the mighty flames,
love one last love,
we still chant our gay song,
himhum, himhum,
we go, we go, we go.

WOMAN AND DEATH

I want
a merry song of women ripe,
a merry song about the grave
to pipe.

I wish
to pack it for the endless road
and sing into the marrow of life
an ode.

The grave
will dun me with a dusty claim,
but think of them and all becomes
the same.

I send
my mother word that love and life
were worth the suffering and
the strife.

Good nights —
our birth and sleep in bawdy bed,
you are the real between the live
and dead.

To woman
I sing my clarion song and brave,
and to her worthy other world,
the grave.

THE OLD TRAMP

1

There he flees,
the old tramp,
in deadly danger
from the wolfteeth of winter.
Heigh ho! my voice falls short.
Ragged and kneedeep in snow
he struggles this way and that.
He stops, his little strength at end.

Heigh ho, he leans against
a wayside cross.
This is not his way, and he is lost.
The cross may mark a grave,
but there are no other signs in this wild.
A white snow-death
rides the whirlwind
into night and fog,
whistling, freezing, and blinding.
This is the end of the road, old tramp,
and the wooden Christ cannot help you.
Heigh ho, life was not given
to the sombre galileans.

2

We lie down and sleep
like an unremembered story,
and God's cold
steals on us in the stealth of sweet dreams.
Heigh ho, we curl up and dream.

3

In a gorgeous miniature palace
the most beautiful girl
is waiting
in perfumed and kiss-scented chambers.

She is a virgin and more gorgeous than life,
intelligent, a restless thoroughbred.
Her holy bedroom
is worth a hundred famous salons.

She is the unattained,
the Gorgeous someone
for whom we willingly suffer damnation
and give up redemption.

She draws the old tramp
into her warm sweet bed,
and the most divine music overflows
the most human night.

4

This is how the old tramp froze to death.

THE CITY GIRL

The holy books confess
in monodies of mournful guilt
that women are more passionate
since cities have been built.

Roses that span and pierce
the marbled walls of ancient Zeus,
the city girl has twined our hearts
in a triumphant noose.

City, I worship you,
not Budapest in equal wise.
A third floor room in Paris once
gave me a great surprise.

A curtain careless girl
in full undress and secret bloom
appeared in tiptoe readiness
for someone's bliss or doom.

The striptease of a destiny,
she gleamed within the window frame
as when above a row of graves
a corposant emits a flame.

No secret pair of eyes
had ever ogled Death like this,
I wailed for every male who stalks
the jungle of the kiss.

In autumn dark I lurked
until the window merged with night,
but this strange pair of Kiss and Death
has never left my sight.

Here they live, Kiss and Death,
sinning within my bosom sealed.
The city girl has come to kill
the flowers of the field.

BENEDICTION FROM A TRAIN

The express is hurtling at full speed,
the sun explodes into the sea,
my memories flash a millisecond,
and I bless you.

"May God bless
all your goodness,
your unresponsiveness,
and all your wickedness.
May your words of torment
return to you in benediction.
May your coldness
leap into flames.
All is at an end.
I have a thousand cares,
and for my folly
the bier is spread.
Well, I bless you,
and meanwhile
kiss me softly,
in silence and peace.
I wish to leave you
with a memory and a kiss
to freeze after warmth,
to be alone,
to feel alone,
to die alone.
May God bless you."

The express is hurtling at full speed,
the sun explodes into the sea,
my memories flash a millisecond,
and I bless you.

How beautiful the town and all which tempts
but casts no more a spell —
the legendary present, future, past,
and girls as well.

How beautiful all alien things on which
only with eyes I dwell —
good spirit, money, chance, success,
and girls as well.

How beautiful that my desires have fled
and will no more compel
and that before me pass, unwanted now,
the girls as well.

Declining Toward God

THE SNOW-WHITE LAWN

This raging red horse
Blood
has dragged me into hell.
A sign flutters,
a snow-white Lawn,
and boldly I want
to become otherwordly, unstained,
immaculate.

I can no longer turn back,
and I curse the tumescence,
the first swelling of desire,
the first impure thought.
Love
which awoke so soon
and memories, memories
let me rest a while.

All my works are a curse,
a shame.
Happy who steeps himself white
in God's grace.
A score of holy monks are dancing.
How blessed the unhappy,
how impure the tulle of life,
how wretched and foul
the Blood.

At the age of thirty four
having lived through it
and overwhelmed by nausea
but knowing much,
I cry as I see
my soul is fluttering
the scarf
of my one and only love,
the snow-white Lawn.

THIS FUGITIVE LIFE

Look, how swiftly flees
the famous lord called life,
like a thieving slave
driven, beaten, pursued
by a lord more mighty than he.
(And with him run in flight
a million little grandchildren,
tiny specks of life;
among them my own,
pattering in tears,
I see.)

Trampling on sheet lightning
of virginal and endless snows,
life runs and runs,
and in its wake are insectlike,
bloody, and monstrous spoors.

Look, drifts of red snow
and a monstrous stalker.
Look, how life runs
into the snow, into the frost,
followed by tiny lives
and bits of death.

Oh, I rise out of my own self
and look upon this chase
like Rembrandt on his paintings
and the gloom which he stroked
into dead colors,
the gloom which glows today.
(I know that I am someone
although with many false beauties,
superstitious reasons and guiles
I entertained
death.
But death is not decisive.
Death, too, is afraid and runs.
My life and death
are two insignificant brothers
of the fleeing ragamuffin hordes.)

On savannahs of sacred snow
the spoors of blood
stalk
the sombre path of my life
like hunters
after forest things.
Here is a great stalker,
these are his marks,
and he is a hundred times more great than death.

Death is a small patch of blood,
a bad hour.
It leaps in a thousand directions,
it points in a thousand directions,
it beckons with a thousand fingers,
this winter's fool, this clown.
It is always a nought.
It comes with an impact on our lives,
and still it is nothing more
than a visiting card,
and still a thousand times
on every run
of the snowy course of life
(of the roving course of my life)
I was followed by this little servant,
this nothing — death.

Perhaps there would be no life
without death,
whereas behind them both
is their mysterious lord,
an ancient, terrible, wild,
and lawless law,
a great and mighty stalker.

And death like a gaudy insect
on freakish spoors of blood,
follows life,
fulfilling the great command
of a lord mightier than himself.

But death is only a hue
on the snows of craven life
(also of my little life),
for look how it capers
like roses on the feverish face
of the sick whom they feed a powder.

O death, I love you
(a hundred times I confess it),
and still you are only
the bloody escort,
the flecked likeness,
of fugitive life
(of my white, frosty
and harassed life also
that flees with life)
after whom incessantly stalks
the great stalker — the unknown.

THE GROWN-UP CHRISTS

Like pregnant mushrooms after rain
and flowers in the florentine morn,
within our day the sacred shoals
of modern world on world are born.

How slow and faltering were the hands
that fashioned us the bible world,
today how finished are the thoughts
that from the brain of man are hurled.

The famous star of Bethlehem
has died untraced by ash or slag,
but on a thousand shining stars
the mind of man has staked his flag.

Our life is but a thought or song
that makes an ugly moment gilt,
creation lives within our soul
where new and newer worlds are built.

The wings of man-made birds avow
as through god-tempting space they cross,
creation is mankind and God
a crown converted into dross.

At any moment he may die
but the eternal is his goal,
for this he is heroic man
and goodness lives within his soul.

When people killed for sake of Christ
in rank and incense-burning times,
within the heart of man alone
God was preserved unstained by crimes.

And in the human heart a flame
leaps up unsullied, brave, and bright;
whatever man who craves creates
becomes a world of finer light.

Forever grows the great intent
that God is not a word dispute,
that on this earth man should receive
the full of every good and truth.

Always more firmly we avow
bread is our due for all the stones,
and always more and more we seek
the secret world of far unknowns.

We sense within our growing soul
the power of the unattained,
the stress for union of the worlds
and kingdoms where no one has reigned.

A million worlds will turn to one
perfection of all joy and grace
and this poor vale of grief become
a garden for the human race.

The living also want their joys
though heaven is not for living man,
but here it shines within our heart,
for it was we who forged the plan.

This Christmas time the grown-up Christs
are walking forth into the dim.
Great ferment, let your music ring,
you great one world, sing forth your hymn.

PRAYER OF TERROR

O cry of terror, ai, ai, ai,
that often makes me wake aghast
from my phantasmagoric nights,
how pleasing you must sound to God.
No prayer excels a shriek that bursts
the rattle of a prison throat.
No oratory invites the Sovran
like oratories of horror's shock.

My raveled dreams are shuddering from
a branding, drowning, kiss, and pox.
A shame, a shadow, and a death,
an intermingling with a tale,
an echo from my waking life,
and urchin-ghosts with tumored eyes
are tightening fast my stricken heart,
and I awaken: ai, ai, ai.

Ai, ai, ai, for whom I was,
whom I no longer dare to be
or if I dared would know not how.
What justice is dispensed on earth
to grant me mercy or to punish?
What greater terror in this world,
more frequent summons to depart
than we receive from screeching life?

The shrieking babe and screaming lover,
the dying man and sage's mouth
wail with the cry of ai, ai, ai
and send their kisses into woe.
And whether sleeping or awake,
on sheeted bed or rotten straw,
they query various thrones of God,
"Is this, in fact, the joy of life?"

THE THUS FAR

The Thus Far speaks, "Amen,
I am your last and furthest Lord.
Thus far, no farther, shalt thou come."
Thus Far is mighty God.

Beneath me is a chasm,
here is the boundary and the end,
while other ends and boundaries
lure to unbottomed pits.

Dumb-struck but with a prayer
I kneel before this mighty Lord.
My soul admits its arrogance,
in truth, I have come far.

And Thus Far speaks, "Now stand."
And foolishly I wait as though
I thought that something would arrive.
Thus Far commanded me.

How sad that he who once
was given faith to sail and soar
is now commanded to a halt
before a deathlike ditch.

How sad this cruel amen,
how sad that all must come to end,
that the no farther should arrive,
Thus Far, this mighty God.

EPIPHANY

I hear the hum of golden sunbeams,
I see the sounds of holy thunder,
and in my mouth your name tastes good.
My God, my God, my God,
today my chaotic soul confessed
you always were the all in all
within my senses,
within my tenderest caresses,
within my sharp and sorrowful glances.
And now I thank you for being present
where I sensed life,
where altars rose and altars fell.
I thank you for the bed prepared for me,
I thank you for my first tear,
I thank you for my sorrowing mother,
for my youth and my sins.
I thank you for doubt and faith,
for love and sickness.
I thank you because to you,
and only you, I owe everything.
I hear the hum of golden sunbeams,
I see the sounds of holy thunder,
and in my mouth your name tastes good.
My God, my God my God,
my soul is lighter for having confessed
you were my life, my sorrow, my kiss, my joy.
And that you will be my death, I thank.

DECLINING TOWARD GOD

> "I am gone like the shadow when
> it declineth: I am tossed up and
> down like the locust." Psalms 109:23

You disappear from my desires,
O God whom I desired and willed;
no longer do I know myself
and ruin chokes my calling you.

I needed you in my sore hours
and sought for you in sombre strife,
but now from my complaints I leave
your name, the fairest of all names.

Saint Fancy, deathless balm of faith,
the realest though you are unreal,
I bow before your holy face
and will that I should will belief.

I am pursued and will not rest
before acquiring faith in you,
because my life is on the dice,
a shadow that is in decline.

And like a locust I am tossed
because the power is yours alone,
because I saw not long ago
I must have faith in no one else.

THE SPRING SUNSET

I am the sunset of a day in spring,
envoy of a faded sun, and dappled skies
invite me to a gentle last caress
for those I love.

So stormless and so soft the world today,
so prone toward embraces are my arms
that with a loving prayer I would enfold
an ugly grave.

Dominoed row on row of faces come
of those who importune a last farewell,
and I release these lips, white faces, eyes,
and snowy necks.

Today I shall release whoever comes.
Although the fallen sun, who sees, may laugh,
the world, behold, deserves a soft caress
and gentle love.

Today I count and cancel with a tear
whatever alms this glorious life once gave,
and on this crossroad I desire no more
what it denied.

The ones who failed to come or who were bad
may now remain away, far off removed —
bad heads, bad girls, bad poets, and bad friends,
vivat, carouse.

Today I know that everyone who lives
shared in my love, even those whom I hurt.
The means I chose were all too mild, but still
the goal was good.

The trespasses and trials of everyone
I always loved as if they were my own;
I still would bless the fair and haughty deeds
if there were some.

I shall still listen to the timeless songs
of every beauty, sorrow, and decay,
but freely and without critique I add
my gentle soul.

I am the sunset of a day in spring,
envoy of a faded sun, and dappled skies
invite me to a gentle last caress
for those I love.

(Now and unto the hour of my death I love
everyone, Amen.)

Unpeace and Death

WITH CHILD BY GOD

This splendor which the winter cannot freeze
is not a changeling left on summer's sod
or autumn's xanthophyllic death.
He is alone in green of splendor
and blooms and blooms
who is with child by God.

Still unsubdued is this chromatic clangor,
the beads of blood and palpitating coals,
the polypetals of defiance,
and for my ears, which hear the bells,
bing bang, bing bang,
the conflagration tolls.

The harsh bell blasts of life whose price was great
must not become the cowards' vapid game,
and though its stress be small of worth,
and though it be a glooming glacier,
huzza, huzza,
in color, clangor, and flame.

UNPEACE AND DEATH

I love to live but intermittent sleep
make it brief.
I love life with a great negation,
but dearly, dearly.

I love the decomposition of dreams
into color,
and the white table where I leave
a spoor of action soaked in blood.

O life of deeds and alienation,
constant quarrels —
kinsmen, friends, and things of beauty
have become all the same to me.

I accept life
with a great negation,
and we shall see who emerges triumphant,
my destiny or I.

Now nothing more can harm me,
and I await the sealer of fulfilment,
the wise and eternally youthful Time,
who whips the lash of law above us.

I surrender, gently and without intent,
to the days.
I live because I live. And God,
if there is one, kisses me with sombre pride.

A LAST THUNDERSTORM

Mirrored,
I see as if present
the thousand works of my green years
covered with mold.
But holier than holy
they are mine, youthful and whole,
ageless,
and younger than the beginning
more everlasting than truth.

Up there on a hilltop
I shall sit no piper of ballads.
Plodding in fours and eights,
the bullocks break ground
evoking an image.

I long to recall
and see this land
green and good.
Hounded, cursed, and loved,
I saw and suffered much.
Deceiving, hurting and stealing from
myself,
I cannot find a wreath
more worthy
than a great thunderstorm
lashed to my soul.
How I loved the storms of my green years
that cradled my birthplace,
how fitting to me now,
one last and lusty thunderstorm.

DEAD SHADOWS HAUNT

Dead shadows haunt my inner eye,
gentle fingers are running through my hair,
but I no longer tremble,
my arms hold eluded embraces,
my legs are hobbled with an unrun chase
for girls who long since ran away,
on my lips a dry and ownerless kiss,
in my ear hoped for but unwhispered words,
and in my nostrils the perfume of springs
puissant no longer to drug the mind.

My God, can one live for long
who does not reach after fresh life
and moves in a cloud of sombre visions?
Can he live who fears the real and dewy fields,
the raw flower and the leaf,
who endures no kiss but only a mocking smile,
the funeral flower of this dead life,
closes his eyes lest he see,
spins himself a hundred different cloaks,
and feels his heart throb terribly at times?

THE SEEDS OF CANAAN

These tremors will pass away
and life will drink a ceremonial wine.
Psalms will resound in a little church.
A snowy Christmas, communion,
and athletic children will come.

An ark will rise on this wild flood,
my wings will dry to a triumphant flight,
and it will pass that I shall only desire
what can be fulfilled
and that I shall desire again and again.

The sluggish crows will turn to doves,
and women with shapely bodies
will longingly wait for me
to release them from their covers,
and many will love me
and I will love them.

I will sow a holy field
with the seeds of Canaan from my soul
which have begun to rot.
I shall be glorious and rejoice
in myself, all things, and earth,
where with blessed hand
I have sown faith, future, and happiness.

If it proves otherwise, it is all the same.

The Unchosen

A MODERN BEUCOLICK

Men plod home from fields
south clear and north ill cloud
ing. Summer desolation,
and a melancholy rhyth
m of the scythe
and smell of poverty on acrid weeds.

A thin world of wheat moan
s into our hush hamlet
three towered.
This too is a world, a complete world,
but man and window stare blan
c.

Men and women count grain
and think shiver
ing on winter. Every hope
in this hamlet born
died on the angelus of the fading twi
light.

Twice ten times old husbandmen knew
the green of summer promise
and sombrely content
wait for
the vale of mourn
ing harvest.

A dogged shepherd
may whirl the curse like a whip,
throw his hat on the ground,
and greet the evening kne
ll
with sour wine he buys on credit.

Young men arrive at night
in fatigue, hate and fear,
and three towers
wan white for new miracles stretch
question
ing into the sky.

THE UNSUNG SUMMERS

Will they remain
eternally unsung and cached,
the melancholy songs
of the sun-seared, sombre Hungarian summers?

Seed-time
is a gash of mute agony,
the dust, a burnt out tear,
and the summer day a cadaverous song.

Who knows resurrection
and the moan of the plowshare?
Who knows the immemorial summer sun
when mockingly it declines?

I cradle my head on dead songs
and seek to waken an earth
with an embrace
as though it were my heart.

I shower
treasures on impoverished summer
like Jesus on a woman who was a sinner
his forgiveness.

But will they remain
eternally unsung and cached,
the melancholy songs
of the sun-seared, sombre Hungarian summers?

I walk the fields,
the subjugated of a thousand revolving seasons,
keeping watch over their sorrows
and waiting simply for their songs.

I stand by a grave. Look close,
for in me the Hungarian summers sleep,
and you cover an eternal summer secret
when you bury me.

THE NEW SPECTER

A Specter walks announced by blasts
who is defiant, handsome, red,
who rose on noon and not on night
and stands before the Lord Himself
with unbared head.

I hear the drone of idle minds
whose dreams are drab and limp,
but well I know who haunts the land,
the great and scarlet presence of
the holy Pimp.

He neither lets himself be loved
nor counts upon a lordly life,
but with the greatest love he gives
himself and all his essence up
to blood and strife.

We often met on walks abroad,
and I would shadowbox and spurn,
but if I left a hundred times,
a thousand times with greater love
I would return.

This is the Specter of the sun
who shines on every honest breast,
who seals the eye and drugs the mind,
and shows that he is greater far
than all the rest.

If you have known a mite of honor
despite a world so false and hollow,
you will confess you never knew
another Specter whom you would
more freely follow.

This well I know we shall lose all,
O sombre sad and faltering race,
and yet this merry mask of red
shall serve again and still again
to mum my face.

This is the only Specter whom
I cannot lightly scare or stone.
I am a Magyar of bitter fate
who with defiance claims — he is
and he alone.

This Specter is unique and new,
a terror for discarded years,
a sign of dread for weak of mind,
accompanied on his youthful way
by senile fears.

Heigh ho, how I despise this life,
how many wars I fell in,
and yet the Magyar land and I
in spellbound trance await the ghost
incarnadine.

May my Lord God destroy and smite
who seeks to keep this new faith dim.
Whomever this new Specter shadows
may he receive the holy spirit,
my God, let him.

THE UNCHOSEN

Because we are unloved
no shambling kings and sages go
around our sombre brown berceau.

We faulted at the start.
The seven fat years we have not seen,
and all our seasons have been lean.

We daubed the doers of good.
We never helped those who despaired,
and we rejoiced when someone erred.

Here are aim, cause, and fate,
a powerful and ancient rule
by which small nations go to school.

We sought for western Goods,
we fell, grayed out in fearsome fight,
and now we bleed into the night.

But still we give ourselves
because a finer tragic plan
does not exist by God or man.

While others rush ahead,
where is a more poetic face
than of this chained and sleepy race?

Odes to Someone

RAISE A GENTLE VOICE

You raise a gentle voice to God,
and he is by your side.

You lose your poor unstable self,
and may God come to help.

The pleasure moments fleet away,
and he arrives in gloom.

This life has offered little joy,
but he has watched with care.

You raise a gentle voice to God,
and he is by your side.

SHAKE UP YOUR HEART

A muteness has mewed up, though filled with light,
this bulging, pregnant likeness of the heavens
that soars in black of silence, tocsin still,
a sign of fear to no one but itself.

Your uses are so rich they hold your tongue,
unfortunate ripe cloud afraid to burst.
Thunder down and accept at last your fate,
shake up your heart, you anguished ego, shake.

If now you drew the bell rope of your heart,
the angel wings of death would moan a chorus
to the sky-scaling rhapsody of life,
and hell would yawn its deepest secrets up.

Beneath cloud caruncles, with strangled heart,
a dark and clotted heart, this bell of blood,
you dodder in the heft of pregnancy
and stay the flood, old toller of the bell.

The cloud is dark, this is the dark of God,
the bell is sombre, this is his sombreness.
Pour out the rain and strike the gonglike bell,
live all the uses of your fate and heart.

Let the sky thunder plunge a noon to night,
and in the holocaustal sound of fate
appeased above a black and furious flood
the stricken bell will peal a final screech.

Notes on THIS FUGITIVE LIFE

1. **A Last Thunderstorm,** Gyula Földessy **(All of Ady's Secrets)**
analyzes the poem as follows: lines 1-4 describe emotions on the tresh-
old of death and of a visit to his birthplace, accompanied by pre-
imagery of all his experiences as a youth; lines 5-9 leap back into the
present and celebrate the immortality of all that furthered his mission:
lines 10-14 open with an echo of a Petőfi song: the plowing is spirit-
ual, related in imagery to **The Seeds of Canaan,** written shortly ear-
lier; and lines 15-29 describe the memories of the past gathering about
the poet like clouds before a storm.

2. **The New Specter.** The Communist Manifesto opens with the
line — "A specter is haunting Europe — the specter of Communism."
Despite some vivid imagery, the poem has a Pinocchio-like wooden-
ness. See the Introduction, page 42-43.

LOVE OF OURSELVES

(1913)

The Returned Flag

THE HOLOCAUSTAL GOD

Victorious on victory's march of death,
I hail you, holy holocaustal God,
the God of gall and fruit of Fury's womb,
the hybris of my heart, great hybris mine.

Often I fought on outer battlefields
and laughed at clashes you had won for me,
and laughed at foe who lay before my feet,
but I have come to sense your holy power.

Who took me from the claws of hawking death
and cupped me fondly in his sheltering hands
or winged me arrowlike into the sky
but you, the ancient hybris of my heart?

My ancient hybris, pagan love of self,
the warning summons and the blood-streaked call,
who looks beyond the chase toward the goal
and loves himself not for his proper sake.

He seldom loves himself for love of self,
or if he does, deservingly and well;
no matter how, but he will never cease,
no matter whom, but he will always love.

Thus the command is made to each his own
but he who has no other God has none
to drive him toward his great and pregnant fate
except his own duped self, his hybris God.

It struck the fancy of my fate to turn
from where I could behold all things that are,
that were and once will be, while all my wars
plunged from an inner to an outer world.

Victorious death march of an inner strife,
great triumph over my most wrathful half,
O missioned task, the secret heart of fire,
the hybris of my heart, great hybris mine.

THE SACRED UNATTAINABLE

Wild swimmery whirls upon a swing of hell,
flaming depths above, below,
soaring descend and descending soar
above our fancy and below the real.
Everywhere
the rigid sign is staked,
mark of unyielding bounds,
because I wait unwaitables,
I wait only unwaitables,
blood red anguish of a blood red hell.

Desire clamors against the gates.
Before my red daubed face a skeleton
lifts a grotesque and prohibitory finger.

Only possibilities around me
and dreamable dreams ethereal.
There is no God to lift my swing
out of its worn and slavish groove,
make my longings seize
upon a something never before seizable
embrace a someone
never before embraceable.
I am blind in flaming depths,
my brain is boiling, my throat is hoarse.
Within this strangling dusk,
you accursed and sacred unattainable,
I thunder your emaciating song.

Heigh ho, life, heigh ho,
whose shirt burns,
heigh ho, life, heigh ho,
who knows and convulses me.
Loft up a great last laugh,
the screw is set
for the final ugly turns.

Heigh ho, life, heigh ho,
more than I
heigh ho, life, heigh ho,
you know how thick we were
and how I seized your steed
as off we rode
against the pounding sky.

Heigh ho, life, heigh ho,
wherever we gad,
heigh ho, life, heigh ho,
I seek not a part
but the whole of us,
the whole of our good,
the whole of our bad.

Heigh ho, life, heigh ho,
whose shirt burns,
heigh ho, life, heigh ho,
who loves the blind believer.
Loft up a great last laugh,
the screw is set
for the final ugly turns.

AWAKENING AND FORGETTING

Slanting arrival of the spring sun,
wake-robin sleep of youth,
splashing bath and hurried dress,
song escaping from a fresh mouth,
the dash to school
or to a field of yellow and blue
in whole-bodied, coltish joy.
The cherry-stained mouth of my playmate,
the hallelujah of life,
my light and lovely self that was,
rested awakenings,
I sometimes look back on you
and reach for poison. Well, let's go.

Furtively,
malevolently and furtively is born
the omnipotent and paralyzing self-love
that living, no matter how,
is better than not living,
that even though paralyzed one may hope
for the image, the lovely illusion,
that one may be content with little,
with lying down instead of waking up,
and that all welling from within —
memory of youth, sorrow, and prayer —
is a greatly great amen
and obligation.

Here is a great and merry time of it,
a gorgeous offering,
a rimeless rime in living verse,
days of youth which return
in old age,
imagination and youth,
the potsherd that scraped the sores of Job.
O stubborn life that we accept,
O compromise and forgetting,
O my lovely self that was
and is no more but wants to be,
awakening and forgetting,
O life that makes believe what it will.

LOVE OF OURSELVES

I search for relics of the past,
my blessed God, my blessed God,
if there are some.
I kiss the picture of a face,
an ancient face
of tortured and of mournful cast,
that is my own.

How all and all we shall dismiss,
how all and all shall stay behind
in times to come.
How we would offer up our lips,
our own good lips,
but worthy is the farewell kiss
for none but us.

A thousand times I shall caress
the only one, the only one
who has remained,
who stayed so good in every place,
in others' place,
worthy although in ruined distress,
my faithful self.

O blessed world on shallows run.
O blessed God, O blessed God,
who gave us leave
that we should gently bask ourselves,
our aged selves,
within the young and godly sun
of your great love.

MY SCARLET KITE

O fleeting moon of increscent youths,
O fleeting youth of decrescent moons,
I know that they will mock and stone
this queer senescent.

Within my maddened self I bear a babe,
boldly I reach my hands into the flame,
boldly I reach for women, honeyed wine,
and deadly weapons.

I skip my scarlet kite into the sky
and have not wearied after thirty springs;
although the moorings broke a thousand times,
I never fretted.

The spell-struck symbols of a virgin peak
shoot arrowy beams within my large, dim eyes.
These keep me a child, this never-never glow
and my own blindness.

Sail, scarlet kite, upon the upper sky.
Escape, but others follow you in flight.
Never a boy who keeps on flying you
with greater fervor.

Mysterious moods perish on the birdlime of fate
spinning down on the sticky mistletoe
in mad masquerade.
Ultimate horror of destiny. O life, orderly and absurd,
that ought to guard this weak, inconstant time with iron fist.
Eternal limitability, lyric string that snaps.
Why do we not live illimitable and free?
Detestable final end. Untidy comma of God.
Why does all submit to a clemency of cold clay?
Why a completion and an end to great desires?
Every wish carries a chromosome of death.
Why do we not like majestic rivers,
laughing and full of laughter,
hosanna down into the sea?
Sombre nausea of love, the nether cup.
Why and why should sorrow heal by morrow?

Prayer for Deception

THE WOMAN HUNT

My inborn sensual and saintly fervor,
I strain at you and with great humor twirl you.
For sumless soft chignons I now prepare
my hero's crown, this insane love.
How self-destroying are my great designs.
How many curious weepables I wait.
How many woman-straying deeds will lead astray.

I am so sick, so beautifully sick.
Waiting for the unbelievable, not the believed,
I rush once more into the world
and seek the steps that lead me down
to the pits of your large blue queer eyes
from where you ascend
like lamp-bearing men.

You blue eyes indeterminate,
dangle your dancing lamps
and show me in their rosy mist
the unattainable great woman
of my soul who bending over me
will scorn my sorrows,
cry at my laughter,
who though not mine belongs to me.

With grievous cries
I perish in your presence,
mysterious and unreal envoys of
the woman.
I love you and need you
like talons grown too long
and aching for the new seized prey.

And still I place my trust in you, blue eyes.
Tomorrow I shall surely be in love.
Direct my eyes upon the true.
Oh, how pursued I am, how much alone.
No one wants my fervor as I would give it.
There is no God, faith, kindness, goodness,
no meek but untamed woman,
no beauty and no worthy chance.

O glossy woman-hunting falsehood,
send me your woman-sister,
the cheating and the life-destroying,
the dear, the virgin, and the false,
O send her, send her.

LETTER OF DISMISSAL

Let break the charm that broke the hundredth time.
You are dismissed once more and for the very last
if you believed that I should always keep you
or that there still was need to be dismissed.
Stricken a hundred times, I throw at you
the ample, lordly robe of my forgetting.
Now clad yourself against the greater cold,
now clad yourself because I pity us
for the great shame of the unequal strife,
for your humiliation and all else.
In a word, by now I pity only you.

How long and how in secret it has been like this.
To gild your fate how many times there sprang
from cheating grace the lovely Leda psalms,
concocted and conveyed for sake of art for art.
I never did receive or take away.
I gently handed you the heresy
of kisses that in mind I kissed with others,
of love acts that in mind I loved with others;
and now I thank you for as many embraces,
I thank you for as many one-time Ledas
as any male may have the power to thank
when stepping over an old and worn-out kiss.

How long since I have tried to look for you
in sand dunes of the past and troubled present.
On your future's slavish womanish path
how long ago I had dismissed you from my mind.
How long I searched for nothing
but to bequeath you something from myself
and my unique poetic, trumped-up charges
that in your orphaned love you might find solace
and claim you also were, not only he
who could not bear the weight alone
and hung some ornaments upon a woman.

From my proud breast which is insatiable and great
I wanted to behold a gentle fall
and not the small revenge of a forsaken female
who in her fury waits in ambush with some man,
and not the mocking of your poor and little self,
for I had placed my Croesus mark on you
and gave you cause for faith that you belonged to me
and that your passing should take place unseen.
I presented you the largest of my embraces
that you would find a joy in them,
and you were nothing but a little question mark
until with my arrival you became fulfilled.

Will you flutter like a dessicated flower
from the leaves of a long tranquil prayer book
or will you flounce about and wear to rags
your purchased nimbus — this despotic, sombre yoke —
and my self-idolizing prayers
which stammer after all for some deserving woman?
I ask of destiny not to let you
presume to cross my starry fate.
Whatever swallows you, a flood or dross,
you live through me because I saw you, but long ago
you ceased to be because I ceased to see you.

THE FARTHER SHORE

Here she undresses, drops her gown,
by now I may not want it.
I enter, take her by the hand,
and show her to the window where
the farther shore is shining.

Beyond the Danube flitting girls.
I hurt beneath this burning,
this womanliness, this all-free,
this present, and this have attained.
The farther shore is shining.

Listen. A fog horn strums, she sobs.
The mating night how frantic.
These apprehenders, little girls,
sense in their blood a moan, a surge,
the farther shore is shining.

BLOOD HARMONIOUS STRIFE

How dense the world appears although
no denseness is upon the trees;
in budding bushes hides a throng
of mischievous mythologies.

The breath of winter still is sharp,
but in unfettered, frisking play,
ho, we would like to sport in nude
upon the tempting grass today.

Upon queer silence come loud cries.
Beneath the bush in hidden bliss,
with feigned endeavor to escape,
the kiss is in pursuit of kiss.

A mask of love is one each face.
Impatience every spirit fills,
and bodies wax now hot now cold
with mad voluptuous fever, chills.

Wonderful, blood harmoniuos strife,
O panting, male melodious call,
when from the old arterial dark
the sweetly scented flowers fall.

O MAGNIFICENT LOVE

O groups of girls unnoticed,
overlooked women,
dear, purchased hetairae,
O females of every rank,
how greatly sad I am,
how greatly in love.
Others rumpled up your beds,
and others sealed your lips,
and others forced on you
the happy yoke,
others, others, not I.

O beginning women,
amorous apprehenders,
with short dresses and school books,
you are the ones who dream
the joy of release,
of the all, of the one, of the unique.
You grow before my aged eyes,
that belong to grownup women.
By mistake alone can you be mine,
and others will taste of you,
because young men are also growing,
others, others, not I.

O magnificent love.
The love for every woman,
the awful impossible,
insane ranting of dreams.
I feel the chills upon my back
when I think of you.
Upon the little streets in pairs
the lovers walk about.
All is fulfilled with a single woman;
the sensible males are so happy,
others, others, not I.

CONVERSATION WITH A WITCH

I

(Have you beheld an angel
in death, my sweetest witch?)
"I saw my lovely self
before I ever lived."

(Have you beheld the sun
and moon in close embrace?)
"I saw a snow white heart
that faded into red."

(Have you beheld the sun
rise in the western night?)
"I saw Silvester's eve
pursue a New Year's Day."

(Have you beheld the fall
of sifting marble rain?)
"I saw upon the skies
a rainbow black as slate."

(Have you beheld a grief
that sprang from proud deceit?)
"I saw an open grave
filled up with deepest love."

(Have you beheld a clock
with moving hands reversed?)
"I saw a seething kiss
that never came to birth."

(Have you beheld the seas
where forests are conceived?)
"I saw your future spouse,
she who will never be."

(Have you beheld, my witch,
the madman loving you?)
"I saw your heart fall down
upon my heart — you doomed."

II

(How heavy on my heart
you lie, my sweetest witch.)
"If I betray you, dear,
you have betrayed me, too."

(I always shall remain
by your fair womanhood.)
"My eyes have caught upon
another man again."

(My soul is overflowing
with your beloved self.)
"Your boring kisses ease
my dark and morbid moods."

(Your loveliness excels
the stars upon the skies.)
"How bad it is on earth,
how bad to be with you."

(Become my wife, my dear,
my faithful, and my own.)
"I am your faithful wife
who left you long ago."

Thus I Weep

PLUNGE INTO THE VOID

I want to plunge with an abominable fall
into the void
and proudly leave behind the accomplished all.

I seek for death alone as beauty's crown,
but death delays
like a local in some dark provincial town.

I would freely yield to judgment day
my captive life,
but fate is scornful and turns away.

Should I be my own jail overseer
and invite
death to approach more near and near?

I revel as the autumn days arrive
and rejoice
in that, now matter how, I stayed alive.

I revel in all the pleasures of earth,
my way is free,
I only wish more days may come to birth.

I want to plunge with an abominable fall
but still alive
receive, desire, live, and surrender all.

Of Youthful Arms

OLD BACHELOR'S LOVE

The wonders of your eighteen years,
your lovely, golden girlishness,
secrets and secrets yet to come,
why offer with your lips' address?

While soft you soothe my aching brow,
gaze in these large and weary eyes.
Today I love you, and studentlike
the joys of kiss rejuvenize.

Today as from a tuberose
my senses at your body swirled;
today I love you, and achingly
I would conceal you from the world.

But if tomorrow you should see
one younger, stronger, comelier,
would you, impassioned, yearned for, dear,
be true and gentle as you were?

I do not call, you want to come;
today I still am used to woe.
Today I am compassionate;
perhaps I still can let you go.

Today you still can safely flee,
stammering at once your curse and prayer.
Alas, let not your gorgeous throat
fall in my fingers' strangling snare.

THE SNOWS OF WINTER

Be glad for the hard seed of my desire,
this late ripening of the miracle,
and forget the puling young,
who are too fast or slow with the act.
You know I say the days to death,
but tomorrow you will give up
what life withheld,
and I am deathly in love with love.

Your cheeky and delicate boys
perform with a twist of the spine
the more easily to run,
but I am sated with earthly pleasures,
and in their place you are the all,
and I am your all.
You fashion faithless plans,
but never, while I live, can you leave.

After so many unremembered loves,
nocturnal struggles and bargains with death,
I wait and long for you,
life, mother, daughter and sister.
Where can you find such complete love?
Stroke my thinning hair
and cry a bit, confused child of Eve.

I forget the reception at the grave
and what I have encountered on earth
because I still have something
I see in your large, yellow eyes.
Be glad, my child. The snows of winter fall
while here I stand in white faith
and desire, offering all to you,
old but more beautiful than a young god.

OF YOUTHFUL ARMS

Flare up, bright Pharos of the slender waist.
Proud tower captive of your youthful years,
with your bright face receive the one who steers
as swagger-featured, aged wanderer
of ancient, secret, and supernal seas.

From faint and holy harbors of strange love,
where are unwound the feeble lamps of heaven,
and burning kisses glow in place of suns,
your frenzied navigator-lover came.
He skipped that in a stolen night of charms,
with kisses, love, and fables he might hide
in the warm harbor of your youthful arms.

Why do you seek aroma on my mouth
of far-away, exotic-scented women?
I kissed each other woman that I might
in proud and lavish bloom appear before you
with the lush garden of my well-versed heart.
Yes, love has opened up a thousand flowers,
which all I plucked and now to you impart.

And while you stroke my aged face, do not
in secret flaunt the treasures of your youth.
Behold, how strong, how sturdy-ribbed my boat.
You scarce were born when it set out for you,
and now it comes from wandering over worlds.
Behold my scintillating diamond-faith;
your inclination for me shines from thence.
Behold this pillaged cup of gold, filled part
with blood and part with your benevolence.

Over our ages with your cunning brain
why do you fret and moil and agonize?
You cannot keep from overtaking me
amid your follies growing old and wise.
And yet the most beloved will be you.
I robbed all other women for your sake.

If mid our kisses cries of woe are borne,
be proud and happy, rejoice and laugh aloud.
They mourn your husband, it is for me they mourn.
And if promiscuous urge should tempt you once,
destroy it — you belong to me alone.
Aye, from the harbor of this honeyed love,
this wonder, beauty, giddiness and good,
there is no God or strength or kiss or Death
that ever can allure my brigand ship.

WHEN SHULAMITE SLEEPS

I tom-peep through the slats of time.
My child, O drowsy Shulamite,
turn up your fresh and dovish bill
and let us stop before the real.
Shh! be still!
Give me, my infant girl,
your mouth.

Yesterday round about this bed
I circled like your elder brother,
but in the moment passions fill
a man you are become a woman.
Shh! be still!
Give me, my infant girl,
your mouth.

I meet with surging juvenescence
your nude and nubile downiness.
How fitting if with girlish will
you now are dreaming of a stranger.
Shh! be still!
Give me, my infant girl,
your mouth.

YOUR SHOULDERS, YOUR SHOULDERS

With dazzled eyes of glory I see you,
as precious, real, vagabond, and home.
I have seen all
which in secret made me brood and rave.
Although I beat on my heart a thousand times,
this beast runs lamely on,
and my eyes alone are true,
honorable, and good.
They move smoothly along your body,
but the snowy whiteness remains,
the gleaming snowy whiteness and warmth
of your shoulders, your shoulders.

Your every word and promise is a lie,
your inciting and defiant nudeness
brings fever and madness,
enrages, conquers, humilates,
and I am ashamed I love you
and your shoulders, your shoulders.
I look at you with glory in my eyes
and foolishly always see you more fair.
I see you
and fall into a blind desire.
If I lived a hundred lives
or a hundred women stood by my door,
your smooth body would remain
for me and me alone
because I worship above all
the white Ararat of my ark,
your shoulders, your shoulders.

GIRL FROM THE GREENWOOD

A girl came out of the greenwood
on a cold autumn afternoon,
looked at me
and dropped a smile and a late September flower.
She was not different from the others,
but the currents of my soul brought her,
the unexpected,
and the nervous movements of her shoulders.
When she left, I was depressed,
when she returned, I revived.
I was ashamed when I missed her
and scolded when she returned.
"Doctor," I told him,
"it comes like a fit of coughing at night,
a hollow reverberation of the heart,
a symptom of some ordinary disease.
She comes from the greenwood
where they came before.
At my season it is not decent or right
to complain about or want a woman."
And I explained to myself
the girl who was created in the greenwood
as the dear, inventive, and painful symbol
of my heroic life.

MORE HONORABLY THAN ANGELS

I wait for her soft hand upon my brow
and close upon my heart as here I lie.
(Has any lover ever wept for you,
sweet nobody, more lovingly than I?)

If but her lips should overrun my face
and plunge upon my throat in hot desire.
(Has any lover ever waited for
more promises from lips of ticklish fire?)

And if my helter-skelter craving should
beclaw her velvet skin and silken head,
(would you, my darling, think it were depraved
to be within this sickly, sorry bed?)

If silence should descend on us in sleep
and I should cry into the soundless gloom,
(would you not whip your flaming scourge upon
the angels who have strayed into our room?)

THE BLACK FLOWER.

You saw a strange black flower
and gathered it in,
the god of lewdness lay his penance
if this was a sin.

You saw a strange black heart
on a market hook;
this was my heart you relished
and in secret took.

I would demand the payment,
coward in my booth,
but you leave and take away the bloodwite,
your girlishness and youth.

Caravan of the Holy Ghost

THE STREET DREAM

This is the straight street of stone
where transpaved death
quickens to blooming dark bats
they throw on the breasts
of hangmen.

This is the straight tooled machine
distending into a cough of ruin
when thousands are moved
and exploiters of other men's lives
tremble in the land.

This is the straight prayer — the curse,
the blaze of blasphemy,
when in raging anguish they build
street barricades,
thrones of brick for the oppressed.

This is the straight city of terror,
a life from death to civilization born
where they prepare the vengeful future,
curse, love, forgiveness,
and every fighter is a Christ.

This is the straight, bold dream
where blue-green meadows grow
and every straight man
is a self-centered lover of men,
and we shall arrive in ships of blood,

CARAVAN OF THE HOLY GHOST

A merchant who is called the Holy Ghost
once placed an order for sore-needed goods;
from far-off corners of the world we come
by lightning, steamer, wheel, and foot.

On camelback we cross Saharan wastes,
our costly goods are somewhat old and patched;
this also was the Holy Ghost's desire,
a bit of future, a bit of past.

Buddha, Moses, and Jesus came with us,
our brains are loaded with the holy Word.
Receive the merchandise as you agreed,
we hunger — pay up, Holy Ghost.

We are the poor, unhappy middlemen,
proud lawmakers and traffickers of thought;
while wealthy men carouse the cup of life
our lot and fate are sandy flaws.

The dawn of every Pentecost was false.
It was a long ten days, an endless wait;
but long ago this caravan deserved
the molten gold and tongues of flame.

Our venerable, drunken, learned heads
ache but for others' sake. The Word misleads,
and running we pass up our happiness
like pleasure hunters by a lovely scene.

We use our vigor and our blood in vain,
and hailstones lashed us from the very first;
the rational for many thousand years
make money and buy up the earth.

We had our fill of eating moody thought.
Ho, Holy Ghost, we will no longer wait;
assailed by storms and jackals, we demand
fulfilment of our long-due claim.

Pay, Holy Ghost, for we are weary of
this sombre, frenzied love we give for nought.
We have arrived and scarlet shadows flash
upon the pentecostal dawn.

Stop screwing, Satan, stop screwing me. The sore
is soft and it still hurts.
Damn, damn, damn.
Because I am Hungarian, my life is tragic and stupid.

Why did your forceps take my laughter, the well-
memorized lines?
Damn, damn, damn.
And again I curse a thousand times the past, the past.

So what, so what if I dare to weep once more,
if my barbarism bursts forth, and the well-groomed laugh at
my unkempt life.

I concealed you in myself like a cowardly thought on
ugly death, in this hateful refuge — like the forest cover
of the last, sick, and dying things.

But now you escape to bank on bank
of black skies.
Damn, damn, damn.
My life is the artesian well of the Hungarian curse.

Stop screwing, Satan, stop screwing me. Your forked rod
has made me teem.
Damn, damn, damn.
All the Hungarian in my life is ugly and dark.

FATE HAS STOPPED

If ever you were real, now come again
you legends, madmen, jesuses,
and coffee-colored magi
with miracles and gifts
to bow before the manger
where the Child is always reborn
and we are born in his birth,
quarrelsome and shivering jesuses,
one perhaps more jesus than the rest.
You legends and madmen, come at last.

In our sober minds
the rational dies, for earth is aflame,
the Milky Way is tracked with blood,
and we see the running hosts,
although we do not know where they run.
How mysterious these runners.
Sometimes we think that fate has stopped
and that our hearts will freeze,
but no, for earth is aflame.

The young are born in horror,
and the dying are unconsoled and mad with rage.
Eternally playful, the sun looks down
on Jesus and the Negro Kings
with equal hauteur,
bestows a solid faith
as well as unreasoning denial,
and makes us divine
although perhaps unconsoled and enraged.

Now fate has stopped and cares are rife.
Old fate, how long will you stand before the abyss?
How long will the sun,
old witness of our anguish, make sombre fools of us,
how long before wise kings or bedlamites
sunder the rags of the Jesus legend
or pull the sun from the sky
and man stand like a god
before the abyss and cry with a curse,
"I shall jump over, let come what will."

WHO SEES ME?

(1914)

Tree of Necessity

NEW HUNNISH LEGEND

Why the advice, the prophecies, the fears?
My gesta stay alive until they die,
the men of now are only viewers of my deeds.

My life extends from farthest far to far,
one life, the sum of many thousand lives,
the timeless Magyar boundary war that never ends.

This is the life of moderate miracles
through which there cuts an ancient constancy,
the new and Hunnish legend of relentless life.

Let weaklings go and copy off their lives,
and having copied burrow in the clod,
my nature and my fate are not a simple rule.

A king must be the king of his own fate.
What do I care how Goethe makes the grade,
how Arany scans, how Petőfi is deified?

For me the storytelling bards are mute,
neither the songs with consummation carved
nor poems offered as a model are my bread.

Within me is the aim of centuries,
the lengthy Magyar wait, God's stricken gift.
My soul is the defiance of a lordly race.

I drummed a synod if I so desired,
and at its head I ordered to appear
a strident Dozsa or a common Jacques Bonhomme.

I championed hundreds but I never changed,
a youth who boldly struck and stood the strikes.
Thus standing, waiting I am always wholly Magyar.

For Magyars I am shackle and release,
protesting faith and missioned veto strength —
the devil take it, *Ugocsa non coronat.*

In grammar school I was already old.
I strove for heaven, stumbling countless times.
To be a schoolboy in old age is my reward.

My cap, my coat, my heart in violent storm
protect me from the raging blasts of winter,
and hailing ice and blame and curse rebound from them.

I made a bargain of my own with death
when taking on myself the lives of millions
I struck toward the new and many gates of life.

I shoved the busy, meddling Grace aside.
I came to overpower, not to charm;
I wanted all but now my nothing fits me well.

I was the Lord, my verse a gaudy crew
that fell with me — this is the servant's lot
when fallen Hunnish lords for their retainers call.

TREE OF NECESSITY

"...Do men gather grapes of thorns
or figs of thistles?" Matthew 7 : 16

My supple branches yield
beneath the harvest fruit,
beneath the harvest yes,
and the derided noes
are etched in yellow rust
upon my leafiness.

O thorn abloom with grape,
O thistle live with fig,
upon a feverish soul
no grape or fig is born,
and like a peaceful serf
I bear the heavy toll.

I did not have the strength
to mock the ordered world
and laugh into the dust
a great remoulding power,
and now I bow before
the honorable must.

O tree alive with fig,
O vine abloom with grape,
in vain I would berate
the garden of this life
because there is for all
a ruthless rule and fate.

I knew not what I was,
I sought to be a blame
and even more a fright,
but see the fair example,
my poor and gentle head
is burgeoning and bright.

I mocked to scorn the yes,
now everyone may pluck
a yes for every no,
and in the house of life
I am no veto flame,
only a fireside glow.

I am the sign of need,
a grave-post of the no,
a sire of ill career,
O piteous, piteous me,
partisan born of rebel,
usurious mutineer.

THE OFFERING OF WISDOM

Hear the order of my virtues, Jehovah.

I believe although I have divorced belief.
I repent although I have not sinned.
I marvel at non-miracles.
I deny the true life.
I hold a lamp to the sun.
I close my eye to the dark.
I give my pennies to the rich.
I smuggle honey into the hive.
I pin roses on the rose bush.
I water cows with milk.
I sprinkle the grape with wine.
I laugh for the pleasure of my enemies.
I sigh for women I do not want.
But above all this I shall also die.

Accept my sacrifice, O Lord.

THE LAST TIME TO PARIS

City of restful restlessness, Paris,
source more deep than love,
how grateful I am you call,
for the aging nomad prepares his wake
and longs to walk once more your streets.

Lightest of my yokes, Paris,
my heart is all-powerful,
my fist hard, my eyes bright,
and my daring ship is steamed up to soar
over new waters.

Paris, how I recall
the frail coach, smooth road,
and rhythmic clip-clop of the horse.
I shut my eyes,
and a sleigh
is flying me into a winter wilderness.
I am walking at even in your woods,
spellbound,
running back into your arms.

Never have I found a warmer embrace,
and ever since I do not live
but wander among sombre forests and old mountains
like an orphan.
Now your love is freed
of my curse, and I have grown young.
Thin, sombre forests, and old mountains,
where I fled the city,
laugh at me for I go
to the city of cities.

Smile on the old nomad, Paris,
call me, urge me, entice me.
Remind me of the vows
I made when I was feverish with love
under your starry nights.

This last time I shall in silence bless you
for being and having been,
and then back again, my heart, old altar,
to guard eternal youth
with a crucifix burning on it.
(Oh, but what if Paris will not let me go?)

Of Ancient Spells

MY AMERICAN COUNTRYMEN

My countrymen, you whom our common curse
has taken from us and dispersed afar,
perhaps too often in your thoughts we are.

But, oh, our Magyar life is overwhelmed,
and from the deluge they alone emerge
whom distant shores from present peril urge.

You far-off Magyars, how I envy you,
for from the very first here all was lost;
you, happy race, are far from ruin tossed.

WINTER'S WHITE TABLE

At winter's white table,
the enormous Hungarian table,
the feast has begun.
Lackeys of poverty serve up
the savory funeral food,
and a million guests wallow in plenty.
A shadow moves in the cup
of coagulated wine-blood.
What a dreadful Communion Supper!
The Winter-King does not appear
to set a table and ask his questions
although many would answer.
Only the guests multiply.
The feast of hunger flows,
and the wine is blond with tears.
When Spring comes,
he will set a table and command order,
and there will be only order here,
skeletons sitting at the table
amid the reign of a pagan silence
at a great imperial feast.

The Lost Families

THE FEMALE PIKES

You are dismissed, my little female pikes.

Because I cannot fill your gluttonous mouths,
I shall no longer bar your way,
the seas are there, strike out and swim.

The catch has grown into a toilsome task,
for every woman,
aging herself and her selected male,
makes good the girlhood that slipped by.
Heigh, female pikes, swim off, devour.

No longer are you mine. You are dismissed,
you also, last and smallest in my heart,
you fancied goldfish, little no one.
The fish which you deserve await.
Perhaps on your voracious mouths will rest
other victims.

You are dismissed, my little female pikes.

PLEA ON A MAY DAY

"... Je sais ton coeur, mon
coeur ..." I send to the
Only Woman.

A red rorschach
infuse the pale flowers and twilight blue
of this wanly written day in May.

Cold dawn
transforms my letter into an alphabet gray.

I would deliver a mystery, a self
who stands here since his fate flashed
in your eyes and suffers
a hundredfold your unsolvable fate —
your secret his fate and your fate his secret.

May is dictating, and I do not know what.
I only know you left
and having looked at me a little while
neither set me free nor put me on trial.

Our secret is a secret, our suit rests,
and our past paralyzes the day.

If I say, "You are the beginning,"
I see on your brow
the tremor of a thousand suspicions,
and your eyes close.

I stand outside shivering,
fearing you will let me in.

You will see me once without mercy,
and mingling with your tears I will know
for whom you weep, how long
you fear, and why you must.

This is May and life.
We are afraid although
the mystery is ours and destiny the brave's.

How accessible were the secret
if you linked your heart to mine.
Do not curse what has happened
and be patient for the slow arrival of happiness.

Weary hearts are beautiful,
and the sobs of lovemaking are blessed.
Do not let my letter make you cry, or the May.
Do not cry because I am crying.

The Bloody Panoramas

THE BLOODY PANORAMAS

Once more in spring, my writings and my soul,
once more from far away you thunder home,
never more whipped or in more wretched time.
No sparkle ever fell in deeper night,
and never was the world more sad than now.
Flaunt the clear skies, my writings and my soul,
and shine upon your youthful friends at home,
for whom we must raise up our wintry heart
when the postillions of the sun call spring.
And even if this aged world is lost,
we still must wait for spring with open arms
because our love is endless and unbound.
We are the one and only joyous mood
where horrors make a little country groan,
our hearts are grave but we are glad of face.

Without — chasms of nations gape at us,
within — abomination and old dark,
reason enough to make the timid die.
Death reaps upon the garden's farther end,
as gravediggers and rogues assault our land.
Fat priests are hawking an Almighty God
and carrion smells are on the breath of spring.
The final judgment comes but we must stand
as though we really thought that we might win.
And everyone, if youthful, shouts and raves —
our heroes over hundred battlefields.

How fair to stand and face a thousand hells
and fight for order in our little land
when great ages, mighty giants, and worlds
scurry about us in a pool of blood
and thrones and ancient dreams begin to shake.
How fair to seek a little country's dream
when underneath a tent of scarlet sky
the panoramas of a hangman play
and when the world would neither note nor care
that Hunnia's dirty stalls are still unclean.
My youthful friends, upon this day of spring
a hundred times more holy than before,
blast forth the bugle-call of our strong soul.

Although the course of history trample us,
still we shall feed the fire within our land
and burn whatever may be old and foul.
Let come what may, collapse or utter ruin,
more wretched days than these can never come.
The world is moving, O my youthful friends,
and here upon this soil we place our feet
and make a vow that it shall also move
and we shall recreate a better life —
else all within this land is doomed. Amen.

THE PEOPLE WHO RESILE

This is the people who resile cringing
from war,
and betray the master
uses the belt.

This people is a beast who labors
for little khans,
never fights
but nurses his listless grudge.

When someone shows force, he sees force.
Born to beating not to beat,
he never uses his powers
or strength against strength.

He was schooled by his masters.
He curses but never kicks,
and once someone has kicked him
it becomes a habit.

Lazy and flabby, he sits there
conned of his heritage, heart, and brain,
and only because a few cry out
does he know he is slapped.

Would that the lord of miracles saw
this pitiful people at last
and gave them
a cruelty of their own.

And their leaders, few remaining,
would cease the broken prayer:
Why fight?
They want a dog's fate. Let it be so.

WAR AND HATE

Song for Christmas

Chained millions
of hungry and anguished mourn,
and they curse
the deceitful legend, the manger,
the falsely anointed, and counterfeit love.

We do not believe in shepherds,
fur-clad rejoicers,
or the star,
only in our sombre strength
grown great.

We open cemeteries
and find accursed graves,
where the glittering star
lured
believers in love.

No longer can they force us to hallelujah
the Jesus of our hangmen.
We show
wounds that incite to hate
and call our hearts to revenge.

We bow our heads
in a dream—the men of red revenge
rise up in long ranks
and step on the hydra-headed Christ
to right the wrongs of centuries past.

We are and remain
the celebrants of hate,
war and hate,
until we kindle for all the world
the symbol of a new and shining Christmas.

Red Autumn Flowers

To Mylitta, the most pagan of
women and goddess, and to the Mylitta
who is the most loving and loved.

YOUR FIERY THRONE

Do not command me lay before your feet
the cold eidola of a life whose fire
has passed beyond the immemorial night.

Do not condemn to death the lifeless flame,
the kisses that once burned from lip to lip
and the desires that flickered up and died.

Deposit your bright throne, the comet-tailed,
upon the solemn ruin of regal stars
and calmly shoot new flames upon the sky.

As you create a towering pyre, build up
a hundred new desires, a city, gold,
a hundred burning new beatitudes

that a new desolation lap all space
and nothing rise around your fiery throne,
only the devastation of your hour.

THIS NEW SPRING

For my little Nobody

The autumn
you case curious but cool
is a mature but not a barren season
on which the snows of winter fill up the curves —
this is the new spring and the new promise.

Give up
your white snowiness on faith and add the fires;
then look about and you will see the barren trees
are live with flowers
and you open on my heart like a great clot of blood.

The season hosannas
and, if with your ermine nearness you will,
my renascent arms
which hold you embraced
will carry you above the lowering autumn clouds.

How small but grown so big in me,
and all that urges, runs, and drives me after you
is a murmuring complaint.
Today you are life and my life,
but, oh, how wintry this new spring.

TO DAWN AT DAWNING

The only mistress I ever left,
the dawn,
paused for me yesterday
erminelike,
while white clouds trembled
on her nervous shoulders.
Ours was the backward glance of lovers
who are out of love.
The city awoke, and blind windows opened
bill-wide like hungering mouths,
and I thought sombrely
somewhere they await the dawn.
My mistress,
if your feet touch the Swiss alps,
repent
and serve as a lover's letter.
This woman also desires to leave.
She is also the dawn.
Tell her to deliver me from evil
and not to leave before she loves.

BLUE DORY

Tomorrow you go and leave
a little piece of death
no larger than yourself,
sweet young thrush of a woman
and lovemaking agonist.
My little blue dory, the seas wait.
You loved although you knew not whom,
and now you will surrender the rest
while in the rail compartment car
I smooth your pillow.
Among stained and spottled people
how good were your blue sails,
my little smart dory.
Remember me
when you have reached the stormy seas.
Hungry waves devour the past
and a future my present
as I kiss your tiny face
that new kisses and fevers
may in jealousy possess you.
Only small loves kill.
Make ready, the steamer blows
and our desires die.
Take with you the happy dreams,
my little blue dory.

WHO LIVES FOR HIMSELF

My song steals whispering into the night,
which holds your fate and mine,
like a biblical
psalm
the kingly David may have sung.

My love steals forth for this little no one
like love of long ago,
because a long dead
life
has shone on many a world and night.

We strike toward a beggars' road
of little cheer.
We live strangely
for each other and ourselves.
How happy is he who lives for himself.

THE THINGS VISIBLE TO MY EYES

I still would have so much to see
upon those avenues, faces, and starlit nights,
and yet I bury the things visible to my eyes
in the red forest of your knotted hair.
My eyes hide before life's face
like eremites of the holy virgin mother
although the present, past and future wait
my visions.
O strange obolus,
red forest, smell of lichens,
little nobody and nothing,
you hide-and-seek of my life,
I shut a universe and my eyes
within your hair
and bury joys imagined
and joys to be that well may never be.

AUTUMN FORESTS

The autumn forests flare and fret
mourning within my heart, Mylitta,
and love
has burst into a million shining suns
of resolve and beauty
in a consummation like the dark of death.

Summer that in me hurt, now hurts no more
and sombrely squanders,
until they die, a hundred thousand hues
on your blondness and the crown
I forged
to grace your young and catlike head.

The dark finger pauses on the dial
and waits for timid approach of lip to lip.
A scent of snow is on the mist.
Our bed
is laid on the heath, and a mournful fret
is strumming from the autumn woods.

Notes on WHO SEES ME?

1. **New Hunnish Legend.** Arany and Petőfi are nineteenth century
Hungarian poets. **Ugocsa non coronat** is the terse Latin message sent
by the county of Ugocsa to the coronation ceremony of Francis Joseph I
at Buda shortly after the Austro-Hungarian Compromise of 1867. All
other Hungarian counties assented to the reconciliation with the em-
peror and with Austria despite wide popular sentiment for complete
national independence in the spirit of 1848 when the revolutionary
leader Louis Kossuth deposed the Hapsburg king. The phrase is ex-
pressive of a spirit of rebellion, reminiscent of a similar spirit in the
old Southern Confederacy and Poland with its **liberum veto.** For Dózsa
see Note 4 to ON ELIJAH'S CHARIOT, page 198.

2. **War and Hate.** See the Introduction, page 42-43.

LEADING THE DEAD

(1918)

Man in Inhumanity

RECOLLECTIONS OF A SUMMER NIGHT

A furious angel upon the sky
drummed an alarm on the sorrowing earth.
A hundred young men died,
a hundred stars shot down,
a hundred virgins wasted away.
A strange,
strange summer's night it was.
Our oldest beehive burst in flame,
our finest filly broke her leg,
and in my dreams the dead were alive.
Our good dog Burkus disappeared,
and Mary our mute servant girl
broke into a strident song.
A strange,
strange summer's night it was.
Cowards boldly noised about,
real and true men hid away,
while cautious robbers stalked the open roads.
We knew that man was frail
and in arrears with love,
but still how strange it was,
this veering of the dead and living world.
The moon had never scoffed like this,
and man was never smaller
than he was upon that night.
A strange,
strange summer's night it was.
Horror possessed our souls
with guileful joy.
A secret, original destiny
stole into every man,
and Thought, a proud youth,
a crippled nobody,
set out with drunken steps
toward a bloody and abominable wedding feast.
A strange,
strange summer's night it was.
I believed, I then believed,
that some neglected God
would spring to life and carry me to death.
Since then I live in the shape
that night has moulded me,
and waiting for God I recall
an appalling night
that sank a world.
A strange,
strange summer's night it was.

MAN IN INHUMANITY

A rifle butted at my breast,
a thing slit in and skinned my heart,
a gibbering genius grabbed my throat,
and mania drip-dropped on my brain.

Rise up, my power, rise up again,
ascending through the dark of earth,
and if this be the hour of hell
or dawn, who cares, rise boldly up
as often in the worlds that died.

And though you sieged a heaven-hell,
what fate more welcome than to be
a man in inhumanity,
risen again but stubborn dead,
a Magyar in an anguished land.

Upon a highway tramped by horror,
and over roof tops, as I wished,
I passed across a world of things.
What cares have fallen on the Magyar.
How ineffective God can be.

A man has risen from the dead
who knows the hell of suffering,
and moves about in walking death
and houses in his frozen heart
the treasures which the living steal
from a more golden yesterday.

Black shrouds of death, I long for you,
recurrent lives, I fear for you
(it ill befits a resurrection)
and mourn my race of fugitives.

And probing in my pounding chest
I feel again, I feel again —
a rifle butted at my breast,
a thing slit in and skinned my heart,
a gibbering genius grabbed my throat,
and mania drip-dropped on my brain.

Once more I live and cry for others —
a man in inhumanity.

EARTH AWAKENING

Stretch and rub your eyes
poor, wrestling child —
you senile and slumbering earth.
An evil has taken you,
a dream incubus.
On your face
march
the murderous armies of horror
and slither a dagger
in your heart.

Stretch and rub your eyes,
wipe in stone muteness
the sweat from your cold brow.
Stare
upon God and others you invented,
your beauty, and the way of miracles
that lead to peace.
But do not let memories well up
because the wrestling child
only counterfeited your dreams.

THE VOICE OF TERROR

The u-lu-lu of trains that wail and pass,
the howl of dogs — this is the scheme of night
that teems with a tumescent multitude
of hordes and packs
because the hordes have filled the darkness up,
and packs have filled the glades and grasses up.

The ai-ai-ai of thin and ancient woods,
white bones of unremembered memories,
the spells and rites of blackness peak into
an eerie strum
because the night has found its proper voice,
and Terror has a polytonal voice.

O life of nights and dogs, the dark and howl,
O fate of soldier hordes and feral packs,
we were the sturdy and unhollowed men
before we came together.
But something has struck hard across the world,
a someone has struck raw across the world.

All separate parts are now a tingling one,
and yet away they rip each on his own —
the sombre trains, the dogs, the hordes, and packs,
but night and woods
and great alarums of the dark remain,
and spectral giggles of a ghost remain.

OF YESTERDAY'S YESTERDAY

My hand waves an encyclical of sorrow,
oh, gestures of unfleshed yesterday,
oh, dead sensuousness of a touch,
oh, small repentances, ye,
oh, yesterday's hopes,
oh, Word of yesterday's yesterday,
noli tangere.

We watched as Man's elite
struck out toward the rainbow bridge
of apotheosis, august
with infinitely new refinements
and stimulations.
and yet, this vainglorious creature
Man is the world itself.

The cup of our self-worship hath overrun
for all to quaff
its grave humors, this precious wine.

Our today is a shivery and shrouded pride.
"Do not fear." "Do not divide."
Small encouragements over assassined, glorious plans
which were life and more
than scattered, falling little men.

Oh, yesterday's circles and holy
dead diagrams, stifled in murderous passageways.

My hand waves an encyclical of sorrow,
oh, gestures of unfleshed yesterday,
oh, dead sensuousness of a touch,
oh, small repentances, ye,
oh, yesterday's hopes,
oh, Word of yesterday's yesterday,
noli tangere.

Oh, time you hooded hangman,
oh, Word of yesterday's yesterday
beautiful in the charm of your evil spell.

THE PROPHET'S CURSE

Abased beyond all degredation
I look upon my spirit, mind, and hide.
Where is the prophet's mad red rage
that storms against the seat of heaven,
or has the levin-brand of curses died?

Who burst into the bounds of hades
as though we did not own the voice and ire
for mission zeal and scorpion scourge?
The murderous elohim had never
laid waste the past like this with sword and fire.

We do not weigh what we have wasted.
Our sense of grief was murdered in its sleep,
and all our deeds are frozen dreams,
and all our visions frozen gestures,
and we have fallen below the uttermost deep.

Sons of an everlasting power
are bleating beastlike on field and sod
while droning prophets stare and dream.
A deeper Hell, a larger Nothing
give him you Great One, oh, give him, you God.

Seed Beneath Snow

CALL TO THE WATCHMEN

O watchmen, keep not the city in vain,
the nights are filled with bolting stars
and fireflies are in the garden.
Memories dwell on parted summers,
a summer in Florence indistinct
with autumn farewells to Lido
and dawn recollections
on a perfumed and tinselled dance floor.
A distant smile,
a troubled and lonely smile
is watching all the beauties,
present and past, which may never pass away,
and all the well-loved living and dead,
O watchmen, keep not the city in vain.

O watchmen, keep not the city in vain,
life lives, desires to live
and does not offer up its beauty
to fall before the charge
of bloody and insensate beasts.
How sorrowful is man,
how horrible the animal cries,
but the star-bolting nights
will not let us forget
the fate of man is splendor spun.
You who still stand upon the lonely posts,
O watchmen, keep not the city in vain.

LETTER FROM THE LIMES

(Érmindszent, June 1914)

Go where weapons gleam.
Rise in battle,
leading my young and faithful troops.
I too have broadcast seed
and pride myself on a prison past.
But what torment
to languish on obscure limes
far from the thrust
of armed wrath.
The daring dies in me inactive
that I stole
into a thousand fighting hearts.
I do not hold my own good place
although who longs more
for the commitment?

Go where weapons gleam
on my fallow steed
before young troops.
I am there in creed and past,
in soul and daring,
and tomorrow perhaps in deed.
The old and worn out rivals
may encounter once more
the fateful hero.
My men,
we must not forget
the first of your brothers.
How good if you see me
not in an image of wasted arms
but like a youthful hero
coming to help you
smite your enemies.

SEED BENEATH SNOW

Steeped in the humors of old creeds,
my torn and tortured self
I gather up
from blood and pain and fire
to stow away with living seeds.

You may still need to see my face,
this tribute from the past,
and I will rise
like a momento dear
for the new world's new human race.

I shall look on a land inflamed
with conquests and defeats
and listen for
the word from chaos born
or hear it by myself proclaimed.

Heroic man declines, sleep falls;
dream good dreams, sunless seer
and my good kind,
until the deathless law
of life and resurrection calls.

Now in this winter of my seed,
numb and besnowed in faith,
I wait for spring
and blasts of heaven to sprout
the seedlings that my truths decreed.

TWO FREEDOM FIGHTERS

My friend, who cares
if wolf or devil should devour?
Devour at last one will.

If a bear, who cares.
This is the sad and ancient tale,
the devouring is the thing.

And sad, who cares
in ample time we did not read
the signature of fate.

My friend, who cares.
The hell, why should we care who eats
our sombre, stupid selves.

THIS LAND ONLY ONCE

This land has only held one wedding feast,
one great and genuine wedding feast,
when the new bridegroom was
George Dozsa,
and on a hero's dawn of spring
the fires of joy lit up a thousand hills.

This land was a volcano only once,
a land of lava only once,
when anger and revenge
joined up,
erupted in a storm of judgment,
and summons came from Dozsas, not from kings.

This land has witnessed daring faith but once,
faith from Moldavia to Rome,
when all our strength and honor
rose up
to wreak destruction and create,
and they unleashed the firebrands on the sky.

This land has known compassionate fate but once,
a fate compassionate and great
because we sent the world
a message
we need today but cannot spark
from a volcano burned to silent ash.

This land has flared in revolution once,
a revolution true and sworn,
making a world of order,
and Dozsa,
the hero of that haughty dawn,
refused to bargain with the people's fate.

This land has known a little hope but once,
a hope, though small, of fire and blood.
We need a newer Dozsa.
He comes,
but, oh, I fear I shall not see him,
or you, my brothers brooding on your lot.

The Lost Horseman

HOUSE AMONG COTTONWOODS

Where cottonwoods are dense
and superstition spells the land,
along mazes of the mastabah
they wake up old
in a world of anesthesia, shadows, and cold.

The sun illumines archeologic profiles,
softens marble floors,
while before silent bedroom doors
the ghost girls chatter
walking unrouged among the dead.

The noonstar dies, chill to sunset.
But at lamp-kindle time
the world dilates on the murmurous diapason
of a warm,
deep, sleepless, and summit rime.

The fireflies are hived in cottonwood,
and in the spellhouse fire shadows
of long kisses, vows, desires, and secrets
flicker up walls
from chambers to servant halls.

When sparks in the cottonwood tangle
and twilight comes in slippered felts,
the enormous mastabah lights up
and melts
in voltage of a hundred thousand insane loves.

This is the hour of paleo-sunsets,
fevers and scarlet forms —
the cypress is transfigured,
and like towering cottonwoods
we surround and veil this house from storms.

THE LOST HORSEMAN

You hear the hollow hoofbeats of
a horseman lost since long ago.
The shackled souls of ghosted woods
and ancient reedlands wake to woe.

And where in patches here and there
a tangled coppice used to thrive,
inaudible and ghostly troops
of wintry tales become alive.

Here is the denseness and the copse,
here are the blunt and brazen songs,
which lurk within the deafened fog
since our brave fathers died in throngs.

The autumn is macabre here;
the dwindling sums of men are small,
and on the hill-encircled plain
November walks in a misty shawl.

And once again the naked plain
is overgrown with reeds and trees,
hiding its bleak November self
in fogs of bygone centuries.

Nothing but secrets, nothing but sires,
nothing but power, nothing but gore,
nothing but reedlands, nothing but woods,
nothing but madmen feared of yore.

Toward a new and tangled path
gallops the horseman lost in night;
he sees no trace of village life,
or even a glimmer of lamplight.

Mute hamlets huddle in their sleep
and dream of days that were more fair,
while from the foggy thickets rush
the aurochs, wolf, and raging bear.

You hear the hollow hoofbeats of
a horseman lost since long ago.
The shackled souls of ghosted woods
and ancient reedlands wake to woe.

Leading the Dead

A HARVEST SONG

The crosses squat on stubble fields,
the crosses grow upon the graves,
the crosses lie upon our hearts,
the crosses stand on battlefields,
but nowhere the owner of the cross.

The crosses are on all the world,
the crosses perch on steeple tops,
the crosses weigh on human kind,
but hear the sky voice: for this world
why did I take the bitter cross.

CORPSE ON A WHEAT FIELD

They left him on a field of snow —
the basil, pink, and southernwood
on his undug grave will never grow.

He will sponge up the earth and rain,
and through his trunk will strike the shoots
of a triumphant seed of grain.

In summer he will turn to mold,
a scarecrow that is fallen to shame
beneath a sandy sea of gold.

His trampling fate now onward beats,
and from him and above him shines
a life which offers hope but cheats.

The sound and shadow are the same
and ours the only autumn change.
The aural chiaroscuroes call
a goodly heart, whereso it be.

The colors, tears, and lusts are old,
the muted melodies remain
and shed mandragora of moods
or gouge the recess of old wounds.

Only the good now dare to live,
and in this autumn day their smiles
are precious babes, the links of life,
whose tears are an awakened corpse.

LEADING THE DEAD

This is the green flat field of our loss
where cumuli
of blood are billowing on the sky,
and I have found my troops,
the ousted from life.

You well-beloved and living lads who wake
as the dead,
how lovingly shines
the sword I raise before your holy lines,
and I have truly found you now.

Comrades more brave
I never knew,
and a cold moonlight
helmets
the heads they found in a new-dug grave.

I waited long in vain,
an orphan and outcast
Cain,
when suddenly my fellows, my fellows arrived,
the humbled in spirit.

Long ago they walked this field with me
in the evening air,
became like my flesh and blood,
and meekly undressed their lives.
Now look how they smile and stare.

We have all become a living one,
and if our souls
should clash we feel the forceful tide.
Above the grave
we understand our varied goals.

What ghostliness is rife,
what strange beauty in the world today.
I lead
a camp of ghostly members
and bid us smile on life.

TOWER OF NIGHT

Moonwan and whitely intumescent
in anxious silence of a summer night
the tower
peers out and waits for sanguine tidings
of flame and ruin and fright.

A monody of silence strangles
the bells and hymns within this voiceless shrine,
and the Lord's
tower arises, stares, and trembles
beneath an awesome sign.

Mysterious swimmers of the heavens,
the misty moon clouds move and drift on high,
the tower
salutes the moon orb, this all-knowing
omnibus of the sky.

The moon has seen unnumbered towers,
it never hurries and is never late,
it glances
in calm upon this little planet
and its unfolding fate.

This sentinel of our salvation
may gleam with blood beneath tomorrow's moon
as once more
we hear proclaimed the ancient motto,
to victory or ruin.

The tower may confess tomorrow
a dedication to the claw and fang,
and the bells,
these iron cubs in spellbound languor,
will ominously clang.

The lonely moon will rumble onward,
so will this vacant and unpeopled earth,
and above
a moonwhite ruin of fallen towers
the peace will come to birth.

(mid-July 1914)

I

Red earth, red autumn, and red cloud.
And yet our thoughts are like the soot,
and yet our thoughts are in a shroud.

Our thoughts today, our thoughts today.
Our thoughts were red in days gone by
and not a clotted, dying gray.

Red was our love in times the best,
red was the paschal pledge of life,
red was the rose upon our breast.

Red were the Indian Summer days,
red were the many little loves,
which after women hotly blaze.

Our blood was always red and wroth,
but now upon the sea it lies
like wine stains on a table cloth.

II

Red were the hangman and the Lord,
and angels came to see us bow —
a flattering and red reward.

Red was the Magyar dream — our bread
had been for long a common food,
not manna from the heavens shed.

Red was the strife that made us pale.
We must make haste with Magyar life,
though we are late, we must not fail.

Our Magyar grief was red and mad.
Truly we were within our truth,
shunning the evil and the bad.

How late we are in our red mood,
and how much poorer by our deeds
than when we only stared and stood.

Red heart, red vintage, and red brain.
Untimely we arrived on earth,
red earth and still a time of bane.

Red dream, red faith, and red caress.
But through the death of countless men
the latest autumn seeks redress.

III

Red earth, red autumn, and red cloud.
And yet our thoughts are like the soot,
and yet our thoughts are in a shroud.

THE MIRROR YAWNS

The mirror yawns
as cravenly I look inside.
We are a long betrothed pair's
farewell,
delays, and tired antagonists.

The mirror yawns.
There was a time when like good friends
we looked with pride both in and out.
The curse
now stands between us like a frost.

The mirror yawns,
and do we know each other now?
How alien have become two friends
who searched
but never could each other find.

The Matured Life

MY AGED LONELINESS

I

Young and unbridled —
proud because he was alone and young,
my youthful issue, loneliness, set out,
This loneliness, was my first triumph,
loneliness, which now has grown old.

How strange is youthful loneliness,
and how he loves himself,
how sombrely he loves himself.

He may be startled without cause,
but wise and powerful he speeds
over the flooded banks of doubt,
loneliness, my youthful loneliness.

II

With the fleeting years
my loneliness began to age,
and painful nothings pricked my heart.
How I sought for a woman
to burst my empty sorrows into bloom
and comfort my loneliness with pain.
But all at once there was no God,
or if there was, that God was not for me.

And still, my aged loneliness,
the hurts will come again,
proudly they will come as in your youth,
begging they will come but not as before
a mocking for the mean.

Those who believed even one whit
in my great and loving loneliness,
my aged loneliness, will always bless you.

III

Once more the hurts will come
and the woman who has changed so much.
Triumph, woman, and haughty loneliness
arrive in lieu of everyone.
And my loneliness, which has grown old,
strikes at the skies with head upraised.
Drunkenly it drinks the wine of life
and dreams of its golden youth.

YOUR INVISIBLE LAWS

I saw your invisible laws, O Lord,
when blithely I sped on again,
when my eyes were bright again,
when the chorus of life
sang in me alone,
and I emerged like a corpse
in the summer of perfection,
and above me a chorus of choruses,
your incompassionate music, rang.

The Summer, and above all my summer,
froze on your little world, my Lord,
like the heart of many a Nazarene saint
inscribed in your Book.

A train bore me
to a hope that was dead in the east.
I was frozen and the world was on fire;
my summer gift was frozen,
and a frantic shower lashed our train.

It was beautiful, awesome, and maybe true.
Your clouds thundered,
your lightning flashed a thousand messages
to the disappearing trees,
and here and there a bolt drove home
and never tried to choose
between the trees that perished and lived.

I saw your invisible laws, O Lord.
What it is you do, you know.

THE MATURED LIFE

The branches of a great and billowy past, the blood-streaked smile of time and my gorgeous years, are bursting in their true foliage.

The great spring of my God Blood has arrived across desires, fears, and yesterday's ghosts.

Life is monstrous and rich, and my hateful, holy sores, like roses in red May, will pop up on the body of the world.

This is the accursed and sombre meaning of my life, the anguish, dizziness, and defiance from where they come.

But covered with foliage I endure this spring, whose arrival is worth it all, and my life is great as the giant grimace of a dream.

EASTER

The snap of caves and crypts,
a voice in sombre corridors —
this is Easter, the sacred and eternal
spring.

Why should he know of blood
when on the snowy boughs
miracles on miracles are born
and every cost recovered?

O Spring, O Easter,
the good cheer of men,
cast tidings abroad
that eternal is the hour of
spring.

Christ awakes and is arisen.
What is more glorious than
the snap of caves and crypts?

MOON FORGIVENESS

Acidulous, the moon shambles above enormous fields, where the hardluck traveller was robbed tens of times.

On his face the dry smile of an old huckster; and below, the field heaves a horrible, sombre sigh and stretches in agony upward,

a scarred field, sterile and niggardly. The moon sprinkles the rotting body with the sardonic silence of cold light.

The corpse sprawls, but on the farther end a girl and her lover in penumbra.

Death seems never to have walked here, and life pricks up his head with a snakish whoop.

Missioned to witness the seminal kiss, the confident moon bursts into light and forgives a hundred transgressions of death.

A SONG ABOUT UNHAPPINESS

Everything we believed in is lost,
lost, lost;
fortunate and happy
the unhappy for himself alone.

Everything is lost, everything we believed in.
The flags we carried to the peaks
are lost
and happy the unhappy.

Happy the unhappy,
and all is lost,
lost, lost, lost.

VALLEY OF THE KRASZNA

In the valley of the Kraszna where villages
are like rosaries,
we took a short ride
in a coach of superstition.
The road was seductive and strange.

We passed through Varsolc
in good cheer
and as became me with courage.
How beautiful are life and land
scudding before the eyes and the soul.

SPRING JOURNEY

(do I live? have I lived?)
Spring, and I decamp on a great journey.
Rivers explode their dams.
My travel bags!
I am free and parched for the world.
Trains with compartment nests
set out like black suns
screaming above the pitch of life,
wakening the world from winter into spring.
The passages to Rome are filling up.
The rich man is steaming up his yacht,
the poor man books a trip at Cook's.
(do I live? have I lived?)

A "Christ is Risen"
bristles in advance of bronze hallelujahs.
Tender moisture and moods
seize on germinal power,
and the seminal sea is somnolent.
Life sets out
and everywhere you hear
a zoharian pizzicato of violins.
Sonatas sway jestfully
between the saraband and the chanson.
Viennese waltzes, gondola lyrics,
Negro ragtime, motets,
the kolo and the csardas embrace,
and all other music is a holy antiphonal
on the dominoed sheet of winter.
(do I live? have I lived?)

A Japanese garden jettisoned its blossoms here;
aroma circles on wings of aroma.
Awakened by the winds of spring,
Nice is full of violets and songs,
and many white villages on the Magyar plains
are full of violets and songs.
Our people are in the fields;
the sweet, parching thirst of life
drives us into song,
and everyone prepares for the new
like an intoxicated hero.
There are dun shadows, but the sun helps
and good words, good faith, a holy will,
and our old colleague — hope.
Our gorgeous dames are roaming.
My travel bags!
Spring, and I decamp on a great journey.
(do I live? have I lived?)

Book of Isaiah

1. Out of Seir I have heard the Lord call, "Watchman, what of the night? Watchman, what of the night?" The radiance of man's divine nature is so vain that a breath of wind will bring the night.

2. How often must we weep the decline of the world with the passing of a joyous love and genius, and how often must great men of the earth grow weak?

3. Why must man, when he rises, always be pulled back by someone whom they call Jehovah, destiny, or fate? Again and again we make ready for the good, make ready to become God, but the Lord rises up in mount Perazim.

4. Why does it humor the Lord to show man mighty aims, a reconciliation with life and the rainbow bridge of peace? Why does he search for our primeval wildness, as when he was wroth in the valley of Gibeon, and incite our fires of wickedness upon one another?

5. No one goes with a great strong sword to see "the piercing serpent, even Leviathan that crooked serpent." And once more the Lord sprays the "vineyard of red Wine" with blood. Oh, why so unloved and so unhappy is man, who longs so much for love and happiness? Watchman, you watch in vain, oh, watchman, we watch in vain, because again and again the face of man shall fall into the mire.

HOSANNA WHO TRUSTS

The human good has always found
a kind of secret Nazareth
from where to steal like tears and rise
for multitudes of sombre men
to swollen rivers bold and clear
that never die a swampy death.

Fear not, O swollen heart of man,
or you, my heart, that never would
allow your palsied self to cry
and swell the banks of sacred streams.
Mankind is worthy of a tear
alone for dreaming of the good.

Swell up, you sacred fountainheads,
O hearts where goodness has withdrawn.
Undam your tears, the pent-up streams.
Hosanna to those who trust and weep,
Hosanna to trusting yesterday,
Hosanna to the sacred dawn.

GAWD'S PUNISHMENT

Are the dead now really dead
here and there and round about?
Was that living or a robbing?
Why
punish then the bare despoiled?

Now I look with dread and pleasure
who is living, who is dead,
what the day and what the night bring,
what
renegade is punishing us.

What is past and what is present?
What arrives on northern winds?
What befalls today, tomorrow?
Why
punished by a past tumescence?

Here and there and round about
are the dead now really dead?
If they sleep within the deep,
who
in the Gawd is punishing us?

"And I saw a woman sit upon a
scarlet coloured beast . . . having
seven heads and ten horns . . . and
upon her forehead was written, Mys-
tery . . ." The Revelation of St.
John the Divine 17

Omega rides and reaps the earth,
she multiplies the sheaves of stubble
and crossed staves,
while men who always sought for stars
are lying prone in undug graves.

Besotten with the blood of saints
she rides upon a scarlet beast
in blood spree,
her every leap a hill of dead,
this woman's name is Mystery.

In purple velvet and scarlet clad
she rides and shrieks and cackles by.
Out goes breath,
and what remains is worse than life,
and what remains is worse than death.

We crack, the Mystery rides and shrieks
as with our hollowed souls we grope,
and she leaps
who from the blood of martyrs drank
and mid the dying reaps and reaps.

". . . And the third angel sounded,
and there fell a great star from
heaven, . . . and the name of the
star is called Wormwood . . . And
the fifth angel sounded, and I saw
a star fall from heaven unto the
earth: and to him was given the
key of the bottomless pit . . . And
in those days shall men seek death,
and shall not find it; and shall de-
sire to die, and death shall flee from
them . . ." The Revelation of St.
John the Divine 8 and 9

For star-plunging, scarlet sounds
of angel trumpets I had lain in wait
until the phantasms arrived,
and miracles that burned my body came
from Fever — eighth of angels.

From ordered paths I snatched myself,
deranged all that my preying eyes had seized.
With hundred lives I mingled mine
so that the dream might bravely buffet me,
the hundred-hued dream terror.

With oriflammes of dreadful awe
the storms of my ensainted years have come.
Within me the unreal and real
seek to become inseparably one
through agonized embraces.

Desire for death and wormwood pass,
I have become complete and like a ghost.
I do not seek forgiveness, dawn;
I have escaped this one, this only yoke —
to all I have submitted.

Why speed? No more can I be late.
The Fever is the world — and I.
For star-plunging scarlet sounds,
these visions worthy of a hundred lives,
bear me above all miracles.

This is the holy idea — a Jesus who was or may have been the Christ and loved mankind.

He said you shall not take up arms against arms and conquer. Jesus was the Christ, the most just.

Mankind has become wicked — indeed we were never better — and mocking of our faith in Christ.

He could be alive today. He is risen who is a Christ, a great, great Lord living justly in other form.

Walk among us, dear Man-God. It is spring, the weeds are growing, and the just man is rare.

You are as I pictured with a heart that is slightly ableed. And still, my ego heart is yours.

Book of Petrarch

THE GREAT BRIDGE

Tall ships that buoy up the vaulting bridge
and rock away across the river of life,
I want to shrive myself before
you women of today and yesterday
and you who rise upon the farther shore.

The male who moves with long and outward steps
will never reach the river's farther bank
unless by linking loves through you.
He will be bright whenever he is false
and false whenever he is bright and true.

I beat a path across the burnished bridge,
and like the lovers of old poesy
I think on women I have known,
not one of whom was dearer than the rest,
not one of whom has ever stood alone.

Forever rolls the bridge. When will I reach
the river's farther shore? I do not know,
but here and there I pause to stay
and gratefully raise up my arms and face
before your gentle rise and rock away.

FULL SCARLET MOON

Behind the hill a full and scarlet moon
arose,
and in the sunset — full three years ago —
my heart,
my sick and silent heart, fell at your feet.

Since then how many others rushed between
and drove,
when by some chance the scarlet moon was full,
toward fire.
Do we still glow or have we burned to ash?

THE VIOLETS I SEQUESTERED

The voltage of a lost and lovely word
which did not strike you down
I feel in icy sadness of this hail,
although it was a single word which missed
the violets I sequestered in the vale,
one word alone which no one else could speak.

You could not even save the name
I pelted with a summer storm of words
that hopscotched on the distant sky
like lightning, too cold among the cryogens
to form one word of forking flame.

This one and only lightning is the sin,
the all and all-destroying nothing.
I was afraid to let you know
how one and good I could have been
beyond the summer solstice and this storm,
but, oh, it never thunderclapped upon
the violets I sequestered in the vale.

Callipareian and destructive,
you wake up,
and I drink a few happy weeks the cup
of philosophy and love.

I live a little
the life of poets and thinkers of Hellene,
who are carried to the empyrean unseen
by rose-nippled temple girls.

What was the most and what the best?
the holy catalepsy,
deep debates on life and beauty,
or the comedies of the kiss?

Hellas sent you
that I might hear the whirring dove
of love
and the manna lips of philosophy.

I lay everyone in a grave
but when they open
for you, the first of women,
I cannot tell whom I bury you as.

THE NOMAD MOON

Strangers in a strange land
where evil men move darkly and make love,
we said good-bye:
good men on parting must embrace
for they seldom ever meet.

I kept watch over us. And have you ever watched
a better two?
How short
the summer shower of our happiness.

You may now regret
our encounter and your adventurous desire,
the goals we sighted and our bold faith.
Do you still believe?
Try and all will be well.

The full moons,
the once together seen,
will pass again like beauty.
Our vow is no odious rack,
and you would turn mad if you knew
the visions that seize me
in the full of a wintry, nomad moon.

Onward, My Ship

MY CALLING

A scale is wedged within my soul,
and like a gleaming, heavy ghost
I see the matters of today
and prayerfully watch and weigh.

And should I stumble into sleep
(my dreams are fitful on these nights),
I always think that I have found
the feel of life is well and sound.

The feel of life is well and sound,
and far away in distant lands
the brooks are splashing to and fro
and running red from my heart's flow.

I feel I stand against the sky,
beneath my feet a solid base
of bronze and granite idols dead —
I stand astride some strange god's head.

I stand, look out, and watch in fear
and never place my trust in time,
and all my hurts and passions fling
upon the plain like floods of spring.

I stand astride some strange god's head,
for this is how I bear with time,
for this is how I bear my heart,
an urn of good and evil art.

This body is a holy tool,
a postman by some devil sent,
who brought the terrors of today
from codes of timeless far away.

THE ASS GOD

How lovely, though invented, that he rode
upon an ass with flowering pomegranate.
The scriptures state
he rode, his heart all thirst, and never thought
about Good Friday.

And ever since with thirsty hearts like his
their way unstrewn by palms
a mighty host of warriors of the good,
mounted on asses and haunted by psalms
travel a faster Calvary of life
and what it offers.

How fair Palm Sunday bids to be tomorrow
when the old legend will unfold again.
Perhaps an ass god
will come with flower and vine
to love and strive for others,
how much we need, we need the asinine.

O Jesus, spring, Jerusalem,
how old, how old this history,
amen, amen.

Confessions of Love

ON THE KALOTA

Stately Magyars in procession from church
are crossing the Kalota river,
and the all-embracing summer sun
almost buoys the bridge with light.
The colors, the colors, the well-loved colors,
the peace of mind in the bright display,
white and red and blooming yellow,
exciting blue and pugnacious brown,
the calm and majestic faces,
the virgin fillets yearning to fall.
The sermon soars from hard peasant heads
and mingles with the scents of summer.
What a pompous procession over the hill.
Oh, cadenced procession, permanence,
security, summer, beauty, and peace.

I am the target of restlessness
from arrowy, girlish eyes,
eyes in which I see myself
a rosy and cheerful rogue of twenty,
eyes more beautiful than ever were,
eyes in which are sealed
my eternally sombre youth —
the attraction, dear pursuit,
excesses until the final blow.
I see my adoring self in these large eyes
and live in them.
The calm of June is in my heart.
The devotion of people proceeding from church
has passed into my soul,
and there is this moment on the Kalota river
security, summer, beauty, and peace.

A chaplet on my brow in morning twilight,
I sail my ship, the truth at last.
The old, determined boatman is so strange,
and I am young with clamor and desire.
My happy ship
rides like a misty fragment of the sky.
The sun is smiling in my eyes of fire
which never saw a more miraculous ship,
or mariner more like the morn.
Desires are flung like seas across our path,
and the ocean is mine.
We sway beneath the gullscream of rhythm,
and on the deck the tamtams beat.
My foremast is the triumph
of girls who madden and yield,
and in my wake the ships
on which I roamed and lay in ambush
for easy conquest and cheap merchandise.
The night seeks for me in vain
because I am a messenger of many dawns,
and still my ship has come at last.
O brigand ships, how lost in mist.
O booties past, how lost your bait.
Which should I want back —
the hungry sloop with flag of green
that was my questioning and anguished youth?
the storm ship that left behind
the siren of ancient songs?
the girling ship, now languid,
and flaunting pennants of a hundred skirts?
or the ugly little brigantine
of fame, philosophy, and rapture?
Look, here upon my breast a girl is lying,
and on the ocean of this life
I am myself. Proudly I guide
into the young, insane and sacred tempests
what alone is worthy —
the fateful and newest vessel of life.

1. **Two Freedom Fighters.** The Freedom Fighters (kurucok) were soldiers in the revolutionary armies of Francis Rákóczi fighting against the Hapsburgs for the nationalist cause in the 17th and 18th centuries (see also Notes 1 and 7 to LONGING FOR LOVE, page 255).

2. **This Land Only Once.** George Dózsa: See Note 4 to ON ELIJAH'S CHARIOT, page 198.

3. **Corpse on a Wheat Field.** The southernwood is **Artemisia abrotanum, in** Hungarian "tree of God", a flowering shrub planted on graves but also the word for a decorated pole that suitors used as a phallic symbol, planting it near the home of the girl or the well which she visits.

4. **Valley of the Kraszna.** For "Kraszna" see Note 12 in Notes on BLOOD AND GOLD, page 151.

5. **Spring Journey.** Written at Csucsa Castle.

6. **On the Kalota.** Along the Kalota river in Transylvania lives an ethnic group of Magyars noted for the distinctiveness and colorfulness of their costumes.

THE LAST BOATS

(1923)

POETS SING IN SPRING

If you feel the spring has come,
stand not in a corner
but under the whip.
Let the snake strike
if you believe and live and die for spring.

I have despaired
and wearied of despair.
We see
not a dream but a conundrum,
not a forgetting but a recollection,
and only they can despair
in spring
who rejected life —
the unwell.

Heigh ho spring, who art
not the same
in Helsinki
as in Ravenna, Irkutsk, or Varad.
I quail under your visitation.

Our sadness has been enough,
and on our meadows
(I, too, have been guilty)
we have too often said
who cares, it is all the same.

Let us gather from spring and ourselves
whatever is dear
and look
with love on one another.

Spring, heigh ho, spring.
Whoever is sad in this Magyar land
let him hold his head up
sombre bold in the bittersweet of diligence.
If spring is not everywhere,
we are.

When the pasha rose
was the sovereign flower,
we stole some for the church
from strange gardens
to see ourselves in bloom,
restless girls and boys,
who saw ourselves as we were
only in church
at prayer, sermon, and in song.

Ho, Holy Ghost,
how youthful you were,
how white the acacias,
how red the Pentecosts.

But the Pentecosts of today
are real and true.
We need no church,
the world is our church.
The Pentecost king knows
what he longs for
and knows
whom he uncovers
and recovers
with new flowers.
How different are
life, desire, and resignation
since the world is a church
and the puffed-up pasha rose
and the acacias
are nothing,
while the true flowers
are sovereign.

The world, the world, the world,
the church, the church, the church,
the girls, the girls, the girls,
I love, I love, I love.

THE HORSES OF NIGHT

My Lord, who drives the horses of the night,
who flicks a moon and lashes on a sun,
I want to look with eyes of faith
upon the dreadful cart wheels of your sky.

Allow my soul to swallow in mute faith
the splendorous secrets of your constancy
and with the faithful's simple heart
believe that all is destined to be so.

Grant each and everyone his own belief
and let the millions also have their truth
and do not let your chosen few
be rapt away by terrors of life and death.

Spin the infinite cart wheels of the sky,
stir up the clouds of dust, our blessed faith,
and never let the great despair
take to the maelstrom's edge your brooding fools.

Gee up, gee up, O horses of the night,
and we, poor souls, the dust of your huge wheels,
in showers of belief and faith
will coalesce to an eternal hymn.

THE GOD OF COWARDICE

Ishten, I was not born or raised to suffer the scream of shrapnel. I believe in mystery, but what is beyond cause or fate?

I look across ancient acres lodged with the bleeding corpses of unnumbered generations.

I never defended the Old, although I am someone as defender, and still I love the die cutter of my life with exultation and only now love him really.

Great hearth of heroic deeds, I know no one else to love, and who could there be but you, Ishten.

I love you in glorious anxiety and dread. I love you unto cowardice, and if I love you, then I love you, and if I love you, then I love you.

EVERYTHING FOR LIFE

Because the son of Adam was wicked does the vengeful Lord God torment his seed with Satan?

Man is not so evil that he must be arrogantly trampled by Satan, his inverse ideal.

We cannot give up the precious jewels and works of life to human anguish.

This race cannot be more savage than all others and devour its own beauties.

Man and Satan cannot but resile from their insane and blood-soaked path.

For both man and Satan pursue one goal — to make life live, to make life live.

IN HONOR OF SAINT ANTON

When I know I am
who I was,
and when mankind
well done and undone,
wallows and raves,
suffers and rages,
let me, the Calvinist,
say a prayer
to Anton of Padua,
the saint.

Holy man
dead
before the ruin
and so wise
he still gives wisdom
to simpletons,
look at me
how I wear the curse.

I was a Saint Anton
of beautiful, careless times,
a rediscovery
of women,
an apostol,
a prophet.
Saint Anton, my forebear,
how sad the past,
how sad, how sad and false,
and everything is false,
perhaps even what I say.

THE FATE OF MY EYES

A world of things unseen once reeled
within these eyes now filled with tears,
desiring no more the once desired.

They now would want a realer world,
but how downcast and shorn these eyes,
who cannot even see the seen.

Now works instead of eyes will see,
O holy eyes for battle born,
blinded before the fight is joined.

THE VISIT

Foundations do not quickly fall,
and on the good and gentle nights
our houses cry and hurt and crawl
for those who long since left.

And when the houses stir and grope
in blinded alleys of their loss,
they seek a secret living hope
in the senescent past.

On quests that always end in vain
they come upon the silent dead,
and yet the houses cry and strain
to make a loving call.

How can they come on those who went?
(It's all the same to me, grant God)
and grant me all the good he meant
should fall unto my lot.

KILL A SOUL

These are times
(they said of old)
to die
or love with fire profane
or kill a soul.

These are times
(I say of now)
these are times
to salute a corpse
or kill a soul.

These are times
(they say of now)
to be and be again
or love with fire profane
or kill a soul.

BEAUTY IS BEAUTY

Oh. what beauty that I am,
oh, what beauty that they are,
oh, what beauty is the real,
oh, what beauty is beauty.

And a man is glorious
if he differs from all else.
Oh, what beauty that I differ,
oh, what beauty is beauty.

Oh, what beauty in today —
more because for me alone
beauty is the ugly's mother,
oh, what beauty is beauty.

COMPLAINT OF A DISSATISFIED YOUTH

Paris, Peking . . . London or Rome?
How boring a habitation this world.
City and village are alike,
and no place is worth
visiting.
Would there only be
something different, some great start.

Who can endure this gray
reflection of lies.
Come, fist,
let this worthless life turn over
and death come, the great doctor,
the awakening after death,
and the terror.
Let something different come.
Revolutions, why are you late?

Blood, blood, blood.
How beautiful mankind will be
after a bath in blood,
and how sound.
Come with your trumpeting angels,
uprisings.
Come with your millions of troops
and rejuvenate this weary
globe.
Come, redeeming arms.
Amen.

THE LAST BOATS

This ocean soul that rolled with freedom's rhythm
runs low and dark
and silhouettes a black rip-tooth
although I always lived by truth, by truth.

The sea was free for every flag to fly.
Our lifeguard boat
would never threaten to capsize
although a wicked fate wished otherwise.

Two tattered sails still slit the dying sea
to stalk and run,
in ambush hide and reappear.
They are morose disgust and dud gray fear.

Why should I leave my ocean to these boats?
Why should I live?
Within their sides I breach a hole
and to the old man secret give my soul.

Dark God, dark fate and dark old man,
you who are not,
leave me. These faithful waters die
and yawn with salty, cold, incurious eye.

Notes on THE LAST BOATS

1. **Poets Sing in Spring.** Várad: see Note 4 to LONGING FOR LOVE, page 255.

2. **The God of Cowardice.** Ishten: see Note 1 to OF ALL MYSTER-IES, page 293.

3. **In Honor of Saint Anton.** Losers of their goods or money appeal for help to Saint Anton. Monte Carlo gamblers who suffered misfortune at roulette repaired to Saint Anton's shrine at Padua.

Selected Bibliography of Ady Literature

by Elemér Bakó

(Library of Congress call numbers included where available)

WORKS BY ENDRE ADY

Collected Works

Ady Endre összes **versei** (Complete Poems). Budapest, Athenaeum, 1930, 544 p.   PH 3202.A35 1930

Ady Endre összes **versei** (Complete Poems). Budapest, Szépirodalmi Kiadó, 1950. 707 p.   PH 3202.A35A17 1950

Ady Endre összes **prózai művei** (Complete Prose Works). Összeállította: Földessy Gyula. Szerkesztő: Koczkás Sándor. Budapest, Akadémiai Kiadó, 1955.   4 PH Hung. 559
(The latest published volume is number 8. The Library of Congress has volumes 1, 3, 4, 6 and 7.) Published under the general series title **Ady Endre Összes Művei** (Complete Works).

Ady, Endre. **Novellák** (Short Stories). 1-2. Összeállította, bevezette és jegyzetekkel ellátta: Bustya Endre. Marosvásárhely, Állami Irodalmi és Művészeti Kiadó, 1957. 2 v.   4 DB Hung 568

Ady Endre összegyűjtött **novellái** (Collected Short Stories). Budapest, Athenaeum, 1939. 517 p.   PH 3202.A35A15

Ady Endre összes **novellái** (Collected Short Stories). Sajtó alá rendezte és jegyzetekkel ellátta: Bustya Endre. Budapest, Szépirodalmi Könyvkiadó, 1961. 1406 p.   PH 3202.A35Z63

Anthologies and Selections

Ady Endre válogatott levelei (Selected Letters). A leveleket válogatta, sajtó alá rendezte, az előszót és a jegyzeteket írta: Belia György. Budapest, Szépirodalmi Könyvkiadó, 1956. 643 p. (Magyar századok).   4 PH Hung. 1048

Ady Endre válogatott cikkei és tanulmányai (Selected Articles and Essays). Sajtó alá rendezte: Földessy Gyula. Budapest, Szépirodalmi Könyvkiadó, 1954. 503 p. (Magyar Klasszikusok) 4 PH Hung.501

Ady, Endre. Ifjú szívekben élek; válogatott cikkek és tanulmányok (Selected Articles and Essays). A válogatás és az Ady-tanulmány Koczkás Sándor munkája. A jegyzeteket Bessenyei György készítette. Budapest, Móra Ferenc Könyvkiadó, 1958. 472 p.

4 PH Hung. 1338

Ady, Endre. A nacionalizmus alkonya (The Twilight of Nationalism). Írták: Koczkás Sándor és Vezér Erzsébet. Budapest, Kossuth Könyvkiadó, 1959. 302 p. 4 DB Hung. 700

Ady, Endre. Válogatott versei (Selected Poems). Szerkesztette: Bölöni György (et. al.). Budapest, Szépirodalmi Könyvkiadó, 1952. 339 p.

PH 3202.A35A17 1952

Individual Editions

Pintér, Jenő. Századunk magyar irodalma (Hungarian Literature of Our Century). For full entry see below. Lists on pages 546 and following individual volumes of Ady's works.

Translations

Magyar Irodalmi Lexikon (Lexicon of Hungarian Literature). For full entry see below. Lists in volume 1 page 17 a total of 34 editions of Ady's poetry translated into 22 languages.

WORKS ABOUT ENDRE ADY

Bibliographies and Biographies

Gulyás, Pál. Magyar írók élete és munkái (The Lives and Works of Hungarian Writers). Megindította: id. Szinnyei József. Új sorozat. Budapest, Magyar Könyvtárosok és Levéltárosok Egyesülete, 1939. v. 1-6 (publication discontinued). "Ady Endre": vol. 1, pages 156-248. PH 3028.G8

Magyar életrajzi lexikon (Hungarian Biographical Lexicon). I.II. Főszerkesztő: Kenyeres Ágnes. Budapest, Akadémiai Kiadó, 1967. 2 v. "Ady Endre": p. 12-13. DB 922.M25

Magyar irodalmi lexikon (Hungarian Literary Lexicon). I-III. Főszerkesztő: Benedek Marcell. Budapest, Akadémiai Kiadó, 1963. 3 v. "Ady Endre": vol. 1, pages 9-18. PH 3007.B4

Tezla, Albert. An Introductory Bibliography to the Study of Hungarian Literature. Cambridge, Mass., Harvard University Press, 1964. XXVI, 290 p. "Ady Endre": p. 174-176. Z 2148.L5T4

Várkonyi, Nándor. **A modern magyar irodalom** (Modern Hungarian Literature). Az életrajzi részeket összeállította: Szabó István. Pécs, Danubia, no date. 466 p. "Ady Endre": p. 189-196.   Z 2148.L5V3

General Handbooks of Hungarian Literary History

Klaniczay, Tibor. **History of Hungarian Literature.** By Tibor Klaniczay, József Szauder and Miklós Szabolcsi. Budapest, Corvina Press, 1964. 361 p. "Endre Ady": p. 192-199.   PH 3012.K513

Magyar Tudományos Akadémia, Budapest. Irodalomtörténeti Intézet. **A magyar irodalom története** (History of Hungarian Literature). Főszerkesztő: Sőtér István. Budapest, 1965-. For Endre Ady, see volumes V. (1905-1919), and VI (1919-).   PH 3012.M33

Pintér, Jenő. **Századunk magyar irodalma** (Hungarian Literature of Our Century). Budapest, "Dr. Pintér Jenőné vállalatának kiadása", 1943. 1428 p. "Ady Endre": p. 491-690.   PH 3012.P57 1943

Szerb, Antal. **Magyar irodalomtörténet** (History of Hungarian Literature). Budapest, Révai, 1943. 536 p.   4 PH Hung. 1324

Szerb, Antal. **Magyar irodalomtörténet.** Budapest, Révai, 1947. 536 p.
     PH 3013.S9

Szerb, Antal. **Magyar irodalomtörténet.** Budapest, Magvető Könyvkiadó, 1958. 538 p. "Ady Endre": p. 476-498.   PH 3013.S9 1958

Special Monographs

Ady, Endre. **Ady Endre az irodalomról** (Endre Ady on Literature). Szerkesztette: Varga József és Vezér Erzsébet. Budapest, Magvető Könyvkiadó, 1961. 450 p.   4 PH Hung. 1674

Ady, Endre. **Ady Endre, 1877-1919.** Szerkesztették: Sára Péter és Pölöskei Ferencné. Budapest, Magyar Helikon, 1957. 169 p. (A Petőfi Irodalmi Múzeum kiadványai, 2).   4 PH Hung. 1169

Ady, Lajos. **Ady Endre.** Budapest, Amicus Kiadó, 1923. 245 p. (A biography of the poet written by his younger brother.)

Ady, Lajosné. **Az ismeretlen Ady** (The Unknown Ady). Budapest, Béta Irodalmi Részvénytársaság, 1942. 412 p. (Appeared as the work of the poet's sister-in-law, wife of Lajos Ady, above; but was ghosted by Zsófia Dénes, see below.)

Bóka, László. **Ady Endre élete és művei** (Life and Works of Endre Ady). I. Budapest, Akadémiai Kiadó, 1955. 319 p. (Author died before completion of Volume II.)

Bölöni, György. **Az igazi Ady** (The True Ady). Budapest, Szépirodalmi Könyvkiadó, 1966. 551 p.

Bölöni, György. **Az igazi Ady** (The True Ady). 1st ed. (Paris, 1934)
     PH3202.A35Z64

473

Bölöni, György. **Az igazi Ady** (The True Ady). 2nd ed. Budapest, Szikra, 1947. 403 p.   4 PH Hung. 142

Bölöni, György. **Az igazi Ady** (The True Ady. 3rd ed. Budapest, **Magvető Könyvkiadó**, 1955. 359 p.

Dénes, Zsófia. **Élet helyett órák** (Hours Instead of Life). Budapest, Pantheon Kiadó, 1939. 269 p. (Described by the author as a "chapter of Ady's life".)

Földessy, Gyula. **Ady minden titkai** (All of Ady's Secrets). Budapest, Athenaeum, 1949. 318 p. (A poem by poem exegesis of Ady's verse.)   PH 3202.A35Z65

Hatvany, Lajos, báró. **Ady: cikkek, emlékezések, levelek** (Ady: Articles, Memoirs, and Letters). Budapest, Szépirodalmi Könyvkiadó, 1959. 2 v.   4 PH Hung. 1463

Hegedüs, Nándor. **Ady elnyeri a főváros szépirodalmi díját** (Ady Wins the Budapest Literature Prize). Budapest, Akadémiai Kiadó, 1959. 59 p. (Irodalomtörténeti füzetek, 26).   4 PH Hung. 1548

Hegedüs, Nándor. **Ady Endre nagyváradi napjai** (Endre Ady in Nagyvárad). Budapest, Magyar Tudományos Akadémia Irodalomtörténeti Intézete, 1957. 463 p. (Új magyar múzeum).   4 PH Hung. 1070

Hegedüs, Lóránt. **Ady és Tisza** (Ady and Tisza). Budapest, 1940. 120 p.

Kovalovszky, Miklós. **Emlékezések Ady Endréről** (Recollections on Endre Ady). 1-2. Gyűjtötte, sajtó alá rendezte és magyarázatokkal kiegészítette: Kovalovszky Miklós. Budapest, Akadémiai Kiadó, 1961. 2 v. (Új magyar múzeum. Irodalmi dokumentumok gyűjteménye, 5).   PH 3202.A35Z75

Lengyel, Géza. **Ady a műhelyben** (Ady in the Workshop). Budapest, Szépirodalmi Könyvkiadó, 1957. 394 p. (An account of Ady's years as a newspaperman up to 1908.)

Lukács, György. **Írástudók felelőssége** (The Responsibility of Literary Men). Moscow, Foreign Language Literature Publishing House, 1944. 93 p.   PH 3017.L8

Nyugat. **"Ady- emlékszám"** (Ady Memorial Issue). Budapest, March 1919. (Includes c. 35 studies on Ady by friends and admirers and a bibliography by Jenő Pintér of studies on Ady which appeared in Hungarian periodicals between 1899 and 1918.)

Révai, József. **Ady.** Budapest, Szikra Könyvkiadó, 1949. 124 p. (A critical evaluation of Ady by a prominent Marxist.)

Révész, Béla. **A teljes Ady-Léda regény** (The Complete Ady-Léda Story). Budapest, Író Könyvkiadó, 1942. 160 p.

Révész, Béla. **Ady Endre.** Budapest, Béta Irodalmi Részvénytársaság, 1924. 160 p.

Révész, Béla. **Ady triológiája** (Ady Trilogy). Budapest, Nova, 1935. 365 p. (Includes the above work and two other studies.)

Schöpflin, Aladár. **Ady Endre.** Budapest, Nyugat, 1934. 214 p.

Szabó, Dezső. **A forradalmas Ady** (The Revolutionary Ady). Budapest, Táltos Könyvkiadó, 1919. 32 p.

Vatai, László. **Az Isten szörnyetege** (The Behemoth of God). Washington, D.C., Occidental Press, 1963. 390 p.   PH 3202.A35Z9

Vezér, Erzsébet. **Ady Endre alkotásai és vallomásai tükrében** (Endre Ady in the Mirror of his Works and Confessions). Budapest, Szépirodalmi Könyvkiadó, 1968. 242 p.

Special Articles, Chapters, References on and to Ady

Bóka, László. **Ady szimbolizmusa** (Ady's Symbolism). Pages 386-417 in his **Tegnaptól máig. Válogatott tanulmányok, esszék, cikkek** (From Yesterday to Today: Selected Studies, Essays, and Articles). Budapest, Szépirodalmi Könyvkiadó, 1958. 580 p.   PH 3017.B6

Bóka, László. **Ady Endre.** Pages 267-287 in his **Arcképvázlatok és tanulmányok** (Profiles and Studies). Budapest, Akadémiai Kiadó, 1962.
          PH 3028.B6

Bóka, László. **Endre Ady the Poet.** Budapest. **The New Hungarian Quarterly,** Vol. III, No. 5, January-March, 1962. Pages 83-108.

Encyclopedia Britannica, **Ady, Endre.** Vol. I. Page 185.

Hazard, Paul. **André Ady Poete Hongrois et Européen.** Paris, Revue D'Historie Comparée XXIVe Année, 1946, Nouvelle Serie, Tome IV, No. 3-4. Les Presses Universitaires de France. Pages 207-224.

Károlyi, Michael. **Memoirs of Michael Károlyi.** Jonathan Cape, London, 1956.

Kirkconnell, Watson. **The Poetry of Ady.** Budapest, **The Hungarian Quarterly,** Vol. III, No. 3, Autumn, 1937. Pages 501-514.

Koestler, Arthur. **Arrow in the Blue: An Autobiography.** New York, Macmillan, 1952-1954. 2. v. (Volume 2, under the title **The Invisible Writing,** contains passages on and references to Ady and his poetry.)

Kosztolányi, Dezső. **Kortársak** (Contemporaries). **Kosztolányi Dezső hátrahagyott művei,** III. kötet. Szerkesztette: Illyés Gyula. Budapest, Nyugat, 1940. "Ady": vol. 1, pages 13-52.   PH 3028.K6

Móricz, Zsigmond. **Válogatott irodalmi tanulmányok** (Selected Literary Studies). Budapest, Művelt Nép Könyvkiadó, 1952. (Contains seven essays on Ady.)

Sőtér, István. **E. Ady.** In his **Aspects et parallélismes de la litterature hongroise.** Budapest, Akadémiai Kiadó, 1966. 291 p. "Ady": p. 246-253.   PH 3017.S6

Szirmay, Henriette (de Pulszky), de. **Andreas Ady und seine Geniewerdung.** In her **Genie und Irrsinn im ungarischen Geistesleben.** München, Ernst Reinhardt, 1935. 212 p.   DB 920.5.S9

Tersánszky, J. Jenő. **Találkozások Ady Endrével** (Meeting with Ady.) In his **Nagy árnyakról bizalmasan** (Confidentially About Great Spirits). Budapest, Magvető Könyvkiadó, 1962. 302 p. Pages 6-27.
                                                    PH 3028.T4

Tóth, Árpád. **Bírálatok és tanulmányok** (Criticism and Studies). Debrecen, 1939. "Ady": pages 84-100. (A study on Ady's relations to his predecessors and the French moderns.)

Vargyas, Lajos. **A magyar vers ritmusa** (Hungarian Prosody). Budapest, Akadémiai Kiadó, 1952. 263 p. (Contains numerous references to Ady.)   PH 3062.V3

Fiction

Dénes, Zsófia. **Akkor a hársak épp szerettek...** (When the Lindens Were in Love). Budapest, Magvető Könyvkiadó, 1957. 294 p.

Dutka, Ákos. **A holnap városa** (The City of Tomorrow). Budapest, Magvető Könyvkiadó, 1955. 255 p.

Krúdy, Gyula. **Ady Endre éjszakái** (Ady's Nights). Budapest, Fehér Holló, 1941. 113 p.   PH 3281.K89A68

Index of Titles

English

483

Hungarian

Hungarian

485

488

490

Ady's birthplace at Érmindszent

Ady's father at his prime

Ady with his mother and wife at the time of World War I.

Léda in 1905

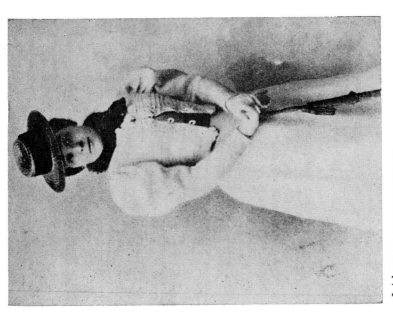

Léda as a young woman

Charcoal drawing
by Dezső Czigány

Ady and fellow poet
Babits

Editorial room of the "Debrecen Morning Daily" (1898)
Ady at the telephone

Ady in 1903

Ady in 1907

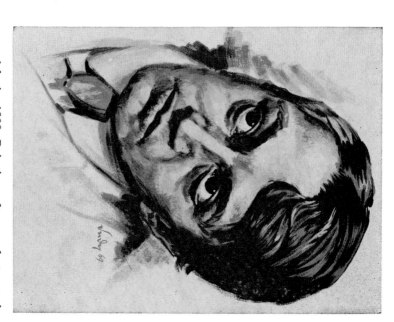

Ady in 1909. Painting after a photograph
by József P. Vudy

Castle at Csucsa

Panorama of Érmindszent

Manuscript of The Peasant Summer

Ady's last photograph

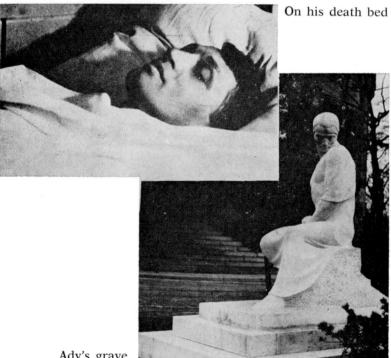

On his death bed

Ady's grave